Total Quality Management

Total Quality Management

John S. Oakland

PhD, CChem, MRSC, FIQA, FSS, MBIM, MASQC, FAQMC

Professor of Total Quality Management
University of Bradford, Management Centre

Butterworth-Heinemann Ltd
Halley Court, Jordan Hill, Oxford OX2 8EJ

 PART OF REED INTERNATIONAL BOOKS

OXFORD   LONDON   GUILDFORD   BOSTON
MUNICH   NEW DELHI   SINGAPORE   SYDNEY
TOKYO   TORONTO   WELLINGTON

First published 1989
Reprinted 1989 (three times)
Reprinted 1990

British Library Cataloguing in Publication Data
Oakland, John S.
    Total quality management.
    1. Quality control.
    I. Title
    658.5′62

ISBN 0 7506 0084 5

Published in the United States of America by
Nichols Publishing Company, PO Box 96, New York, NY 10024

Library of Congress Cataloging-in-Publication Data
Oakland, John S.
Total quality management.
    1. Quality control.   2. Production management – Quality control
    3. Quality assurance.   I. Title
    TS156.O24 1989   658.5–dc20   89–32160

ISBN 0 89397 348 3

Printed in Great Britain by
Redwood Press Limited, Melksham, Wiltshire

For Susan, Jane and Robert

Contents

Preface

The 'industrial revolution' took place in the last century. Perhaps the 'computer revolution' happened in the early 1980s, but we are now, without doubt, in the midst of the 'quality revolution' – a period of change affecting every type of business, enterprise, organization, and person.

In any competitive economy, continuous cost reduction and quality improvement are essential if an organization is to stay in operation. Competitiveness is measured by three things: quality, price and delivery. The theory behind the costs of quality shows that, as quality improves, costs fall through reduction in failure and appraisal costs. Satisfying the customer in terms of quality *and* price will clearly benefit market share. The absence of quality problems also removes the need for the 'hidden operations' devoted to dealing with failure and waste, and delivery performance benefits from increased output and higher productivity.

We cannot avoid seeing how quality has developed into the most important competitive weapon, and many organizations have realized that total quality management (TQM) is the new way of managing for the future. TQM is far wider in its application than assuring product or service quality – it is a way of managing the whole business or organization to ensure complete customer satisfaction at every stage, internally and externally.

This book is about how to manage in a total quality way. It is structured around just twelve words:

- Understanding
- Commitment
- Organization
- Measurement (costs)
- Planning
- Design
- System
- Capability
- Control
- Teamwork
- Training
- Implementation

Under these headings, the essential steps for the successful introduction of TQM are set out in a meaningful and practical way. Aimed at directors and managers in industrial, commercial, and service organizations, the book guides the reader through the language of TQM and sets down a clear way to proceed for the whole organization.

Many of the gurus appear to present different solutions to the problems of quality management and control. In reality they are all talking the same 'language' but they use different dialects. The basic principles of defining quality and taking it into account throughout all the activities of marketing, invention, design, development, purchasing, production, operations, distribution, and finance are common. Quality has to be managed – it does not just happen. Understanding and commitment by senior management, effective leadership and teamwork are fundamental parts of the recipe for success. The author has used his unique research and consultancy experience to take what is to many a jigsaw puzzle and assemble a model for total quality – the rewards of which are greater efficiencies, lower costs, improved reputation and greater market share.

In addition to helping senior managers to develop total quality management within their organizations, this book will meet the requirements of all students who need to understand the part quality plays in their courses on science, engineering, or management. Those engaged in the pursuit of professional qualifications in management of quality assurance, such as membership of the Institute of Quality Assurance, the American Society of Quality Control, or the Australian Organisation for Quality Control will make this book an essential part of their library.

With its companion book, *Statistical Process Control, Total Quality Management* documents a comprehensive approach which has been used successfully in many organizations throughout the world.

The author would like to thank his close colleague Dr Roy Followell for the sharing of ideas and help in their development. The book is the result of many years of collaboration in assisting organizations to introduce good methods of quality management and embrace the concepts of total quality. He is most grateful to Barbara Shutt who single-handedly converted a patchwork quilt of scribble into an error-free typescript, and indebted to Susan, Jane and Robert who put up with a 'distant' husband and father for nearly a year.

1 Understanding quality

1.1 What is quality?

The air hostess pulled back the curtain across the aisle and set off with a trolley full of breakfasts to feed the early-morning travelling business people on the short domestic flight into an international airport. Having stopped at the row of seats marked 1ABC, she passed the first tray onto the lap of the gent sitting by the window. By the time the second tray had reached the lady beside him, the first tray was on its way back to the air hostess with a complaint that the bread roll and jam were missing. She calmly replaced it in her trolley and reached for another – which also had no roll and jam.

The calm exterior of the girl began to evaporate as she discovered two more trays without a complete breakfast. Then she found a good one and, thankfully, passed it over. This search for complete breakfast trays continued down the aeroplane and caused the inevitable delays, so much so that several passengers did not receive their breakfasts until the plane had begun its descent. At the rear of the plane could be heard the mutterings of discontent. 'Aren't they slow with breakfast this morning?' 'What is she doing with those trays?' 'We will have indigestion by the time we've landed!' It is interesting how the problem was perceived by many to be one of delivery or service. The air hostess, who had suffered the embarrassment of being the purveyor of defective product and service, was quite flushed as she returned to the curtain and almost ripped it from the hooks in her haste to hide. She was heard to say through clenched teeth, 'What a bloody mess!'

A problem of quality? Yes, probably, but where? The passengers suffered from it on the aircraft, but down in the bowels of the organization was a little man whose job it was to assemble the breakfast trays. On this day the system broke down – perhaps he ran out of bread rolls, perhaps he was called away to refuel the aircraft, perhaps he didn't know or understand, perhaps he didn't care.

Three hundred miles away in a chemical factory . . . 'What the Hell is quality control doing? We've just sent 3000 gallons of lawn weedkiller to CIC and there it is back at our gate – they've returned it as out of spec'.'

This was followed by an avalanche of verbal abuse, which will not be repeated here, but poured all over the shrinking Quality Control Manager as he backed through his office door, followed by a red-faced Technical Director advancing menacingly from behind the bottles of sulphuric acid racked across the adjoining laboratory.

'Yes, what is QC doing?' thought the Production Manager, who was behind a door two offices along the corridor, but could hear the torrent of language now being used to beat the QC man into an admission of guilt. He knew the poor devil couldn't possibly do anything about the rubbish that had been tested, but why should he volunteer for the unpleasant and embarrassing ritual now being experienced by his colleague – for the second time this month. No wonder the QC Manager had been studying the middle pages of the *Telegraph* on Thursday – what a job!

Do you recognize the situations above? Do they not happen every day of the week – possibly every minute somewhere in manufacturing or the service industries? Is it any different in banking, insurance, the health service? The inquisition of checkers and testers – the last bastion of desperate systems which try in vain to catch mistakes, stop defectives, hold lousy materials, before they reach the customer – and woe betide the idiot who lets it pass through!

Two everyday incidents, but why are events like these so common? The answer is the acceptance of one thing – *failure* – to do it right the first time, every time at every stage, and lack of understanding of another – *quality*.

Why do we accept failure in the production of artifacts, the provision of a service, or even the transfer of information? In many walks of life, we do not accept it. We do not say, 'Well, the nurse is bound to drop the odd baby in a thousand – it's just going to happen.' We do not accept that.

'Is this a quality watch?' Pointing to my wrist I ask a class of students – undergraduates, postgraduates, experienced managers – it matters not. The answers vary:

'No, it's made in Japan'
'No, it's cheap'
'No, the face is scratched'
'How reliable is it?'
'I wouldn't wear it'

My watch has been insulted all over the world – London, New York, Paris, Sydney, Brussels, Amsterdam, Bradford! Very rarely am I told that the quality of the watch depends on what the wearer requires from a watch – a piece of jewellery to give an impression of wealth or a time piece which gives the required data, including the date, in digital form? Clearly these requirements determine the quality.

Quality is often used to signify 'excellence' of a product or service – we talk about 'Rolls-Royce quality' and 'top quality'. In some engineering companies, the word may be used to indicate that a piece of metal conforms to certain physical dimension characteristics often set down in the form of a particularly 'tight' specification. If we are to define quality in a way which is useful in its management, then we must recognize the need to include in the assessment of quality, the true requirements of the 'customer'.

Quality then is simply *meeting the requirements* and this has been expressed in many ways by other authors:

'fitness for purpose or use' Juran.
'the totality of features and characteristics of a product or service that bear on its ability to satisfy stated or implied needs' BS 4778, 1987 (ISO 8402, 1986) *Quality Vocabulary: Part 1 International Terms*.
'the total composite product and service characteristics of marketing, engineering, manufacture, and maintenance through which the product and service in use will meet the expectation by the customer' Feigenbaum.

There is another word that we should define properly – reliability. 'Why do you buy a Volkswagen car?' 'Quality and reliability', comes back the answer. The two are used synonymously, often in a totally confused way. Clearly, part of the acceptability of a product or service will depend on its ability to function satisfactorily over a period of time, and it is this aspect of performance which is given the name reliability. It is the ability of the product or service to continue to meet the customer requirements. Reliability ranks with quality in importance, since it is a key factor in many purchasing decisions where alternatives are being considered. Many of the general management issues related to achieving product or service quality are also applicable to reliability.

It is important to realize that the 'meeting the customer requirements' definition of quality is not restrictive to the functional characteristics of products or services. Anyone with children knows that the quality of some of the products they purchase is more associated with satisfaction in ownership than some functional property. This is also true of many items, from antiques to certain items of clothing. The requirement for status symbols accounts for the sale of some executive cars, certain bank accounts and charge cards, and even hospital beds! The requirements are of paramount importance in the assessment of the quality of any product or service, and quality is the most important aspect of competitiveness.

The ability to meet the customer requirements is vital, not only between two separate organizations, but within the same organization. There exists in every department, every office, even every household, a series of suppliers and customers. The typist is a supplier to her boss – is

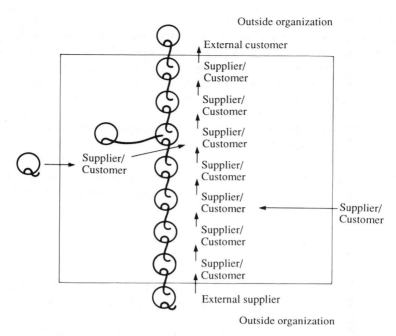

Figure 1.1 *The quality chains*

she meeting his requirements? Does he receive error-free typing set out as he wants it, when he wants it? If so, then we have a quality typing service. Does the air hostess receive from her supplier in the airline the correct food trays in the right quantity?

Throughout and beyond all organizations, whether they be manufacturing concerns, banks, retail stores, universities, or hotels, there is a series of quality chains (Figure 1.1) which may be broken at any point by one person or one piece of equipment not meeting the requirements of the customer, internal or external. The interesting point is that this failure usually finds its way to the interface between the organization and its outside customers, and the people who operate as that interface – like the air hostess – usually experience the ramifications.

A great deal is written and spoken about employee motivation as a separate issue. In fact the key to motivation *and* quality is for everyone in the organization to have well-defined customers – an expansion of the word, beyond the outsider that actually purchases or uses the ultimate product or service, to anyone to whom an individual gives a part, service or information; in other words the results of his or her work.

Quality has to be managed – it will not just happen. Clearly it must involve everyone in the process and be applied throughout the organization. Some people in customer organizations never see, experience, or touch the products or services that their companies purchase, but they do see things like invoices. If every fourth invoice from a certain supplier carries at least one error, what image of quality is transmitted?

Failure to meet the requirements in any part of a quality chain has a way of multiplying and failure in one part of the system creates problems elsewhere, leading to yet more failure, more problems and so on. The price of quality is the continual examination of the requirements and our ability to meet them. This alone will lead to a 'continuing improvement' philosophy. The benefits of making sure the requirements are met at every stage, every time, are truly enormous in terms of increased competitiveness and market share, reduced costs, improved productivity and delivery performance, and the elimination of waste.

1.2 Meeting the requirements

If quality is meeting the customer requirements then this has wide implications. The requirements may include availability, delivery, reliability, maintainability and cost effectiveness, amongst many other features. The first item on the list of things to do is to find out what the requirements are. If we are dealing with a supplier/customer relationship crossing two organizations, then the supplier must establish a 'marketing' activity charged with this task. The marketeers must, of course, understand not only the needs of the customer, but also the ability of their own organization to meet the demands. If my customer places a requirement on me to run a mile (ca 1500 metres) in four minutes, then I know I am unable to meet this demand, unless something is done to improve my running performance. Of course, I may never be able to achieve this requirement. Within organizations, between internal customers and suppliers, the transfer of information regarding requirements frequently varies from poor to totally absent. How many executives really bother to find out what their customers' – their secretaries' – requirements are? Can their handwriting be read; do they leave clear instructions; do the secretaries always know where the boss is? Equally, do the secretaries establish what their bosses need – error-free typing, clear messages, a tidy office? These internal supplier/customer relationships are often the most difficult to manage in terms of establishing the requirements. To achieve quality throughout an organization, each person in the quality chain must interrogate every interface as follows:

Customers
● Who are my immediate customers?
● What are their true requirements?

- How do or can I find out what the requirements are?
- How can I measure my ability to meet the requirements?
- Do I have the necessary capability to meet the requirements? (If not, then what must change to improve the capability?)
- Do I continually meet the requirements? (If not, then what prevents this from happening, when the capability exists?)
- How do I monitor changes in the requirements?

Suppliers
- Who are my immediate suppliers?
- What are my true requirements?
- How do I communicate my requirements?
- Do my suppliers have the capability to measure and meet the requirements?
- How do I inform them of changes in the requirements?

Design and conformance

To understand how quality may be built into a product or service, at any stage, it is necessary to examine the two distinct, but inter-related aspects of quality:

- Quality of design
- Quality of conformance to design

Quality of design

We are all familiar with the old story of the tree swing (Figure 1.2), but in how many places in how many organizations is this chain of activities taking place? To discuss the quality of, for example, a chair it is necessary to describe its purpose – what is it to be used for? If its use involves watching TV for three hours then the typical office chair will not meet the requirements. The difference between the quality of the TV chair and the office chair is not a function of how it was manufactured, but its *design*. Quality of design is a measure of how well the product or service is designed to achieve its stated purpose. The beautifully presented gourmet meal will not necessarily please the recipient if he or she is travelling on the highway and stopped for a quick bite to eat. The most important feature of the design, with regard to achieving quality, is the specification. Specifications must also exist at the internal supplier/customer interfaces to pursue company-wide quality. For example, the company lawyer asked to draw up a contract by the sales manager requires a specification as to its content:

- Is it a sales, processing or consulting type of contract?

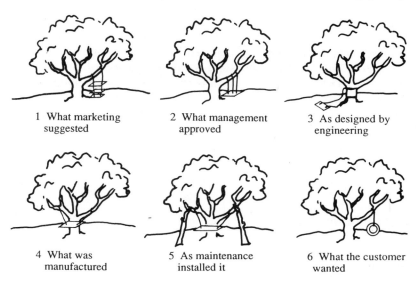

1 What marketing
  suggested

2 What management
  approved

3 As designed by
  engineering

4 What was
  manufactured

5 As maintenance
  installed it

6 What the customer
  wanted

Figure 1.2   *Quality of design*

- Who are the contracting parties?
- In which countries are the parties located?
- What are the products involved? (if any)
- What is the volume?
- What are the financial (e.g. price, escalation) aspects?

The financial controller must issue a specification of the information he or she needs, and when, to ensure that foreign exchange rate fluctuations do not cripple the company's finances. The business of sitting down and agreeing a specification at every interface will clarify the true requirements and capabilities. It is the vital first stage for a successful total quality effort.

There must be a corporate understanding of the company's quality position in the market place. It is not sufficient that marketing specifies the product or service, 'because that is what the customer wants'. There must also be an agreement that the producing departments can achieve that requirement. Should they be incapable of doing so, then one of two things must happen, either the company finds a different position in the market place or substantially changes the operational facilities.

Quality of conformance to design

This is the extent to which the product or service achieves the quality of design. What the customer actually receives should conform to the design, and operating costs are tied firmly to the level of conformance achieved. Quality cannot be inspected into products or services, the customer satisfaction must be designed into the whole system. The conformance check then makes sure that things go according to plan.

A high level of inspection or checking at the end is often indicative of attempts to inspect in quality. This will achieve nothing but spiralling costs and decreasing viability. The area of conformance to design is concerned largely with the quality performance of the actual operations. The recording and analysis of information and data play a significant role in this aspect of quality and here statistical methods must be applied effectively.

1.3 The basic concepts

Every day two men who work in a certain factory scrutinize together the results of the examination of the previous day's production, and commence the ritual battle over whether the material is suitable for despatch to the customer. One is called the Production Manager, the other the Quality Control Manager. They argue and debate the evidence before them, the rights and wrongs of the specification, and each tries to convince the other of the validity of his argument. Sometimes they nearly break into fighting.

This ritual is associated with trying to answer the question: 'Have we done the job correctly?' correctly being a flexible word depending on the interpretation given to the specification on that particular day. This is not quality *control*, it is *detection*, postproduction, wasteful detection of bad product before it hits the customer. There is a widespread belief that to achieve quality we must check, test, inspect or measure – the ritual pouring on of quality at the end of the process. This is nonsense, but it is frequently practised. In the office one finds staff checking other people's work before it goes out, validating computer input data, checking invoices, typing, etc. There is also quite a lot of looking for things, chasing why things are late, apologizing to customers for lateness, and so on, waste, waste, waste.

To get away from the natural tendency to rush into the detection mode, it is necessary to ask different questions in the first place. We do not ask whether the job has been done correctly, we ask first: 'Are we capable of doing the job correctly?' This has wide implications and this book is devoted largely to the various activities which are necessary to ensure that the answer is yes. However, we should realize straight away that such an answer will only be obtained using satisfactory methods, materials, equipment, skills and instruction, and a satisfactory 'process'.

What is a process?

A process is the transformation of a set of inputs, which can include actions, methods and operations, into desired outputs, in the form of products, information, services or, generally, results. In each area or function of an organization there will be many processes taking place. For example, a finance department may be involved in budgeting processes, accounting processes, salary and wage processes, costing processes, etc. Each process in every department or functional area can be analysed by an examination of the inputs and outputs. This will determine the action necessary to improve quality.

The output from a process is that which is transferred to somewhere or to someone – the customer. Clearly to produce an output which meets the requirements of the customer, it is necessary to define, monitor and control the inputs to the process, which in turn may be supplied as output from an earlier process. At every supplier-customer interface then, there resides a transformation process (Figure 1.3). Every single task throughout an organization must be viewed as a process in this way.

Once we have established that our process is capable of meeting the requirements, we can address the next question, 'Do we continue to do the job correctly?' which brings a requirement to monitor the process and the controls on it. If we now re-examine the first question: 'Have we done the job correctly?' we can see that, if we have been able to answer the other two questions with a yes, we *must* have done the job correctly – any other outcome would be illogical. By asking the questions in the right order, we have removed the need to ask the 'inspection' question and

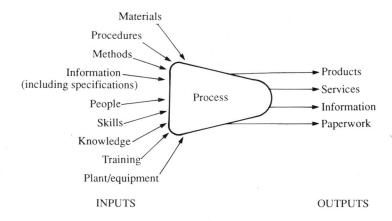

Figure 1.3 *A process*

replaced a strategy of *detection* with one of *prevention*. This concentrates all the attention on the front end of any process, the inputs, and changes the emphasis to making sure the inputs are capable of meeting the requirements of the process. This is a managerial responsibility.

These ideas apply to every transformation process, which must be subject to the same scrutiny of the methods, the people, skills, equipment and so on to make sure they are correct for the job. A person giving a lecture, whose overhead projector equipment will not focus correctly, or whose teaching materials are not appropriate, will soon discover how difficult it is to provide a lecture which meets the requirements of the audience.

The control of quality clearly can only take place at the point of operation or production – where the letter is typed or the chemical made. The act of inspection is not quality control. When the answer to, 'Have we done the job correctly?' is given indirectly by answering the questions on capability and control, then we have assured quality and the activity of checking becomes one of quality assurance – making sure that the product or service represents the output from an effective system to ensure capability and control. It is frequently found that organizational barriers between departmental empires encourage the development of testing and checking of services or products in a vacuum, without interaction with other departments. These will be discussed in Chapter 3.

Quality control then is essentially the activities and techniques employed to achieve and maintain the quality of a product, process, or service. It involves a monitoring activity, but also concerns finding and eliminating causes of quality problems so that the requirements of the customer are continually met.

Quality assurance is broadly the prevention of quality problems through planned and systematic activities (including documentation). These will include: the establishment of a good quality management system and the assessment of its adequacy, the audit of the operation of the system, and the review of the system itself.

1.4 Market demand

The 'marketing' function of an organization must take the lead in establishing the quality requirements for the product or service. Having determined the need, marketing should define the market sector and demand. This will determine product or service features such as the grade, price, quantity, timing, etc. For example, a major hotel chain, before opening a new hotel or refurbishing an old one, will need to consider its location and accessibility, before deciding whether it will be predominantly a budget, first-class, business or family hotel.

Marketing will also need to establish customer requirements by reviewing the market needs, particularly in terms of unclear or unstated expectations or preconceived ideas held by customers. Marketing is responsible for determining the key characteristics which determine the quality of the product or service in the eyes of the customer. This may, of course, involve the use of market research techniques, data gathering, and analysis of customer complaints. If possible, quasi-quantitative methods should be employed giving proxy variables which can be used to grade the characteristics in importance, and decide in which areas superiority over competitors exists. It is often useful to compare these findings with internal perceptions of quality.

If these ideas are also used within an organization, then the internal supplier/customer interfaces will operate much more smoothly. An example of preconception is the distribution manager who believed that trucks arrived at the factory to collect goods at random times during the day. An analysis of easy-to-collect data showed in fact that 80 per cent arrived between 12 noon and 2.00 p.m., when an excellent lunch was available, not only for employees but for all site visitors. This time also happened to coincide with the weakest staff provision in the gate and warehouses due to lunch breaks being taken!

All the efforts devoted to finding the nature and timing of the demand will be pointless if marketing fail to communicate the requirements promptly, clearly, and accurately to the remainder of the organization. The marketing function should be capable of supplying the company with a formal statement or outline of the requirements for each product or service. This constitutes a preliminary set of specifications which can be used as the basis for service or product design. The information requirements include:

1 Characteristics of performance and reliability, these must make reference to the conditions of use and any environmental factors which will be important.
2 Aesthetic characteristics such as style, colour, smell, taste, feel, etc.
3 Any obligatory regulations or standards which govern the nature of the product or service.

Marketing must also establish systems for feedback of customer information and reaction, which should be designed on a continuous monitoring basis. Any information pertinent to the product or service should be collected and collated, interpreted, analysed, and communicated to improve the response to customer experience and expectations. These same principles must also be applied inside the organization for continuous improvement at every transformation process interface to be achieved. If one department of a company has problems recruiting the correct sort of staff, and Personnel have not established mechanisms for gathering, analysing, and responding to information on new employees, then frustration and conflict will replace communication and cooperation.

One aspect of the analysis of market demand which extends back into the organization is the review of market readiness of a new product or service. Items which require some attention include assessment of:

1 the suitability of the distribution and customer service systems,
2 training of personnel in the 'field',
3 availability of spare parts or support staff,
4 evidence that the organization is capable of meeting customer requirements.

All organizations receive a wide range of information from customers through invoices, payments, requests for information, letters of complaint, responses to advertisement and promotion, etc. An essential component of a system for the analysis of market demand is that this data is channelled quickly into the appropriate areas for action and, if necessary, response.

There are various techniques of market research which will not be described in detail in this book for they are well documented elsewhere. It is worth, however, listing some of the most common and useful general methods which should be considered for use, both externally and internally:

1 customer surveys
2 quality panel techniques
3 in-depth interviews
4 brainstorming and discussions
5 role rehearsal and reversal
6 interrogation of trade associations

The number of methods and techniques for researching market demand is limited only by imagination and funds. The important point to stress is that the supplier, whether the internal individual or the external organization, keeps very close to the customer. Market research, coupled with analysis of complaints data, is an essential part of finding out what the requirements are and breaking out from the obsession with inward scrutiny which bedevils quality.

1.5 Quality in all functional areas

For an organization to be truly effective, every single part of it must work properly together. Every part, every activity, every person in a company affects, and is in turn affected by, others. Errors have a way of multiplying and failure to meet the requirements in one part or area creates problems elsewhere, leading to yet more errors, yet more problems and so on. The benefits of getting it right first time everywhere are enormous.

Everyone experiences – almost accepts – problems in working life. This causes people to spend a large part of their time on useless activities, correcting errors, looking for things, finding out why things are late, checking suspect information, rectifying and reworking, apologizing to customers for mistakes, poor quality and lateness. The list is endless and it is estimated that about one-third of our efforts are wasted in this way.

Quality, the way we have defined it as meeting the customer requirements, gives people in different functions of an organization a common language for improvement. It enables all the people, with different abilities and priorities, to communicate readily with one another, in pursuit of a common goal. When business and industry were local, the craftsman could manage more or less on his own. Business is now so complex and employs so many different specialist skills that everyone has to rely on the activities of others in doing their jobs.

Some of the most exciting applications of TQM have materialized from departments which could see little relevance when first introduced to the concepts. Following training, many examples from different departments of organizations show the use of the techniques. Sales staff can monitor and increase successful sales calls; office staff have used TQM methods to prevent errors in word-processing and improve inputting to computers; customer service people have monitored and reduced complaints; distribution have controlled lateness and disruption in deliveries.

It is worthy of mention that the first point of contact for some outside customers is the telephone operator, the security people at the gate, or the person in reception. Equally the paperwork and support services associated with the product, such as invoices and sales literature, must match the needs of the customer. Clearly TQM cannot be restricted to the 'production' areas without losing great opportunities to gain maximum benefit.

Managements which rely heavily on exhortation of the workforce to 'do the job right the first time', or 'accept that quality is your responsibility', will not only fail to achieve quality but will create division and conflict. These calls for improvement infer that faults are caused only by the workforce and that problems are departmental when, in fact, the opposite is true – most problems are interdepartmental. The involvement of all members of an organization is a requirement of company-wide quality improvement. It must involve everyone working together at every interface to achieve perfection. And that can only happen if the top management is really committed to quality improvement.

2 Commitment and policy

2.1 The total quality management approach

'What is quality management?' Something that is best left to the experts, is usually the answer to this question. But this is avoiding the issue because it allows executives and managers to opt out, to avoid getting involved. Quality is too important to leave to the 'quality controllers', it cannot be achieved on a company-wide basis if it is left to the experts. Equally dangerous, however, are the uninformed who try to follow their natural instincts because they 'know what quality is when they see it'. This type of intuitive approach will lead to serious attitude problems which do no more than reflect the understanding, and knowledge of quality that is present in an organization.

The organization which believes that the traditional quality control techniques, and the way they have always been used, will resolve their quality problems is wrong. Employing more inspectors, tightening up standards, developing correction, repair, and rework teams does not promote quality. Traditionally, quality has been regarded as the responsibility of the QC department, and still it has not yet been recognized in some organizations that many quality problems originate in the service or administration areas.

Quality management is far more than shifting the responsibility of inspection from the customer to the producer. It requires a comprehensive approach which must first be recognized and then implemented if the rewards are to be realized.

Today's business environment is such that managers must plan strategically to maintain a hold on market share, let alone increase it. Consumers now place a higher value on quality than on loyalty to their home-based producers and price is no longer the major determining factor in consumer choice. Price has been replaced by quality and this is true also in industrial, service, hospitality, and many other markets.

Total quality management (TQM) is an approach to improving the effectiveness and flexibility of businesses as a whole. It is essentially a way of organizing and involving the whole organization; every department, every activity, every single person at every level. For an organization to be truly effective, each part of it must work properly together, recognizing that every person and every activity affects, and in turn is affected by, others.

TQM is a method for ridding people's lives of wasted effort by involving everyone in the processes of improvement; improving the effectiveness of work so that results are achieved in less time. The methods and techniques used in TQM can be applied throughout the organization. They are equally useful to finance, sales, marketing, distribution, development, manufacturing, public relations, personnel, to every one of a company's activities. TQM needs to gain ground rapidly and become a way of life in many organizations.

2.2 Commitment to quality

To be successful in promoting business efficiency and effectiveness, TQM must be truly company-wide and it must start at the top with the Chief Executive, or equivalent, the most senior directors, and management, who must all demonstrate that they are serious about quality. The middle management have a particularly important role to play, they must not only grasp the principles of TQM, they must go on to explain them to the people for whom they are responsible, and ensure that their own commitment is communicated. Only then will TQM spread effectively throughout the organization. This level of management must also ensure that the efforts and achievements of their subordinates obtain the recognition, attention and reward that they deserve.

At the introductory stage, it is necessary for everyone in the organization to examine their feelings with respect to quality. Do they want to improve their activities, the company, the prospects for success? It cannot be said too often that to be successful TQM must involve everyone in all departments.

If the Chief Executive of an organization accepts the responsibility for and commitment to a quality policy, this action alone will offer a broad approach extending well beyond the accepted formalities of the disciplines required in the quality assurance function. It creates in turn responsibilities for interaction between the marketing, design, producing, purchasing, distribution and service functions. Within each and every department of the company at all levels, starting at the top, basic changes of attitude will be required to operate TQM. If the owners or directors of the organization do not recognize and accept their responsibilities for the initiation and operation of TQM, then these necessary changes will not happen. Controls and techniques are important in TQM, but they are not the primary requirement. It is more an attitude of mind, based on pride in the job, and requiring total commitment from the top, which must then be extended to all employees at all levels and in all departments.

Senior management commitment must be obsessional, not lip service. It is possible to detect real commitment, it shows on the shop floor, in the offices – at the point of operation. Going into organizations sporting poster campaigning for quality instead of belief, one is quickly able to detect the falseness. The people are told not to worry if quality problems arise, 'just do the best you can', 'the customer will never notice'. The contrast of a company where total quality means something can be seen, heard, felt. Things happen at this operating interface as a result of *real* commitment. Material problems are corrected with suppliers, equipment difficulties are put right by improved maintenance programmes or re-placement, people are trained, change takes place.

2.3 Policy on quality

A sound quality policy, together with the organization and facilities to put it into effect, is a fundamental requirement, if an organization is to begin to implement TQM. Every organization should develop and state its policy on quality, together with arrangements for its implementation. The contents of the policy should be made known to all employees. The preparation and implementation of a properly thought out quality policy, together with continuous monitoring, makes for smoother production or operation, minimises errors and reduces waste.

Everyone, from executives to the youngest and newest entrants in the organization, has a part to play in TQM, and one of the principal aims of an effective quality policy is to ensure that quality becomes everyone's concern. The traditional approach to many transformation processes, of depending on 'production' to make the product and 'quality control' to inspect it and divert that output which does not meet the requirements, is wasteful, because it allows time and materials to be invested in products or services which are not always saleable. This postproduction inspection is expensive, unreliable and uneconomical.

The more effective strategy of avoiding waste by not producing unsale-able output in the first place sounds sensible and obvious to most people. It is often captured in slogans such as: 'quality – right first time'. This type of campaigning is, however, not enough on its own. What is required is an understanding of the elements of a systematic control system which is designed to the prevention of products or services which do not conform to requirements. Management must be dedicated to the ongoing im-provement of quality, not simply a one-step improvement to an acceptable plateau. These ideas must be set out in a *quality policy* which requires top management to:

1 establish an 'organization' for quality;
2 identify the customer's needs and perception of needs;
3 assess the ability of the organization to meet these needs economically;
4 ensure that bought-out materials and services reliably meet the required standards of performance and efficiency;
5 concentrate on the prevention rather than detection philosophy;
6 educate and train for quality improvement;
7 review the quality management systems to maintain progress.

The quality policy must be publicized and understood at all levels of the organization.

Given below are six examples of good company quality policies. Each have their own style and impact and, hopefully, are consistent with the other policies within the companies.

Quality policy A

1 Quality improvement is primarily a task and responsibility of management as a whole.
2 In order to involve everyone in the company in quality improvement, management must enable all employees – and not only the employees in the factories – to participate in the preparation, implementation and evaluation of activities.
3 Quality improvement must be tackled and followed up systematically and in a planned manner. This applies to every part of our organization.
4 Quality improvement must be a continuous process.
5 Our organization must concentrate more than ever on its customers and users, both outside and inside the company.
6 The performance of our competitors must be known to all relevant units.
7 Important suppliers will have to be more closely involved in our quality policy. This relates to both external and internal suppliers of goods as well as of resources and services.
8 Widespread attention will be given to education and training. Existing education and training activities will be assessed, also, with regard to their contribution to the quality policy.
9 Publicity must be given to this quality policy in every part of the company in such a way that everyone can understand it. All available methods and media will be used for internal and external promotion and for communication.

10 Reporting on the progress of the implementation of the policy will be a permanent point on the agenda in review meetings.

Quality policy B

The board considers the quality aspects of our business to be of great importance, as only products and services leading to lasting customer satisfaction safeguard the continuity of the company.

Management practices and employee work activity will, without exception, promote on-time delivery of products to our customers, which are in conformance with requirements and competitively priced. In addition, the company is committed to a policy of 'right first time' and to a policy of continuous improvement in the quality of products and services.

Site Quality Manuals will be prepared accurately and adequately to describe the application of this corporate quality programme.

The requirements of the quality programme shall be fully applied by all company personnel.

Quality policy C

- The goal of the organization is to achieve superior external and internal customer satisfaction levels. Each employee's commitment to quality improvement and management's further commitment to implementation of supporting managerial and operating systems is essential to realizing that goal.
- Quality is defined by the customer; the customer needs products and services that, throughout their life, meet his or her needs and expectations at a cost that represents value.
- Quality excellence can best be achieved by preventing problems rather than by detecting and correcting them after they occur.
- All work that is done by company employees, suppliers and product outlets is part of a process that creates a product or service for a customer. Each person can influence some part of that process and therefore, affect the quality of its output and ultimate customer's satisfaction with our products and services.
- Sustained quality excellence requires continuous improvement. This means, regardless of how good present performance may be, it can become better.
- People provide the intelligence and generate the actions that are necessary to realize these improvements.
- Each employee is a customer for work done by other employees or suppliers, with a right to expect good work from others and an obligation to contribute work of high calibre to those who, in turn, are his or her customers.

• Each activity is responsible for reviewing its existing systems and procedures and for revising them, as required, in line with this policy statement.

Quality policy D

General statement:
Customer satisfaction is vital – the company must meet the requirements in terms of products and service.

There is a need, therefore, to establish the customer requirements and respond quickly and effectively.

The policy of the Company:
To provide high-quality products and services that fully meet the customer requirements. The Company believes in the concept of customer–supplier working together for continual improvements in quality.

The statement from the Board:
The organization for quality – A director has been given responsibility for quality improvement. The responsibility for quality throughout the Company must, however, remain with the individual.

Marketing will strive to determine the quality requirements and will respond to changes. There will be an effective Marketing/Production interface to achieve products that fully meet requirements. The performance of the Company's competitors will be known to all operating units.

Specifications which describe the requirements will be established. An understanding of the performance requirements will be translated into technical specifications. This will require effective collaboration between Marketing, Research and Development and Production.

Purchasing will assure that bought-out materials and services reliably meet the required standards of performance and efficiency. Suppliers will be closely involved in the quality policy.

Documentation – written procedures for all aspects of the Company's operations will be established and maintained. Records of all relevant data will be kept and used to meet the objectives of the policy.

Process control – the company has a philosophy of prevention of failure and it will establish programmes which encourage the control of key process variables, and move away from the simple detection of errors and failure.

Standards of production – consistency of products and service is a prime objective of the Company policy. This will be assisted by the establishment of standards for all aspects of production.

External and internal failure to achieve the requirements will be critically examined and corrective action taken to prevent recurrence.

Quality-related costs, particularly those related to nonconformance to requirements, will be recorded and examined to identify critical areas for improvement.

Distribution of products and service will be managed to achieve reliable storage, transport and distribution to meet the customer requirements.

Education for quality will start at the most senior management of the Company and all personnel will be made aware of the aims of quality improvement. Education and training needs will be established and widespread attention will be given to fulfilling them. All employees will participate in the training programme.

Reviews – regular reviews of the management systems will take place to maintain progress and implementation of the quality policy.

Publicity will be given to the quality improvement in every part of the organization.

Quality policy E

The Company is dedicated to a quality policy which will ensure that its products and services meet the requirements of its customers at all times.

It is the Company's intention to become and remain the market leader with respect to the quality of its products and services.

The Company believes in the concept of customer and supplier working together in pursuing this policy and in continually striving for improvements in quality.

All the Company's employees must have a positive commitment to quality and respond quickly and effectively to achieve the performance standards required of them and to 'get it right first time'.

The quality policy is based on four fundamental principles:

1 The definition of quality is conforming to requirements, having specified very carefully the needs of our customers, our suppliers and our own processes.
2 The system of quality management concentrates on prevention, looking at our processes, identifying the opportunities for error and taking action to eliminate them.
3 The standard of quality is 'no failures', everyone understanding how to do their job, the standards required, and doing it right first time.

4 The measurement of quality is the cost of nonconformity and the eventual cost of getting it right.

Each department will develop its own quality policies based on these principles, taking into account its own particular circumstances.

To ensure the policy is fully implemented each department is responsible for specifying the customers' requirements (which could be another department within the Company), preparing adequate procedures, and for providing the facilities to see that these requirements are met.

The quality policy involves all employees and the principles and objectives will be communicated as widely as possible. Practical assistance and training will be given, where necessary, to ensure the relevant knowledge and experience is acquired for successful implementation of this policy.

Quality policy F

Total quality is meeting customers' requirements
- both external and internal
- for all products and services
- all the time

This requires:
- total involvement of all employees
- total management commitment
- customer and supplier working together
- objectives, standards and systems which conform to the commitment to total quality

It is achieved by:
- conforming to requirements
- prevention not detection
- getting it right first time
- measuring quality performance (including costs)

Total quality is to be a permanent feature of the Company's life. It will be implemented, monitored, nurtured and maintained by having an ongoing quality improvement programme.

2.4 Achieving the 'mind set'

Any organization which accepts failure in its operations will inevitably proceed to try to inspect in quality, to detect and stop defective work reaching the customer. Any inspection or checking process will be nothing more than a filter, dividing the failure between external failure –

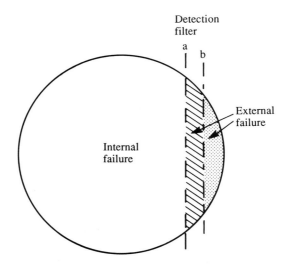

Figure 2.1   *The acceptance of failure and its detection*

that which still reaches the customer and causes complaints, returns, claims, lost business, etc. – and internal failure – that which has to be repeated, scrapped, reworked, repaired, rechecked, etc. (Figure 2.1a). In this situation, the common reaction to customer returns or complaints is to shift the filter to the right by more inspection and detection (Figure 2.1b), resulting possibly in a reduction of external problems, but increasing the internal ones.

The replacement of detection by the totally different strategy of prevention, through better input and process control, will apply pressure to the outside of the failure circle causing a shrinkage of both internal and external difficulties. As the circle contracts further and further through adoption of never-ending improvement, the picture becomes one of a target, the centre of which is zero failure – error-free transformation processes (Figure 2.2). If the concept of zero failure is not adopted, at least as the target, then it certainly will never be achieved.

The impact of TQM on an organization is firstly to ensure that the management adopt a strategic overview of quality. The approach must focus on developing the prevention mentality. It is easy to underestimate the effort that is required to change attitudes and approaches. Many people will need to undergo a complete change of 'mind-set' to unscramble their intuition which rushes into the detection/inspection mode to solve quality problems; 'we have a quality problem, we had better check every letter, take two samples out of each sack, check every widget twice', etc.

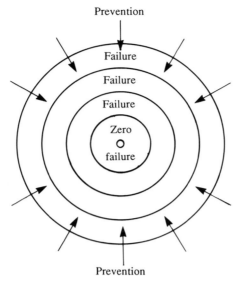

Figure 2.2 *The prevention of failure*

The correct mind set may be achieved by looking at the sort of barriers which exist in key areas. Staff will need to be trained and shown how to reallocate their time and energy to searching for causes of problems, and correcting the causes, not the symptoms, hopefully once and for all. This will require of management a positive, thrusting initiative to promote the 'right first time' approach to work situations. Through quality improvement teams, which will need to be set up, these actions will reduce naturally the inspection–rejection syndrome. If things are done correctly first time round, the usual problems which create the need for inspection for failure will disappear. There will be a shift away from the error consciousness.

The management of many firms may think that their scale of operation is not sufficiently large, that their resources too slim, or that the need for action is not important enough to justify implementing TQM. Before arriving at such a conclusion, however, it is suggested that the existing quality performance should be examined by asking the following questions:

- Is any attempt being made to assess the costs arising from errors, defects, waste, customer complaints, lost sales, etc.? If so, are these costs minimal or insignificant?
- Is the standard of quality management adequate and are attempts made to ensure that quality is given proper consideration at the design stage?

- Are the company's quality systems, documentation, procedures, operations, etc., in good order?
- Have personnel been trained in how to prevent errors and quality problems? Do they anticipate and correct potential causes of problems, or do they find and reject?
- Do job instructions contain the necessary quality elements, are they kept up-to-date, and are employees doing their work in accordance with the instructions in the most economical way?
- What is being done to motivate and train employees to do work right the first time?
- How many errors, defects, how much wastage occurred last year? Is this more or less than the previous year?

If satisfactory answers can be given to most of these questions, an organization can be satisfied that it is already well on the way to using adequate quality procedures and management. Even so it may well find that the introduction of TQM causes it to reappraise quality activities throughout. If answers to the above questions indicate problem areas, it will be beneficial to review the top management's attitude to quality. Time and money spent on quality-related activities are *not* limitations of profitability, they make significant contributions towards greater efficiency and enhanced profits.

Control

The effectiveness of an organization and its people depends on the extent to which each performs his/her role and moves towards common goals and objectives. Control is the process by which information or feedback is provided so as to keep all functions on track, being the sum total of the activities which increase the probability that the planned results will be achieved. Control mechanisms fall into three categories, depending upon their position in the managerial process:

Before the fact	Operational	After the fact
Strategic plans	Observation	Annual reports
Action plans	Inspection and correction	Variance reports
Budgets	Progress review	Audits
Job descriptions	Staff meetings	Surveys
Individual performance objectives	Internal information and data systems	Performance review
Training and development plans	Training programmes	Evaluation of training

Many organizations use after-the-fact controls, causing managers to take a reactive rather than a proactive position. Such 'crisis-orientation' needs to be replaced by a more anticipative one in which the focus is on preventive or before-the-fact controls.

Attempting to control performance through systems, procedures, or techniques external to the individual is not an effective approach since it relies on 'controlling' others; individuals should be responsible for their own actions. An externally based control system can result in a high degree of concentrated effort in a specific area if the system is overly structured, but it can also cause negative consequences to surface:

1 Since all rewards are based on external measures, which are imposed, the 'team members' often focus all their efforts on the measure itself, i.e. to have it set lower (or higher) than possible, to manipulate the information which serves to monitor it, or to dismiss it as someone else's goal not theirs. In the budgeting process, for example, distorted figures are often submitted by those who have learned that their 'honest projections' will be altered automatically anyway.
2 When the rewards are dependent on only one or two limited targets, all efforts are directed at those, even at the expense of others. If short-term profitability is the sole criterion for bonus distribution or promotion, it is likely that investment for longer-term growth areas will be substantially reduced by those involved. Similarly, strong emphasis and reward for output or production may result in lowered quality.
3 The fear of not being rewarded, or even being criticized, for performance that is less than desirable, may cause some to withhold information that is unfavourable but nevertheless should be flowing into the system.
4 When reward and punishment is used to motivate performance, the degree of risk taking may lessen and be replaced by a more cautious and conservative approach. In essence, the fear of failure replaces the desire to achieve.

The following situations have been observed by the author and his colleagues within companies which have taken part in research on quality management:

1 Goals are imposed which are seen or known to be unrealistic. If the goals perceived by the subordinate are in fact accomplished then the subordinate has proved himself wrong. This clearly has a negative effect on the effort expended, since few people are motivated to prove themselves wrong!
2 Where individuals are stimulated to commit themselves to a goal, and where their personal pride and self-esteem are at stake, then the level

of motivation is at a peak. For most people the toughest critic and the hardest taskmaster they confront is not their immediate boss, but themselves.

3 Directors and managers are often afraid of allowing subordinates to set the goals for fear of them being set too low, or loss of control over subordinate behaviour. It is also true that many do not wish to set their own targets but prefer to be told what is to be accomplished.

TQM is concerned with moving the focus of control from outside the individual to within; the objective being to make everyone accountable for their own performance, and to get them committed to attaining quality in a highly motivated fashion. The assumptions a director or manager must make in order to move in this direction are simply that people do not need to be coerced to perform well, that work is natural, and that people want to achieve, accomplish, influence activity, and challenge their abilities. If there is belief in this, then only the technique remains to be discussed.

Total quality management is user driven, it cannot be imposed from outside the organization, as perhaps a quality system standard or statistical process control. This means that the ideas for improvement must come from those with knowledge and experience of the methods and techniques. And this has massive implications for training and follow-up. TQM is not a cost-cutting or productivity improvement device and it must not be used as such. Although the effects of a successful programme will certainly include these benefits, TQM is concerned chiefly with changing attitudes and skills so that the culture of the organization becomes one of preventing failure and the norm is operating right first time.

3 Organization for quality

3.1 Personnel and the organizational structure

A company in the mechanical engineering industry had developed the outline organizational structure shown in Figure 3.1. The great big crack down the middle did not appear on the paper version, only in the reality. Contrary to some opinion, the way we set down an organization on paper *does* affect the way people behave. It casts them in roles, sets them with or against others, and even provides them with short-term objectives. When the role of the quality function clearly appears on paper as a high-ranking police force, set up to stop defective produce reaching the external customer, it is usually a reflection of the message which has been transmitted to the producing departments – output, output, output. It is this message alone which causes responsible, honourable people in production or operations to behave in a quite peculiar way and try to send or transfer to the customer defective material, poor service, error-ridden information, paperwork, invoices, etc., in order to reach output targets. Human beings will respond, like any other animals, to various stimuli. If these are all related to quantity then quality will be seen to be of secondary importance.

Unfortunately, this will have far more wide-ranging effects than merely creating conflict between the producers and 'quality control'. It will strip the whole organization of the opportunity to manage quality at every interface, at every level, within and across all functional areas.

Clearly, the only point at which the responsibility for quality can lie is with the department or person that actually does the job. Abdication of this responsibility can be generated easily by the creation of a separate and elitist army of inspectors, checkers, measurers and testers. To make sure that the responsibility stays where it belongs, it is first necessary to arrange the people in their roles on the organogram. Of course, this simple act will not ensure a quality-ever-after life together, but it will give people and the organization a chance.

The organization of many companies reflects their concentration on the relatively narrow area of inspection or checking oriented quality assurance. The very title 'quality manager' is a misnomer when it is

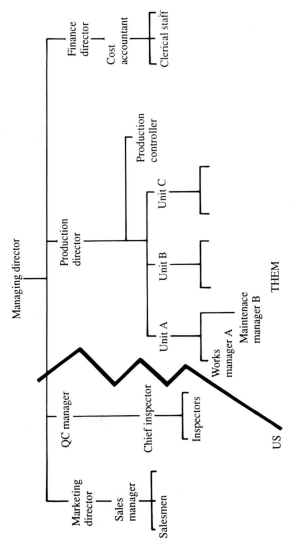

Figure 3.1 *The US and THEM organization for quality*

associated solely with the management of product or service quality. There is no way that one person or one department can manage quality, but one person, the chief executive, must take on the overall responsibility. A major thrust of TQM is to have the quality department spending more time helping to prevent rather than inspecting or correcting errors. Resources can then be redeployed from firefighting activities and the organizational culture can gradually change to reflect the error-free-work method of operation.

To transform quality into a strategic business planning and management dimension, a new role must be created for the quality function, a role which is similar to that of a navigator on a ship. After preparing a course for the chief executive, the captain, the navigator 'manages' the route and the progress. When the ship is off course, he does not stride onto the bridge, elbow the helmsman in the ribs and start turning the ship's wheel. That is not his role. He is the provider of systems and guidance but responsibility lies firmly and squarely on the shoulders of the captain and each of his colleagues for doing their job right the first time.

3.2 Define responsibilities

The establishment of positive quality policy objectives within an organization must be accompanied by the clear allocation of responsibilities within the management structure. It is generally accepted that the primary operational responsibility for ensuring that the quality chain does not break must rest with line management, and in particular there are two key areas which require attention:

1 Senior executive level. Direct responsibility for the general management of quality should be included in the duties of one of the senior executives in the same way that a director may be allocated overall responsibility for production, marketing, or safety. Undivided line management responsibility for quality often stops at some point in the middle-management ladder, further up the responsibility tends to become diffused and uncertain. Quality must be treated like any other major managerial function, with a clear line of responsibility and command running up to an accountable individual at the top of the organization.

2 First-line supervision level. The other critical level is the supervisor who is 'on the spot' and in a position to know whether the supplier/customer interfaces are working satisfactorily in practice, and his/her influence can be dramatic. The promotion of quality is first and

foremost a matter of efficient management. The first level supervision has a responsibility to:

- instruct subordinates in the appropriate methods and procedures;
- inform them of likely causes of errors or defects and the preventive methods necessary;
- supervise the arrangement of such methods and instructions in the quality system;
- initiate any steps necessary to improve methods, equipment, materials, conditions, in the work area for which he/she is responsible.

Line managers and supervisors can improve their effectiveness as 'instructors' if they themselves have been trained in 'how to instruct'.

As with other areas, such as productivity and safety, real progress in quality is impossible without the full cooperation and commitment of all employees. If they are to accept their full share of responsibility, however, they must be able to participate fully in the making and monitoring of arrangements for achieving the requirements at their place of work. Some organizations have arrangements whereby all employees in a particular unit meet periodically for discussions about quality – sometimes called 'quality circles' (see Chapter 12). This 'total involvement' approach stresses the need for the participation of every individual employee.

The feeling of responsibility must be engendered in all employees to:

- follow the agreed written procedures;
- use materials and equipment correctly and as instructed;
- draw attention to existing or potential quality problems and report all errors, defects and waste;
- suggest ways in which risks of errors or quality problems could be reduced;
- assist in the training of new entrants and young people, particularly by setting a good example.

An effective method of achieving general cooperation, interest and involvement in quality should be established by formal arrangements for *quality improvement teams*. This will vary from organization to organization and depend on particular circumstances on the site, e.g. its size and location, the composition of the workforce, and processes operated (see Chapter 12).

Department purpose analysis

'Quality is everyone's business' is an often-quoted cliché, but 'everything is everyone's business', and so quality often becomes nobody's business.

The responsibility for quality begins with the determination of the customer's quality requirements and continues until the service or product is accepted by a satisfied customer. The 'department purpose analysis' (DPA) technique, developed by IBM, helps to define clearly the real purpose of each department with the objective of improving performance. It leads to an understanding and agreement on the key activities of each group. The department can then liaise with its immediate 'suppliers' and 'customers', often internally, to identify potential or actual problem areas and simultaneously carry out an analysis of what proportion of time is spent on the key activities.

Group discussions, during the DPA process usually yield many good ideas for improvement, either eliminating wasteful activity, or improving the quality of output from the department. Everyone becomes and should then remain aware of the prime purpose of the department, and the focus on efficiency and reducing waste usually carries through to all work activities. The manager of the department, who should run the exercise, must understand the DPA process and why it is necessary and important. He/she needs to be open-minded towards change and to encourage departmental staff to question whether all their activities add value to the product, service, or business. One of the greatest barriers to improvements through DPA is the '. . . but we've always done it that way . . .' response.

The basic steps of DPA are:

1 Form the DPA group.
2 Brainstorm to list all the departmental tasks (see Chapter 10).
3 Agree which are the five main tasks.
4 Define the position and role of the departmental manager.
5 Review the major activities and for each one identify the 'customer(s)' and 'supplier(s)'.
6 Consult with the customer(s) and supplier(s) completing a suitable questionnaire, an example of which is given on pages 32 and 33.
  This is very similar to the list of questions suggested in Chapter 1 for interrogating any customer/supplier interface.
7 Review the customer/supplier survey results and brainstorm how improvements can be made.
8 Prioritize improvements to list those to be tackled first, and plan how.
9 Implement the improvement action plan, maintaining encouragement and support.
10 Review the progress made and repeat the DPA.

As with any new group activity, some successes are desirable early in the programme, if the department is to build confidence in its ability to make improvements and solve problems. For this reason, DPA should

Department purpose analysis (DPA) questionnaire

Part 1

Function/Business Unit	Dept:	No:

Task Ref.	Task list	Proportion of time taken
1 2 3 4 5 6 7 8 9 10 11 12 13 14 15		
Misc.		
	Total (must be <100%)	

confine itself, initially at least, to resolving issues which are within its control. It is unlikely, for example, that a sales team will be successful in getting a product redesigned in its first improvement project. Experience at IBM shows that, as confidence builds through continued management encouragement, the DPA groups will tackle increasingly difficult business problems, with an increasing return of the investment in time.

Such an analysis will lead to specific duties associated with the various management functions identifiable within the organization. An example of the output from the first part of step 6 of a DPA is given below. Some of the activities are shared and, therefore, appear under several functions:

Marketing

- Determination of customer requirements.
- Gaining knowledge of the competitors' quality performance.

Part 2

Activity	Dept No.	Date

Customer

Have you seen your customer recently to determine their needs?

Yes   No

What are they?

How do you/should you measure your output quality?

What is the impact of non-conformity?

Supplier

Have you seen your supplier recently to determine your needs?

Yes   No

What are they?

How do you/should you measure your input quality?

What is the impact of non-conformity?

- Setting of product and service specifications.
- Analysis of customer complaints, returns, sales staff reports, warranty claims, and product liability cases.
- Downgrading of products or services for sale as seconds, etc.

Research and development and design

- Designing or inventing the product or service to meet the customer requirements.
- Setting of appropriate specifications (including purchased materials, processes, products and services).
- Preproduction and prototype trials.
- Design and specification of inspection and checking equipment.
- Analysis of some rework and rectification problems.
- Downgrading of products and services.
- Analysis of products or service complaints and warranty claims.

Production or operations

- Agreeing specifications.
- Preproduction and prototype trials.
- Training of operations and associated personnel, including supervisors, foremen, etc.
- Special handling and storage during production or operation.
- Supervision and control of quality at all stages.
- Line or process control.
- Finished product or service control.
- Analysis of scrapped, reworked, rectified, replaced and downgraded products and services.

Purchasing

- Vendor rating and supplier approval.
- Procuring of materials and services which meet the requirements of the organization.

Service (including after sales and technical)

- Product and service specification and performance evaluation.
- Preproduction and prototype product or service evaluation.
- Analysis of customer complaints and returns.

Stores, transport and distribution
- Special handling and storage.

- Receiving and checking of materials, bought-out items and services.
- Checking and despatching of finished products and replacement goods.
- Receiving, checking and sorting of returned products for replacement or repair.

Quality assurance or management
- Quality planning.
- Quality advice and expertise.
- Management of the quality systems.
- Training of personnel.
- Analysis of customer complaints, warranty claims and product liability cases.

A quality management system based on the fact that all functions share responsibility for quality, provides an effective method of acquiring and maintaining the desired performance standards. The 'quality department' should not assume direct responsibility for quality but should support, advise and audit the work of the other functions, in much the same way as a financial auditor performs his duty without assuming responsibility for the profitability of the company.

The responsibility for actual control of quality during the operation of the transformation process, whether that be the production of artefacts, delivery of a service or the passing of information internally, rests squarely on the shoulders of the operators of the process. They must ensure that all the appropriate concepts and techniques are applied to this task. Organizationally, this means that staff carrying out the work must be given the tools to enable the requirements to be met. The control of quality involves the quality of input materials, methods, equipment, processes and the appropriate instructions designed for the purpose of preventing failure. To enable the responsibility to be met, organizations must use every device practicable to prevent, detect and correct errors that occur. This implies that, to achieve the control of quality, the variables which may affect quality and which can result from the actions of human beings, the nature of materials, and the performance of equipment, must all be controlled.

The process of performance management

Managers are in control only when they have created a system and climate in which their subordinates can exercise self-control. Mechanisms may then be created to provide clear performance standards in all areas, backed by appropriate job descriptions and training, to ensure those standards are achieved. The process of performance management consists then of:

1 clarifying responsibilities;
2 developing performance indicators and objectives;
3 preparing action plans.

1 *Clarifying responsibilities*

If job descriptions have been written for the organization, they may serve as a starting point for clarifying each individual's role. It should be emphasized, however, that these need to be updated and reviewed with each subordinate to ensure their relevancy. The format of job descriptions is not of critical importance although they must be standardized for a particular organization. They should contain a statement of the overall purpose, reporting relationships, responsibility and priorities. Agreement must be reached on the priorities – frequently managers or directors expect the major emphasis to be on activities, 2, 5, 6, 7, when the subordinate perceives the critical areas to be 1, 3, 4 and 8.

Organizational problems which require role clarification will not be resolved by the introduction of job descriptions alone. Some of the other factors which prevent groups functioning smoothly are:

  (i) poor communication of information to other departments, groups or individuals in time for it to be useful;
 (ii) lack of understanding of where decisions are taken or goals set;
(iii) low involvement of other departments, groups or individuals in reaching decisions;
(iv) lack of appreciation of the role of other departments, groups or individuals in reaching goals or targets;
 (v) failure to identify and use systems, methods, or techniques for specific activities;
(vi) absence of corrective action, following identification of weaknesses and problems;
(vii) lack of recognition of role of training and follow-up.

To address some of these problems a responsibility chart should be developed for the organization. An example is given on page 37, which identifies levels of authority, responsibility, and inter-relationships with all the management team members.

W Performs the work. Includes decision making necessary in the performance of the work and uses appropriate techniques.
A Must approve action taken or decision made.
C Must be consulted before action is taken or decision made. Advice significant, but not binding.

Responsibility Chart

	1	2	3	4	5	6	7	8	9	10	11
1 Manages the corporation to achieve profit and other stated goals.	W										
2 Establishes and executes overall operating policies for the company.	W	C			C				C	C	
3 Establishes overall company financial, sales, and production goals.	W	C							C	C	
4 Prepares quarterly operating statements.	N								W		N
5 Maximizes sales volume consistent with company policy and profitability.	S	W	D								
6 Supervises field people.		S	W	C							
7 Hires immediate subordinates.	W	W			W			W	W	W	
8 Operates plant to produce quality product at minimum costs to meet schedules.	S				W						
9 Maintains projected level of production.					W						
10 Determines inventory levels.	N		C		A	W		C			
11 Purchases capital equipment upon receipt of purchase requisition.	A				C		C	W	C		

1 General Manager
2 Marketing–Sales Manager
3 Field Sales Manager
4 Sales Service Manager
5 Manufacturing Manager
6 Production Control Supervisor
7 Plant Superintendent
8 Purchasing Manager
9 Controller–Office Manager
10 Personnel Manager
11 Cost Accountant

D   Makes decisions on those matters submitted to him to resolve internal conflicts.

N   Must be notified via direct communication of actions taken and decisions made by 'W' person.

S   Supervises but does not perform the work. Plans, organizes and coordinates work: maintains contact with those doing the work. Trains and instructs employees.

The important aspect of this method is its team-building impact within each operational group. All participants have the opportunity to review their current roles, seek to change those aspects for which they perceive valid cause, and become more involved in those areas where they feel their inputs would have merit.

2 *Developing performance indicators and objectives*

Although the responsibilities clarify what is to be performed, they do not define how well the tasks are expected to be performed. Performance indicators, therefore, are the means by which performance will be evaluated. To be meaningful they must be:

(a) Measurable. Indicators must lead to performance objectives which are quantifiable and tangible. Achievements in these areas must be recordable, verifiable, and observable. Areas such as quantity or quality of output, time schedules, costs, ratios, or percentages would be examples of measurable indicators.

(b) Relevant. Indicators must serve as a linkage between specific areas of responsibilities and the individual performance objectives to monitor achievement. They must describe what is the expected role of the position – the critical areas of performance.

(c) Important. Indicators need not be defined for every area of responsibility. They should be developed for those activities which have a significant impact on the results for the individual, department, and the organization.

The establishment of performance objectives provides clear direction and communication of expected levels of achievement. The process is a joint one – an interaction between the manager and his/her subordinates. If full commitment on the part of both parties is to be realized, the targets should be negotiated in the form of a performance 'contract'. Once the indicators have been agreed, the specific results desired need to be decided. The greater the participation, the greater the motivation to achieve. Agreed performance objectives should, therefore, contain the following ingredients:

(a) Participatively developed

(b) Challenging but attainable

(c) Clear statements of performance expectations

(d) Within the individual's scope of control

(a) *Participation* An interaction which leads to mutual agreement provides a good exchange of ideas between the manager and his/her subordinates. The results are not a compromise but should be the outcome of a persuasive but logical presentation of why such an outcome is plausible. Discussions should be analytical, not emotional, and deal with both sides of an issue if there are significant differences. The crucial factors in examining the advantages of this approach are:

Involvement → Commitment → Personal → Higher drive
                                 responsibility   to achieve

rather than:

Imposition → Lack of → External → Lower drive
                   acceptance responsibility to achieve

(b) *Challenge* A well-set performance objective is one which is attainable but yet requires stretching. The achiever sets targets which involve moderate risk. When the likelihood of success is 65 per cent to 85 per cent, the inner sense of challenge is at its peak. As this probability decreases or increases from this range, the motive to achieve is reduced. The former makes the risk too great, since the target becomes perceived as unrealistic and self-esteem is lowered. The latter sets the risk as too low and if success is 'guaranteed', the pay-off value attached to attainment is reduced.

When individuals press for objectives which are either too low or too high, they tend to be motivated more by a fear of failure than the need to achieve. Those in this category either want the target to be fail-safe and, hence, be assured of success or else want to set a target so high that no-one really takes their goals seriously.

To deal most effectively with either of these personalities, the performance objectives which are established should be of three levels: minimally acceptable, above average, and excellent. A person need not negotiate the minimal acceptable level since this is the least level of performance to maintain employment. The other levels can be discussed to arrive at realistic but challenging targets. Once they have been agreed upon, the choice of which path to follow is that of the subordinate – and the rewards can be similarly distributed.

(c) *Clarity of expectation* The target should be objectively expressed and be tied to a specific time framework. Expressions such as 'approximate, minimum, maximum, adequate, none, 100 per cent, or as soon as possible' are vague and should be avoided. Descriptive, evaluative terms such as 'frequently, seldom, usually, etc., are also open to misinterpretation.

(d) *Scope of control* The performance of the responsibility must be within the limits of authority that have been delegated. An individual cannot be reasonably held responsible for activities that cannot be directly controlled or influenced. For example, a production manager's performance objective of reviewing and accounting for the variation between budgeted and actual performance by the fifth working day of the month may not be adequately expressed, since the input for review may originate in data processing or accounting, rather than the manager's own department. If this is so, he may have no control over the budgeting data being available in time for a review on that date. A better indicator might be the time from receipt of the input to the submission of the analysis and recommendation.

3 *Preparing action plans*

The process of planning is dealt with in detail in Chapter 5. It is clear that some form of action plan, perhaps in the form of a bar chart or Gantt chart (see also Chapter 7), is required to enable the objectives to be reached. The plans should stipulate action by the individuals concerned and be reviewed periodically against the milestones set down.

Improvements can only take place in relation to established standards with the improvements then being incorporated into the new standards. Peformance standards in operational areas must be complemented by standards in all functional areas. *Competitive benchmarking*, one of the most transferrable aspects of Rank Xerox's approach to total quality management, measures a company's operations, products and services against those of its competitors in a ruthless fashion. It is a means by which targets, priorities and operations can be established that will lead to competitive advantage. The concept requires every counterpart to 'benchmark' itself against the counterpart in the best competing companies. This includes a scrutiny of all aspects of:

marketing and sales
design
production operations
costs
distribution
after-sales service
organizational aspects
technology

within the department. The task is to work out what has to be done to make improvements on the competition's performance in each of these areas.

At regular (say weekly) meetings, managers discuss the results of the competitive benchmarking, and on a daily basis, departmental managers discuss quality problems with staff. One afternoon may be set aside for the benchmark meetings followed by a 'walkabout' when the manager observes directly the activities actually taking place and compares them mentally with the competitors' operations.

The process has ten major stages and these are all focused on trying to measure comparisons of competitiveness:

Plan
- Select department(s) for benchmarking
- Identify best competitor
- Identify benchmarks
- Decide information and data collection methodology

Analysis Compare the company and its competitors using the benchmark data

Develop Set performance level objectives
Develop action plans to achieve goals
Improve Implement specific actions

Review Monitor the results and improvements
Review the benchmarks

Benchmarking is very important in the administration areas, since it continuously measures services and practices against the equivalent operation in the toughest direct competitors or organization renowned as leaders in the area, even if they are in the same organization.

Technologies and conditions vary between different industries and markets, but the basic concept of quality management and the financial implications are of general validity. The objective should be to produce, at an acceptable cost, goods and services which conform to the requirements of the customer. The way to accomplish this is to use the TQM approach in the operating departments of: marketing, design, production or operations, quality assurance, purchasing, sales and others – nobody should be exempt. TQM is not a separate science or a unique theory of quality control; rather a strategic approach which generates the 'total' quality approach through individual and departmental responsibility.

3.3 The quality function and the quality manager

In many organizations, management systems are viewed in terms of the internal dynamics between marketing, design, production, distribution, accounting, etc. A change is required from this to a larger system which also encompasses and integrates the business interests of customers and suppliers. Management needs to develop an in-depth understanding of these relationships and how they may be used to cement the partnership concept. The quality function should be the organization's focal point in this respect and should be equipped to gauge internal and external customers' expectations and degree of satisfaction. It should also identify quality deficiencies in all business functions and promote improvements.

The role of the quality function is to make quality become an inseparable aspect of every employee's performance and responsibility. The transition in many companies from quality departments with line functions will require careful planning, direction, and monitoring. Quality professionals have developed numerous techniques and skills focussed on product or service quality. In many cases, there is a need to adapt these to broader applications. The first objectives for many 'quality managers' will be to gradually disengage themselves from line activities, which will then need to be dispersed throughout the appropriate operating departments. This should allow quality to evolve into a 'staff' department, at a senior level and to be concerned with the following throughout the organization:

- encouraging and facilitating quality improvement;
- monitoring and evaluating the progress of quality improvement;
- promoting the 'partnership' in quality, in relations with customers and suppliers;
- planning, managing, auditing, and reviewing quality systems;
- planning and providing quality training and counselling or consultancy;
- giving advice to management on the
  - establishment of quality systems and process control;
  - relevant statutory/legislative requirements with respect to quality;
  - quality improvement programmes necessary;
  - inclusion of quality elements in all job instructions and procedures.

Quality managers have an initial task, however, to help those who control the means to implement this concept – the leaders of industry and commerce – to really believe that quality must become an integral part of all the organization's operations.

The author has a vision of quality as a strategic business management function that will help organizations to change their cultures. To make this vision a reality, quality professionals must expand the application of quality concepts and techniques to all business processes and functions, and develop new forms of providing assurance of quality at every supplier–customer interface. They will need to know the entire 'production cycle' of products or services, from concept or raw materials to the ultimate end user. An example of this was observed in the case of a company manufacturing pharmaceutical seals, whose customer expressed concern about excess aluminium projecting below and round a particular type of seal. This was considered a cosmetic defect by the immediate customer, the health service, but a safety hazard by a blind patient – the *customer's customer*. The prevention of this 'curling' of excess metal involved changing practices at the mill which rolled the aluminium – at the *supplier's supplier*. Clearly the quality professional involved with this problem needed to understand the supplier's problems and the ultimate customer's needs, in order to judge whether the product was fit for use.

The shift in 'philosophy' will require considerable staff training in many organizations. Not only must people in other functions acquire quality-related skills, but quality personnel must change old attitudes and acquire new skills, replacing the inspection, calibration, specification-writing mentality with knowledge of defect prevention, wide-ranging quality systems design and audit. Clearly, the challenge for many quality professionals is not so much making changes in their organization as recognizing the changes which are required in themselves. It is more than an overnight job to change the attitudes of an inspection police force into those of a consultative, team-oriented improvement force. This emphasis on prevention and improvement-based systems elevates the role of quality professionals from a technical one to that of general management. A narrow departmental view of quality is totally out of place in an organization aspiring to TQM, and the typical quality managers will need to widen their perspective, and increase their knowledge to encompass all facets of the organization.

To introduce the concepts of operator self-inspection required for TQM, will require not only a determination to implement change but sensitivity and skills in industrial relations. This will depend very much, of course, on the climate within the organization. Those whose management is truly concerned with cooperation and concerned for the people will engage strong employee support for the quality manager or director in his catalytic role in the quality improvement implementation process. Those with aggressive, confrontational management will create for the quality professional impossible difficulties in obtaining support from the 'rank and file'.

Many organizations have realized the importance of the contribution which a senior, qualified quality manager can make to the prevention strategy. Smaller organizations may well feel that the cost of employing a full-time quality manager is not justified, other than in certain very high risk areas. In these cases a member of the management team should be appointed to operate on a part-time basis performing the quality management function in addition to his/her other duties. To obtain the best results from a quality manager, he/she should be given sufficient authority to take necessary action to secure the implementation of the organization's quality policy, and must have the personality to be able to communicate the message to all employees including staff, management and directors. Occasionally the quality manager may require some guidance and help on specific technical quality matters, and one of the major attributes required is the knowledge and wherewithal to acquire the necessary information and assistance.

3.4 Personnel selection

To obtain the appropriate people for the organization and to carry out the tasks necessary for TQM, the phases and activities of the selection procedure listed opposite and on page 46 should be followed:

A, B and C are products of the initial conceptual phase of a selection procedure (i.e. developing a person specification). In the subsequent recruitment, screening and selection phases predictive information (D) is collected, compared for 'fit' (E) with the person specification and a decision (F) is made.

3.5 Councils, committees and teams

To devise and implement a total quality management programme takes considerable time and ability. It must be given the status of a senior executive project. The creation of cost-effective quality improvement is difficult because of the need for full integration with the organization's operating philosophy and management systems. It may require an extensive review and maybe substantial revision of existing systems of management and ways of operating. Fundamental questions may have to be asked, such as: Do the managers have the necessary authority, capability, and time to carry this through?

Any review of existing management and operating systems will inevitably open many cans of worms and uncover problems that have been successfully buried and smoothed over, perhaps for years. Authority must be given to those charged with following TQM through with actions

Phases	Activities

Developing a person specification

Job analysis conduct a systematic analysis of the job to identify the specific tasks it entails and how they should be performed.

Job description write a full and accurate statement of what the job entails, indicating the activities/responsibilities of any incumbent and expected standards of performance.

Person specification develop a statement of the 'qualifications' required of any applicant (e.g. education, experience, personal characteristics) using the job description.

Recruitment

Advertise the job in an attractive manner through the appropriate media providing sufficient information to attract suitable applicants and to deter unsuitable ones.

Application form design a form to be completed by applicants which will provide the essential biographical and other data needed to determine their suitability, distribute copies to applicants with additional information about the job.

Screening

Use the 'topping and tailing' method to eliminate from further consideration applicants who lack appropriate qualifications, or who are too highly qualified, based upon data from application forms etc. Draw up a short-list.

Test applicants using valid and reliable psychological tests known to predict 'qualifications' in the person specification. (These tests may be used to aid initial screening but they must be administered by 'qualified' personnel.)

References obtain 'structured' references from referees on the suitability of applicants for the job. (Could be obtained for initial screening or after the interview.)

Selection

Interview applicants on short-list to check and clarify information already collected; obtain additional information from face-to-face encounter; answer questions; influence applicants (possibly) by persuading them of their suitability or otherwise for the job.

Decide which applicant(s), if any, is(are) suitable by matching information obtained from the application form, tests etc., with the requirements of the person specification, looking in particular for evidence of both the capacity and willingness to work to the required standards. The 'objective' information (e.g. educational qualifications past work record), should be given the greatest weight when making the decision.

Induction and training

Induction arrange an appropriate welcome and familiarization with the organization for all new employees, emphasizing the total quality approach.

Training in the systematic management of the work activities of new employees, when necessary, so that the information, attitudes, technical skills and other essential behaviours needed to perform their jobs effectively are acquired.

The key processes in this procedure may be represented as follows:

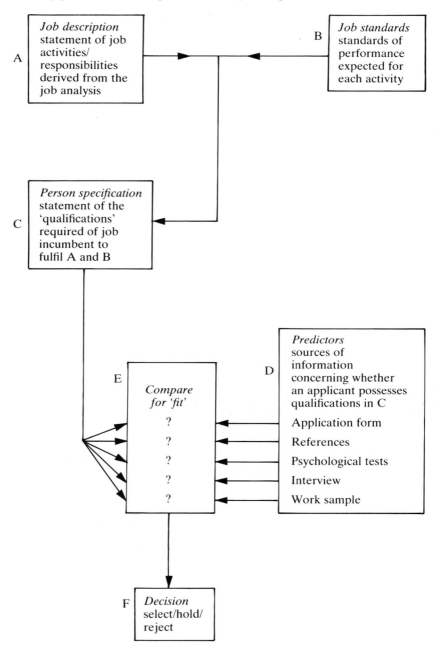

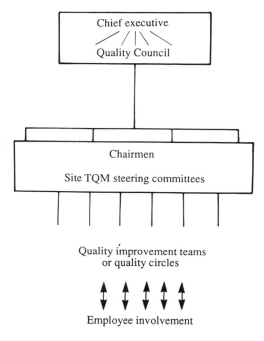

Figure 3.2 *Employee involvement through the TQM structure*

that they consider necessary to achieve the goals. The commitment will be continually questioned and will be weakened, perhaps destroyed, by the failure to delegate authoritatively.

The following steps are suggested in general terms. Clearly, different types of organizations will have need to make adjustments to the detail, but the component parts are the basic requirements. A disciplined approach to the organization of TQM may be established in a quality council and 'site' steering committees (Figure 3.2). The council should meet at least monthly to review strategy, implementation progress, and improvement. It should be chaired by the chief executive who must attend every meeting, illness alone should cause postponement. The council members should include the top management team and the chairmen of a number of site TQM steering committees, depending on the size of the organization. The objectives of the council are to:

- provide overall strategic direction on TQM for the organization;
- establish plans for TQM on each 'site';
- review and revise quality plans for implementation.

Each site TQM steering committee should also meet monthly, shortly before the council meetings. Every senior manager on a site should be a member of at least one steering committee. This system provides the 'top-down' support for employee involvement in quality through either a quality improvement team or a quality circle programme. It also ensures that the commitment to TQM at the top is communicated effectively through the organization.

The two-tier approach of council and steering committees allows the former to concentrate on quality strategy, rather than become a senior problem-solving group. Problem awareness is assured, however, if the steering committee chairmen are required to present a status report at each meeting. Detailed suggestions for running QITs are provided in Chapter 12.

In large organizations it may be necessary to make several specific appointments or to assign details to certain managers. Typically, the following actions may be deemed to be necessary:

1 Assign a TQM project manager
   This person will be responsible for the planning and implementation of TQM. He or she will be chosen first for project management ability, rather than detailed knowledge of quality assurance matters. Depending on the size and complexity of the organization, and its previous activities in quality management, the position may be either full or part-time, but it must report directly to the chief executive.

2 Appoint a quality management advisor
   A professional expert on quality management will be required to advise on the 'technical' aspects of planning and implementing TQM. This is a consultancy role and may be provided from within or without the organization, and may be full- or part-time. This person needs to be a persuader, philosopher, teacher, advisor, facilitator, reporter and motivator. He or she must clearly understand the organization, its processes and interfaces, be conversant with the key functional languages used in the business, and comfortable operating at many organizational levels. On a more general level, this person must fully understand, and be an effective advocate and teacher of TQM, be flexible and become an efficient agent of change.

Throughout a TQM programme, each function must develop its own conscience, and focus its efforts on quality improvement. Each needs to be given the encouragement, tools, and responsibility to achieve the requirements at the next interface.

4 Measurement (costs) of quality

4.1 Cost-effective quality management

Manufacturing a quality product, providing a quality service, or doing a quality job, one with a high degree of fitness for purpose, is not enough. The cost of achieving that quality must be carefully managed so that the long-term effect of quality costs on the business is a desirable one. These costs are a true measure of the quality effort. A competitive product or service based on a balance between quality and cost factors is the principal goal of responsible management. This objective, which is highlighted in Figure 4.1, is best accomplished with the aid of competent analysis of the costs of quality. The balance works like this: as quality goes down, costs go up, and as quality improves, costs will fall.

The analysis of quality costs is a significant management tool which provides:

- a method of assessing the overall effectiveness of the management of quality;
- a means of determining problem areas and action priorities.

The costs of quality are no different from any other costs in that, like the costs of maintenance, design, sales, production, and other activities, they can be budgeted, measured and analysed.

Having specified the quality of design, the operating units have the task of matching it. This comprises activities which will incur costs that may be separated into the categories of failure costs, appraisal costs and prevention costs. Failure costs can be further split into those resulting from internal and external failure.

Internal failure costs

These costs occur when the results of work fail to reach designed quality standards and are detected before transfer to the customer takes place. Internal failure includes:

Waste the activities associated with doing unnecessary work as the result of errors, poor organization, the wrong materials, etc.

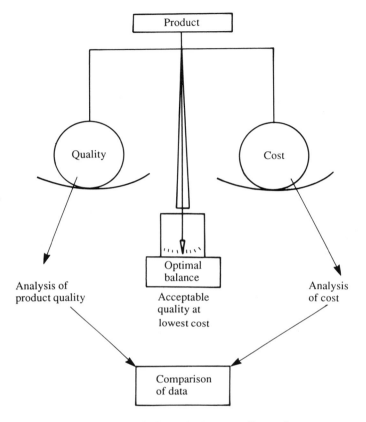

Figure 4.1 *The balance between quality and cost*

Scrap defective product which cannot be repaired, used or sold.

Rework or rectification the correction of defective material or errors to meet the requirements.

Reinspection the re-examination of products or work which has been rectified.

Downgrading product which is usable but does not meet specifications and may be sold as 'second quality' at a low price.

Excess inventory to cope with the 'reject factor' which is frequently built in.

Failure analysis the activity required to establish the causes of internal product or service failure.

External failure costs

These costs occur when the product or service from a process fails to reach design quality standards and is not detected until after transfer to the consumer. External failure includes:

Repair of either returned products or those in the field.

Warranty claims failed products which are replaced under guarantee.

Complaints all work and costs associated with handling and servicing of customers' complaints.

Returns the handling and investigation of rejected or recalled products, including freight charges.

Liability the result of product liability litigation and other claims, which may include change of contract.

External and internal failures produce the 'costs of getting it wrong'. Order re-entry, retyping, unnecessary travel and telephone calls, conflict, are just a few examples of the wastage or failure costs often excluded. The organization must be aware of the costs of getting it wrong. The financial management need to get some idea how much failure is costing, each year.

Appraisal costs

These costs are associated with the evaluation of purchased materials, processes, intermediates, products and services to assure conformance with the specifications. Appraisal includes:

Inspection checks and tests of incoming material, process set-up, first-offs, running processes, intermediates and final products, services, and includes product or service performance appraisal against agreed specifications, including reinspection.

Quality audits to check the quality system is functioning satisfactorily.

Inspection equipment the calibration and maintenance of equipment used in all inspection activities.

Vendor rating the assessment and approval of all suppliers, both of products and services.

Appraisal activities result in the 'costs of checking it is right'.

Prevention costs

These are associated with the design, implementation and maintenance of the total quality management system. Prevention costs are planned and are incurred prior to actual operation. Prevention includes:

Product or service requirements the determination of requirements and the setting of corresponding specifications for incoming materials, processes, intermediates, finished products and services.

Quality planning the creation of quality, reliability, operational, production, supervision, inspection and other special plans (e.g. preproduction trials) required to achieve the quality objective.

Quality assurance the creation and maintenance of the overall quality system.

Inspection equipment the design, development and/or purchase of equipment for use in inspection work.

Training the development, preparation and maintenance of training programmes for operators, supervisors, staff, and managers.

Miscellaneous clerical, travel, supply, shipping, communications and other general office management activities associated with quality.

Resources devoted to prevention give rise to the 'costs of doing it right the first time'.

Clearly this classification of cost elements may be used to interrogate any internal transformation process. Using the internal customer requirements concept as the standard for failure, these cost assessments can be made wherever information, data, materials, service or artefacts are transferred, from one person or one department to another. It is the 'internal' costs of lack of quality that lead to the claim that approximately one third of *all* our efforts are wasted.

The relationship between the so-called direct costs of prevention, appraisal, and failure costs and the ability of the organization to meet the customer requirements is shown in Figure 4.2. Where the ability to match a quality acceptable to the customer is low, the total direct quality costs are high, the failure costs predominating. As ability is improved by modest investment in prevention and possibly appraisal, the failure costs drop, initially very steeply. There may be an optimum operating level at which the combined costs are at the minimum, but the author has not yet found one organization in which the total costs have risen following investment in prevention.

So far little has been said about the often intractable indirect quality costs associated with customer dissatisfaction, and loss of reputation or

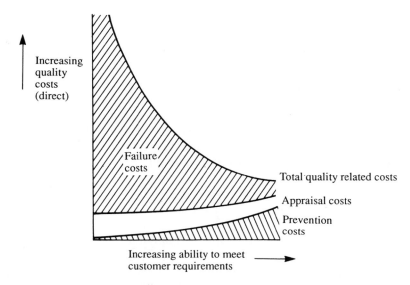

Figure 4.2 *Relationship between direct costs of quality and organizational capability*

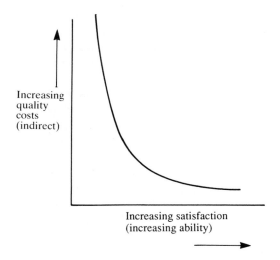

Figure 4.3 *Relationship between indirect costs of quality and customer satisfaction*

goodwill. These costs reflect customer attitude towards an organization and may be considerable. Figure 4.3 portrays the relationship between indirect quality costs and the organization's ability to provide customer satisfaction. It shows that when a critical level of dissatisfaction occurs, confidence and sales decline rapidly, increasing the indirect costs of quality.

It is worthy of note that indirect costs may move the desired operating point further to the right, indicating the need for the never-ending-improvement approach to customer satisfaction. Indirect quality costs, like direct costs, may be lowered by relatively small increases in prevention costs which subsequently reduce external failure – the cause of customer dissatisfaction and loss of reputation.

4.2 Data and sources

Costing quality, or rather non-quality, is something which organizations must pursue to make improvements in competitiveness. An assessment of the failure costs will create the thrust needed for a successful quality improvement programme. In the service sector the costs of failure or non-quality are sometimes difficult to measure, sometimes intangible, but they usually exceed the 10–15 per cent of turnover usually quoted. They may be as high as 35–40 per cent.

In finding costs, one of the major pitfalls is isolating only those things which can be measured. The less easily quantified areas tend to be ignored or forgotten. Measuring only tangible items, such as scrap, wasted materials, direct labour for reworking, mending or redoing is a mistake which many organizations make. It leads to the conclusion that the cost of failure is low – this is always far from the truth. Use of formulae which fail to provide the true costs of quality will generate complacency and lethargy, particularly in the non-producing areas such as finance, personnel, legal services, computer systems, public relations, and purchasing.

The bulk of the costs associated with getting it wrong often lies in the non-producing sectors of an organization – the people who never touch the product or provide the service. A major source of such failure costs are the activities of the salesforce and marketing, who are responsible for defining the customers' requirements in terms sufficiently specific to develop suitable designs from which producing departments can operate. This applies very much in non-manufacturing industries where the customer needs are potentially more difficult to define, and yet very noticeable when they are absent.

This type of communications problem can lead to cost creating difficulties in other parts of the organization. For example, materials management problems frequently accompany poor marketing information. Companies with inventories as high as turnover may restrict their investigations to the systems for inventory control, never getting to the real causes of high stocks, and all the time the competitive edge is being blunted due to high operating costs. Such companies can go out of business with full order books.

Progressive managers, always anxious to reduce costs, should be looking closely at the costs involved in achieving and maintaining conformance to a predetermined design quality. Most of those who have attempted to do so have found ample scope for economies. It is necessary for effective management control that these expenditures be detailed and displayed. Yet efforts to discover the extent of quality costs prevailing in many organizations have met with frustration for a variety of reasons. Quality costing tends to cut across normal accounting methods and cannot simply be secured by asking the accounting department for them. This may well elicit the response, 'We don't keep the books that way'.

The information must be pieced together using the 'books' where possible and resorting to estimates and finding new data when necessary. Successful quality costing involves working closely with the accountants and with the supervisors of the various departments to evaluate and estimate the costs associated with various activities. The author and his colleagues have designed a quality cost proforma (Table 4.1, pages 56–9) which is offered as a basis for modification to meet specific requirements of the user's own operations. It is based primarily on each department's contribution to quality costs, and secondly, on the prevention, appraisal and failure cost categories. This approach may enable the extraction of quality costs with less difficulty than by previously suggested methods. It is not fully comprehensive, further cost areas may need to be added and some of the sections may be omitted, some may be too small to warrant inclusion, too difficult to isolate from a larger category, or not determined with sufficient accuracy to be valid. Particular care must be taken to avoid double counting.

Many useful documents and reports may exist within an organization and these should aid the quality costing process, for example:

- Labour or equipment utilization reports.
- Material usage and review reports or records.
- Field or salespeople's reports.
- Analysis of credit notes.
- Analysis of rework, repair, replacement, or refund records or authorizations.
- Salaries and wages analyses.

Table 4.1 Proforma for quality costs

	Salaries and wages	Consumable materials	Capital equipment depreciation	Others	Total
Quality assurance					
Prevention costs					
Quality planning					
Training personnel					
Appraisal costs					
Receiving and process appraisal					
Final product appraisal					
Failure costs					
Internal failure					
External failure					
Research, design and development					
Prevention costs					
Setting specifications (incl. services, materials, processes and products)					
Pre-production and prototype trials					
Appraisal costs					
Inspection equipment					
• maintenance of					
• designs and specifications for					
Failure costs					
Rework and rectification					
Downgrading of products and services					
Product or service complaints and warranty claims					

Table 4.1 contd

	Salaries and wages	Consumable materials	Capital equipment depreciation	Others	Total
Production/operations					
Prevention costs					
Training – including supervisor training					
Preproduction and prototype trials					
Special handling and storage during production or operations					
Supervision of quality at all stages					
Appraisal costs					
Line or process inspection (by production/operations personnel)					
Finished product inspection or service checking (by production/operations personnel)					
Failure costs					
Full cost of scrap or wasted effort					
Rework or rectification					
Replacement of rejected product or repeating service					
Downgrading of products, materials and services					
Marketing and sales					
Prevention costs					
Setting of product or service specifications					
Appraisal costs					
Analysis of degree of acceptance of goods and services					

Table 4.1 contd

	Salaries and wages	Consumable materials	Capital equipment depreciation	Others	Total
Failure costs					
Downgrading of products and services					
Customer complaints, liaison and compensation					
Warranty claims and replacements or refunds					
Purchasing					
Prevention costs					
Supplier approval					
Appraisal costs					
Vendor rating					
Service department					
Prevention costs					
Product or service specification evaluation					
Preproduction and prototype trials					
Planning of in-process control procedures					
Appraisal costs					
Finished product or service performance evaluation					
Failure costs					
Customer complaints					
Product or customer service					
Returned material investigations and repairs					
Stores, transport and distribution					
Prevention costs					
Special handling and storage					

Table 4.1 contd

	Salaries and wages	Consumable materials	Capital equipment depreciation	Others	Total
Appraisal costs					
Receiving and checking materials, bought-out items or services					
Checking and despatching finished products and/or services					
Failure costs					
Sorting of reject finished goods in stock					
Receiving and checking returned reject goods					
Checking and despatching replacement goods					
Material control					
Failure costs					
Scrap material control					
Ordering of material or services for rework and rectification					
Ordering of material or services and finished goods for replacement					
Maintenance and engineering					
Prevention costs					
Prototype processes and equipment					
Planning and maintenance of plant and inspection equipment					
Appraisal costs					
Equipment reliability monitoring					
Failure costs					
Investigations and repairs following complaints, return of goods and warranty claims					
Total quality costs					

- Production or operations costing reports.
- Scrap reports.
- Travel expense claims.
- Inspection, check, test, verification records.

A pilot study should establish the preliminary figures from a small area of a company or a single product line or service operation. The aim of the pilot programme is to determine the scope of the work and to gain management approval and commitment to a total quality costing system. The quality costs categories and the cost elements to be used should also be defined at this stage. A first estimate of the costs of quality in an organization may be made by combining data from such reports with estimates derived from discussions with appropriate managers and supervisors. Each assumption and estimate used in this first quality cost computation should be published in a document which is circulated to selected managers. This will produce heated arguments about whether certain costs are part of quality costs. It is unimportant whether these 'grey' items are included or not, provided that there is consistency in including or excluding the debatable categories, the opportunities for reducing costs are not affected.

4.3 Assumptions, risks and benefits

Some assumptions

One danger in recording and reporting quality costs is that managers become too concerned with accuracy in their determination – a number crunching exercise which will consume resources disproportionately. For many organizations or their parts, particularly the non-profitmaking ones, it may be sufficient to assess the amount or proportion of time spent on work related to errors and their appraisal. This can always be equated to financial measures later. In quality costing, as in all areas of management, the skewed Pareto distribution[1] applies and it is likely that 20 per cent of the cost elements result in 80 per cent of the total costs. Clearly, the isolation of this 'vital few' will focus attention on the areas in need of improvements. The following may be done to gather pertinent quality cost data throughout the whole organization:

- The percentage of time spent by each person is categorized as appraisal, internal failure, or prevention, the individuals being asked initially to give estimates of the percentages for each category.

See *Statistical Process Control* John Oakland, Heinemann 1986.

- The percentage of total costs expended for each category is determined for each month.

The percentage values characteristic of most organizations without TQM are, failure about 65 per cent, and appraisal about 25 per cent of the total quality related costs, with prevention much lower at 10 per cent.

Quality costs may be 'normalized' if a standard costing system[2] is established. This neutralizes any inflation effects. For each category, an index of the quality cost per £1000 or $1000 standard cost may be calculated using the formula:

$$\text{Category index} = \frac{\text{Quality cost in category}}{\text{Standard cost}} \times 100$$

For example, if the December standard cost of production was £2 250 000, and the total prevention cost for December was £39 250, the 'prevention index' is:

$$\text{Prevention index} = \frac{39\ 250}{2\ 250\ 000} \times 100 = 1.7\%$$

Calculation of separate index values for scrap, rework or repeated work, may show trends in the value of the 'scrap index' (in terms of standard cost). Analysis of various improvement programmes or changes should show whether the results manifest themselves in the percentage of total costs attributable to failure. It is essential that the preventive cost category is also monitored throughout any study period.

There are several methods that may be used to analyse quality costs. The objective of the exercise is to observe any trends and to relate the results to the management turnover and style. A complete analysis would include an assessment of the effects of any reorganization in personnel, increased work loads, or changes in communication methods, including the introduction of quality management systems. Any changes from appraisal to prevention should be recorded and their effects noted. There are other indicators that should be included in the analysis, some with both advantages and disadvantages, e.g. fluctuations in total output. In this case the various indices give a better idea of quality cost trends as they are normalized. Weak quality assurance programmes, or management which believes that tighter control means more measuring to detect and redo faulty work will be highlighted by this type of index-quality related cost system.

[2] See *Production and Operations Management* Keith Lockyer, Alan Muhlemann and John Oakland, Pitman 1988.

Risks

Quality costs must not become a measure of competition between departments. This will serve to bury the real issues and causes of quality problems, which often lie between people or departments. The competitive use of quality costing will prevent individuals or managers from taking ownership and responsibility for failure; particularly if its resolution will have a more favourable impact on someone else or another department. Cooperation rather than competition is the essential component in reducing costs through TQM.

These comments also apply to the setting of goals. As stated in Chapter 3, if they are to be used they should be:

- clearly stated;
- measurable;
- achievable;
- agreed upon and not imposed.

It is important to realize that the cost measurement process is like any other process and will improve with use and experience. Hence, it is most likely that the second and third assessment of quality costs will be more accurate than the first and capture more sources of cost. It is not uncommon for senior management to interpret this as a deterioration of things, which may also correspond with the introduction of TQM! Clearly, like must be compared with like, and factors of time, use, and experience must be considered in the interpretation of quality cost data.

Benefits

There is no short cut to reducing the costs of quality, but once the workforce recognize that these high costs are reducing the organization's competitiveness they will become involved and committed to making total quality part of their working lives. The loss of the competitive edge through not meeting the customer requirements, sustaining high costs, or failing to deliver reduces the number of options for man-management. When shown, most workforces recognize the logical arguments that growth and job security derive from maintaining or increasing sales which brings us back to the competitive edge. In this way, a demonstrated overall high percentage quality-related cost figure will often catalyse a TQM programme.

Some of the first actions that might result from this are:

- The initiation of a special study to determine error or defect sources, training needs, etc. This will, of course, initially increase prevention costs.

- Special efforts to improve communication at the internal supplier/ customer interfaces and between departments such as marketing, design, production/operations, and purchasing.
- The continued collection, analysis, and reporting of quality cost information by personnel in finance and quality management.
- The establishment and maintenance of quality objectives, in terms of costs, for the entire organization and for specific areas.

Perhaps the most important benefit which will be derived is the appreciation by top management that they construct the quality image of the whole operation. It may come as a surprise to some managers to read that such lessons may be learned from a simple quality cost reporting system, but the implementation of a quality-related cost programme will be truly effective only if it measures the real quality costs within the organization. As stated, many organizations will have true quality costs in excess of 15 per cent of sales revenue and an effective quality cost programme can reduce this considerably, thereby making a direct contribution to profits.

Total direct quality costs, and their division between the categories of prevention, appraisal, internal failure and external failure, vary considerably from industry to industry and from plant to plant. The average figure for quality-related costs of ten per cent of sales turnover, means that in the average organization there exists a 'ghost operation', amounting to approximately one-tenth of capacity. This is devoted to producing errors, waste, scrap, rework, correcting errors, replacing defective goods and so on. Thus, a direct link exists between quality and productivity and there is no better way to improve productivity than to convert this ghost resource to truly productive use. A systematic approach to the introduction of TQM will accomplish this.

4.4 The quality cost system and management

Good working knowledge of all the processes involved and experience of the organization's accounting systems are essential for the successful management of a quality cost system. The costs cut across conventional accounting boundaries in most companies so it is important to set down the objectives of the system at the start. This will avoid difficulties later and influence the strategy employed.

The main aim of the system, initially, may be to identify high cost problem areas, in which case approximate costs will suffice. Subsequently, the system should broaden and perhaps set a percentage cost-reduction target on the organization's total quality-related costs. This eventually requires the identification and measurement of all the contributing cost elements in order to be sure that the costs are actually reduced and not simply transferred elsewhere.

The key words, prevention, appraisal, internal failure and external failure, and the detailed check lists are helpful, but do not replace the need for knowledge and experience of the business and the whole operation.

The system

The checklist of quality cost elements in Table 4.1 stresses that total quality costing involves much more than the check, inspection and test functions. Every person, in every department of an organization, bears the responsibility for ensuring that the 'customer's' requirements are met, and the costs associated with making sure they are must be included. Prevention costs, especially in small companies, are the most difficult to identify and slavish adherence to the checklist may result in a great deal of effort being expended in chasing insignificant costs.

The stages in establishing a quality costing system are:

- Identify the cost elements using the checklist.
- Begin the collection of quality cost data.
  (More work at these two stages is needed in organizations that do not already have departmental costing systems than in those that have.)
- Calculate the costs attributable directly to the 'quality function', including staff costs, pension costs, portion of accommodation costs – rent, rates, insurance, heating, lighting, security, etc., canteen, office services and administration costs, etc.
- Calculate costs incurred by all other departments and organizations in a similar manner.

The above should be entered in a 'memorandum account' of quality-related costs, as should the results of the remaining steps:

- Calculate the costs of the 'budgeted' failure. For example, it may be company practice to begin producing 1100 articles for every 1000 actually required, to be certain of achieving that number.
- Calculate the internal costs of unplanned failure, for which there is no allowance in the initial planning. Related costs may include material scrapped and repeated work, and they should be found either in the accounts of the department causing failure or the one rectifying. Wherever they lie, the costs should be noted in the memorandum account.
- Identify and calculate the costs of failures which fall between departments, including time spent on investigations by the quality and other departments. These costs will rarely appear in existing systems, and an initial estimate may need to be made.

Reporting

Data extracted from source documents should be coded for easy tabulation so that all cost data is reported by code. The use of coding permits consistency of collection regardless of the source or size of the costs. Where actual costs cannot be directly associated with specific elements, it may be necessary to make an allocation by arbitration. If these costs are significant, the necessary records should be established, in order to record the data factually.

Quality costs should be collated and reported by the 'quality department' based on data collected by the accounts department. The separate roles most likely to be established are that the accounts department collect quality costs data, produce an operating report, allocate quality costs to agreed accountable areas, and provide comparative bases for quality cost assessment. The quality department analyse quality costs and take appropriate controlling action by investigating causes, and making recommendations for improvement, coordinate interdepartmental activity to achieve quality costs objectives, pursue a policy for quality cost reduction and control, and arbitrate on the allocation of responsibility for quality failure costs.

Important aspects of the management of the quality cost system are the valuation of scrapped products and allocation of overhead costs. It is important to reach agreement early in the exercise on whether scrap products should be costed as materials plus added value to the point in the process they had reached, or whether they should be valued at the cost when completed, and whether the cost to produce or the selling price be used. It has been found satisfactory by Dale[3] and his colleagues, in many small/medium-sized companies, to value scrapped products at the materials cost to the point of scrapping, plus half the direct labour costs (including overhead) which would have been incurred if the product had been processed to completion.

It will also be necessary to have a policy on how overhead costs should be included in the quality costing system. Many quality-related costs are normally included as part of the overhead, whilst others are treated as direct costs and attract a proportion of overheads. Failure to clarify this issue can lead to a gross distortion of the picture derived from quality-related cost analyses. It is also easy to fall into the trap of double counting.

Following identification of where costs are incurred and their magnitude, action can be taken to control and reduce them. Quality costs should be collected and reported separately and not absorbed into a variety of overheads, or otherwise hidden, for example, debits in one area that are balanced by credits in another. A financial report should be

[3] University of Manchester, Institute of Science and Technology (UMIST).

presented to management to provide an accurate statement of the costs of failure, and the costs of operating quality controls. In order to have sufficient impact, this report should be presented separately but in a similar style to other management accounts, and should be supported by financial ratios and trend analysis related to the business of the company, to enable management to allocate the relevant financial resources. It is essential that the classification of costs data is relevant, and consistent with other accounting practices within the company so that comparisons may be made between costing periods or related activities.

The report format and frequency will depend upon the nature of the business and the level of management to which the information is presented. The reports must be relevant to the business objectives and should therefore have a consistent basis against which true comparisons can be made. Several measurement bases for the quality cost reports may be useful for presentation. They should represent the business from different viewpoints and be sensitive to changes. The following bases may be appropriate:

- labour cost;
- total cost;
- sales or turnover;
- value added;
- unit.

Quality cost per unit produced or generated has many advantages, but it is always necessary to take into account the effect of product mix, volume and value. The most generally used base is sales volume or turnover which has the great advantage of being understood by all as a measure of an organization's activity. A change in the quality cost:sales ratio can be immediately converted into an effect on the organization's pretax profitability. For a given industry, the profit:sales ratio is one of the indices of financial success so its close relationship to the quality costs:sales ratio is another reason for favouring sales volume as the base for quality cost reporting.

Known or forecast changes, such as any of the following, can affect the choice of base:

1 direct labour to be replaced by automation;
2 the use of alternative materials or methods of processes affecting costs;
3 changes in selling prices, distribution costs, market demand, product mix, or gross margins.

In reporting quality costs, the scope for misinterpretation of the findings should be considered very carefully. For the overview, a bar-chart presentation is often the least troublesome. A typical one is shown

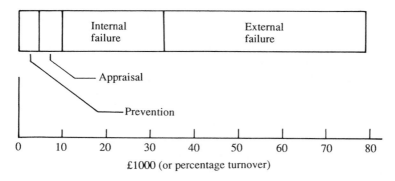

Figure 4.4 *Quality costs bar chart presentation*

in Figure 4.4. This provides an effective method for establishing the significance of quality costs by comparison with other costs that are normally reported regularly within the company. The relationships between the total quality costs and the costs of prevention, appraisal and failure, are clearly seen. Ideally, quality costs should be recorded and reported on a regular period basis on a running scoreboard. An annual once-off survey is a poor alternative.

4.5 Summarizing

Quality cost reductions cannot be dictated by management, they have to be earned through the processes of total quality management. The identification of quality problems – areas of significantly high quality costs – must be conducted within the framework of an appropriate company quality policy.

The approach adopted by a particular organization will depend on many factors, but there are common elements to all successful quality cost systems. These include the following:

1 Management commitment; real commitment of the management to finding the true cost of quality throughout the organization.
2 A quality costing system; the design and implementation of a system for the identification, reporting and analysis of quality costs.
3 Quality costs management; the formation of a quality costs management team responsible for overall direction, and coordination of the quality cost system and for ensuring that realistic targets are set and met.
4 Training; the inclusion of quality costing as an integral part of all

training schemes to enable everyone to understand the financial implications of quality.

5 Quality costs promotion; the presentation of significant quality costs in readily understandable terms to all personnel, e.g. displays of defective products carrying price tags, or charts of errors and their costs. If possible, the promotion material should indicate courses of remedial action.

6 Quality costs participation; the introduction of suitable schemes for achieving maximum participation of employees in this area, including means for promoting, initiating, receiving, discussing, appreciating and actioning ideas. Quality cost action groups, 'quality circles', corrective action teams, or quality improvement groups, organized throughout the company may well meet this purpose (see Chapter 12).

5 Planning for quality 1 – flow charting, quality planning and JIT

5.1 Flow charting

In the systematic planning or examination of any process, whether that be a clerical, manufacturing, or managerial activity, it is necessary to record the series of events and activities, stages and decisions in a form which can be easily understood and communicated to all. If improvements are to be made, the facts relating to the existing method must be recorded first. The statements defining the process should lead to its understanding and will provide the basis of any critical examination necessary for the development of improvements. It is essential, therefore, that the descriptions of processes are accurate, clear and concise.

The usual method of recording facts is to write them down, but this is not suitable for recording the complicated processes which exist in any organization. This is particularly so when an exact record is required of a long process, and its written description would cover several pages requiring careful study to elicit every detail. To overcome this difficulty certain methods of recording have been developed and the most powerful of these is flow charting. This method of describing a process owes much to computer programming where the technique is used to arrange the sequence of steps required for the operation of the program. It has a much wider application, however, than computing.

Certain standard symbols are used on the chart and these are shown in Figure 5.1. The starting point of the process is indicated by a circle. Each processing step, indicated by a rectangle, contains a description of the relevant operation, and where the process ends is indicated by an oval. A point where the process branches because of a decision is shown by a diamond. A parallelogram contains useful information but is not a processing step. The arrowed lines are used to connect symbols and to indicate direction of flow. For a complete description of the process all operation steps (rectangles) and decisions (diamonds) should be connected by pathways to the start circle and end oval. If the flow chart cannot be drawn in this way, the process is not fully understood.

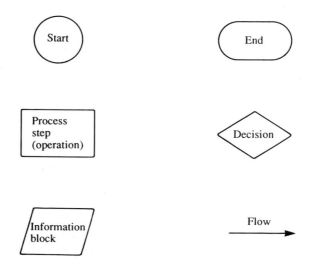

Figure 5.1   *Flow charting symbols*

It is a salutary experience for most people to sit down and try to draw the flow chart for a process in which they are involved every working day. It is often found that:

1 the process flow is not fully understood;
2 a single person is unable to complete the flow chart without help from others.

The very act of flow charting will improve knowledge of the process, and will begin to develop the teamwork necessary to find improvements. In many cases the convoluted flow and octopus-like appearance of the chart will highlight unnecessary movement of people and materials and lead to commonsense suggestions for waste elimination.

Example of flow charting in use

Improving a travel procedure
Description of the original process
(The process is described for a male employee, clearly it applies equally to females.)
The process starts with the employee explaining his travel plans to his secretary. The secretary then calls the travel agent to inquire about the possibilities and gives feedback to the employee. The employee decides if the travel arrangements (e.g. flight numbers and dates) are acceptable

and informs his secretary who calls the agent to make the necessary bookings or examine alternatives. The administrative procedure, which starts as soon as the bookings have been made, is as follows:

1 The employee's secretary prepares the travel request (which is in four parts A, B, C and D) and gives it to the secretary. The request is then sent to the employee's manager who approves it. The manager's secretary sends it back to the employee's secretary.
2 The employee's secretary sends copies A, B, and C to the agent and gives copy D to employee. The travel agent delivers the ticket to the employee's secretary together with copy B of the travel request. The secretary endorses copy B for receipt of the ticket, sends it to Accounting, and gives ticket to employee.
3 The travel agent bills the credit card company, and sends Accounting a proforma invoice with copy C of the travel request. Accounting matches copies B and C, and charges the employee's 181 account.
4 Accounting receives the monthly bill from the credit card company, matches against the travel request, books and pays the credit card company.
5 The employee reports the travel request on his expense statement. Accounting matches and books to balance the employee's 181 account.

The total time taken for the administrative procedure, excluding the correction of errors and the preparation of overview reports, was 23 minutes per travel request.

The flow chart for the process is drawn in Figure 5.2. A quality improvement team was set up to analyse the process and make recommendations for improvement, using brainstorming and questioning techniques. They made the following proposal to change the procedure. The preparation for the trip remained the same but the administrative steps, following the bookings being made, became:

1 The travel agent sends the ticket to the secretary, along with a receipt document which is returned to the agent with the secretary's signature.
2 The agent sends the receipt to the credit card company which bills the company on a monthly basis with a copy of all the receipts. Accounting pays the credit card company and charges the employee's 181 account.
3 The employee reports the travel on his expense statement, and Accounting books to balance the employee's 181 account.

The flow chart for the improved process is shown in Figure 5.3. The proposal reduced the total administrative effort per travel request (or per travel arrangement, because the travel request was eliminated) from 23 minutes to 5 minutes.

The details which appear on a flow chart for an existing process must be

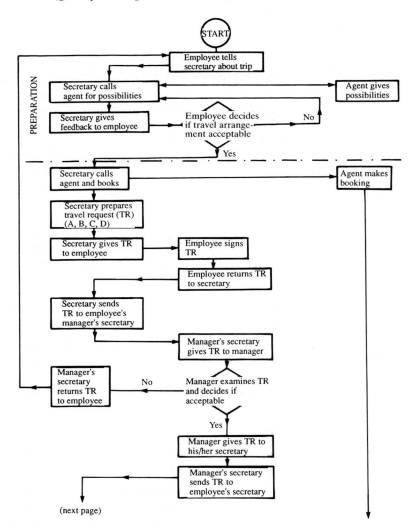

Figure 5.2 *Original process for travel procedure*

obtained from direct observation of the process, not by imagining what is done or what should be done. The latter may be useful, however, in the planning phase, or for outlining the stages in the introduction of a new concept. Such an application is illustrated in Figure 5.4 for the installation of statistical process control charting systems (see Chapters 10 and 11). Similar charts may be used in the planning of quality management systems.

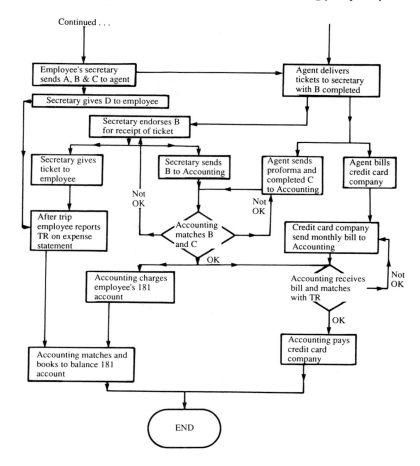

Figure 5.2 *contd*

It is surprisingly difficult to draw flow charts for even the simplest processes, particularly managerial ones, and following the first attempt it is useful to ask whether:

- the facts have been correctly recorded;
- any over-simplifying assumptions have been made;
- all the factors concerning the process have been recorded.

The author has seen too many process flow charts which are so incomplete as to be grossly inaccurate.

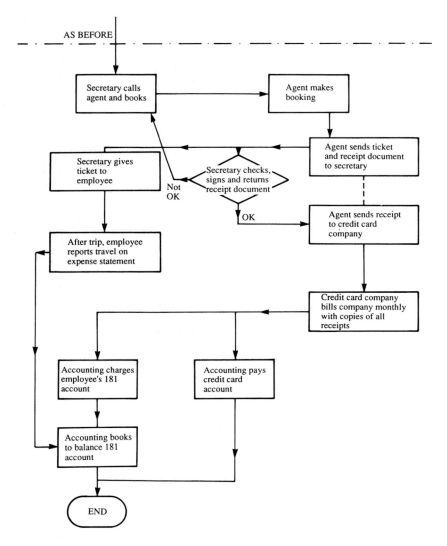

Figure 5.3   *Improved process for travel procedure*

Detailed flow process charts and flow diagrams
(as used in industrial engineering)

The recordings of detailed facts about a process is achieved by the use of five standard symbols, which together represent all the different types of activity or event likely to be encountered. These are shown on a detailed

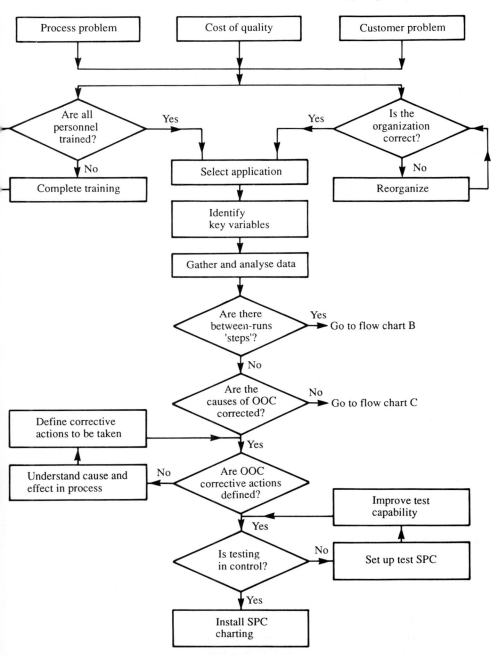

Figure 5.4   *Flow chart (A) for installation of SPC charting systems*
The author is grateful to Exxon Chemical International for permission to use and modify this chart.

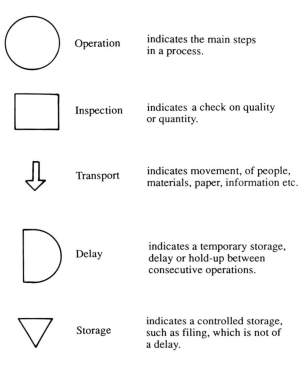

Figure 5.5   *Symbols used for detailed flow process charts and flow diagrams*

flow process chart and a flow diagram which together give a complete picture of the 'shape' of the flow and its components. The symbols provide a convenient, easily communicated shorthand and international language, saving much time and writing which helps to show exactly what happens, or needs to happen, in the correct sequence. The symbols are shown in Figure 5.5.

The charts and diagrams may be of four basic types:

1 *Person* recording what people actually do,
2 *Material* recording how material is handled or treated (including paperwork),
3 *Equipment* recording how equipment is used,
4 *Information* recording how information flows and to whom or where.

An example of a material type flow process chart and flow diagram, using the symbols, is given in Figures 5.6 and 5.7. This describes the authorization to investigate following an insurance claim.

The flow diagram shows the original layout of the property loss department of the company. The path of movement of the claims

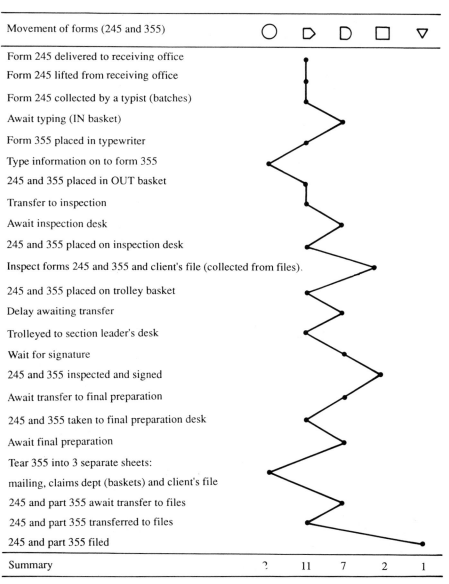

Movement of forms (245 and 355)	○	▷	◻	▽
Form 245 delivered to receiving office				
Form 245 lifted from receiving office				
Form 245 collected by a typist (batches)				
Await typing (IN basket)				
Form 355 placed in typewriter				
Type information on to form 355				
245 and 355 placed in OUT basket				
Transfer to inspection				
Await inspection desk				
245 and 355 placed on inspection desk				
Inspect forms 245 and 355 and client's file (collected from files).				
245 and 355 placed on trolley basket				
Delay awaiting transfer				
Trolleyed to section leader's desk				
Wait for signature				
245 and 355 inspected and signed				
Await transfer to final preparation				
245 and 355 taken to final preparation desk				
Await final preparation				
Tear 355 into 3 separate sheets:				
mailing, claims dept (baskets) and client's file				
245 and part 355 await transfer to files				
245 and part 355 transferred to files				
245 and part 355 filed				
Summary	?	11	7	2	1

Form 245   Claims department request
Form 355   Authorization to investigate

Figure 5.6 *Flow process chart; method for completing form to authorize investigation*

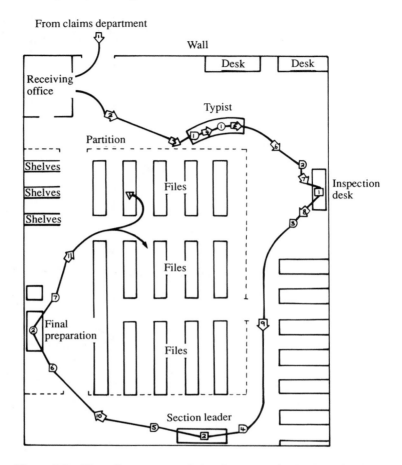

From claims department

Wall

Desk

Desk

Receiving office

Typist

Partition

Shelves

Shelves

Files

Inspection desk

Shelves

Files

Final preparation

Files

Section leader

Figure 5.7 *Flow diagram; completing form to authorize investigation*

department request (form 245) from the point of delivery to the filing system is shown by the broad line. It will be noticed that the symbols for the various activities have been inserted at the proper places. This enables anyone looking at the diagram to imagine more readily the activities to which the forms are subjected.

A study of the flow diagram in Figure 5.7 shows immediately that the forms take a very long and roundabout path on their journey to the files. This could not have been seen from the flow process chart alone (Figure 5.6). The chart, however, enables the various activities to be recorded and summarized in a manner not conveniently possible on the diagram.

A critical examination of the two together is required, using a questioning technique which follows a well-established sequence to examine:

the *purpose* for which
the *place* at which
the *sequence* in which } the activities are undertaken
the *people* by whom
the *method* by which

with a view to { *eliminating*
combining
rearranging } those activities
or
simplifying

The questions which need to be answered in full are:

Purpose	What is actually done? (or what is actually achieved?)	*Eliminate* unnecessary parts of the job
	Why is the activity necessary at all?	
	What else might be or should be done?	

Place	Where is it being done?	*Combine* wherever possible and/or REARRANGE operations for more effective results or reduction in waste
	Why is it done at that particular place?	
	Where else might or should it be done?	

Sequence	When is it done?	
	Why is it done at that particular time?	
	When might or should it be done?	

People	Who does it?	
	Why is it done by that particular person?	
	Who else might or should do it?	

Method	How is it done?	*Simplify* the operations
	Why is it done in that particular way?	
	How else might or should it be done?	

Questions such as these, when applied to the insurance authorization, raise many points demanding explanation, such as:

Question   Why are the inspection, section leader and final preparation points so far apart?
Answer   Because they happen to have been put there.
Question   Where else could they be?
Answer   They could be all together.
Question   Where should they be?
Answer   Together at the present inspection point.
Question   Why do the forms and client's file have to go all round the building to reach the filing system?
Answer   Because the door to the files is located at the opposite end from the delivery point.

No doubt if the flow diagram and the flow process chart are examined carefully there will be many other questions to ask. There is evidently much room for improvement. This is a real-life example of what happens when a series of activities is started without being properly planned. Examples with as much waste of time and effort can be found in offices all over the world.

The solution arrived at by the staff in this insurance company can be seen in the Figures 5.8 and 5.9. It is clear that among the questions they asked were those suggested above. The section leader's and final preparation desks have now been placed beside the inspection desk so that the forms and file can be passed from hand to hand for inspection, signing and final preparation. It is evidence that the investigators were led to ask the question 'Why do the forms and client's file have to go all round the building to reach the filing system?' Having received no satisfactory answer, they decided to make a new doorway into the files opposite the desks, so that the files could be taken in by the shortest route.

It will be seen from the summary on the new flow process chart (Figure 5.8) that the 'inspections' have been reduced from two to one, the 'transports' from eleven to six and the 'delays' (or temporary storages) from seven to two. The distance travelled was reduced from 56.2 to 32.2 metres.

Summarizing then, a flow chart is a picture of the steps used in performing a function. This function can be anything from a process step to accounting procedures, even preparing a meal. Lines connect the steps to show the flow of the various functions. Flow charts provide excellent documentation and are useful troubleshooting tools to determine how each step is related to the others. By reviewing the flow chart it is often possible to discover inconsistencies and determine potential sources of variation and problems. For this reason, flow charts are very useful in

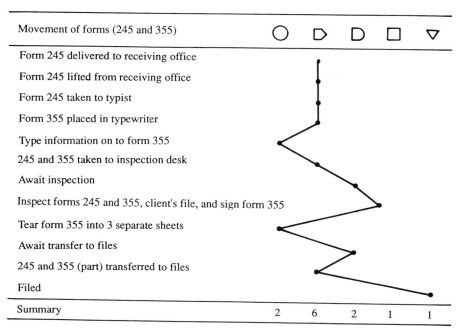

Figure 5.8 *Flow process chart; improved method for completing form to authorize investigation*

process improvement when examining an existing process to highlight the problem areas. A group of people, with the knowledge about the process, should follow the simple steps:

1 Draw a flow chart of existing process.
2 Draw a second chart of the flow the process could or should follow.
3 Compare the two to highlight the changes necessary.

5.2 Quality planning

Systematic planning is a basic requirement for effective quality management in all organizations. For quality planning to be effective, however, it must be part of a continuous review process which has as its objective zero errors or defectives, through a strategy of never-ending improvement. Before an appropriate total quality management system can be developed, it is necessary to carry out a preliminary analysis to ensure that a quality organization structure exists, that the resources required will be made available, and that the various assignments will be carried out. This

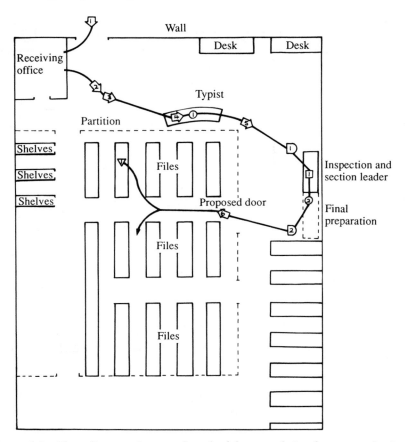

Figure 5.9 *Flow diagram; improved method for completing form to authorize investigation*

analysis has been outlined in the flow chart of Figure 5.10, from which the answers to the questions will generate the appropriate action plans.

In quality planning, it is always necessary to review existing programmes within the organization's functional areas and these may be compared with the results of the preliminary analysis to appraise the strengths and weaknesses in quality throughout the business or operation. Having done this, the required systems and programmes may be defined in terms of detailed operating plans, procedures and techniques. This may proceed through the flow chart of Figure 5.11 which provides a logical approach to developing a multifunctional total quality management system.

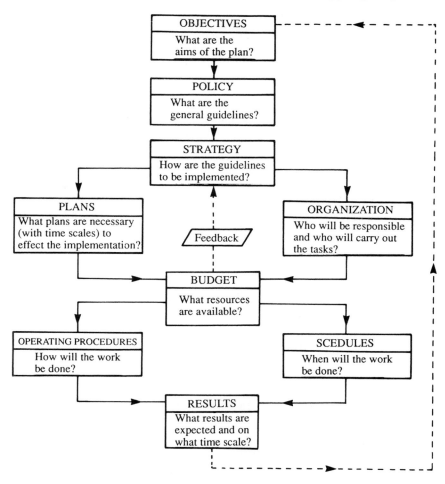

Figure 5.10 *Preliminary analysis for quality planning*

A quality plan

A quality plan is a document which is specific to each product, activity or service (or group) that sets out the necessary quality-related activities. The plan should include references to any:

- purchased material specifications;
- quality control procedures;
- product formulation or service type;
- process control;

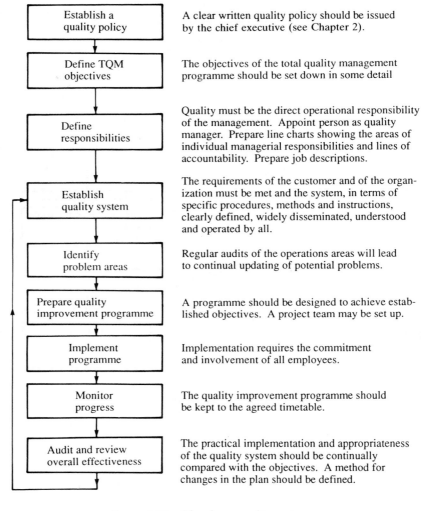

Establish a quality policy	A clear written quality policy should be issued by the chief executive (see Chapter 2).
Define TQM objectives	The objectives of the total quality management programme should be set down in some detail
Define responsibilities	Quality must be the direct operational responsibility of the management. Appoint person as quality manager. Prepare line charts showing the areas of individual managerial responsibilities and lines of accountability. Prepare job descriptions.
Establish quality system	The requirements of the customer and of the organization must be met and the system, in terms of specific procedures, methods and instructions, clearly defined, widely disseminated, understood and operated by all.
Identify problem areas	Regular audits of the operations areas will lead to continual updating of potential problems.
Prepare quality improvement programme	A programme should be designed to achieve established objectives. A project team may be set up.
Implement programme	Implementation requires the commitment and involvement of all employees.
Monitor progress	The quality improvement programme should be kept to the agreed timetable.
Audit and review overall effectiveness	The practical implementation and appropriateness of the quality system should be continually compared with the objectives. A method for changes in the plan should be defined.

Figure 5.11   *Plan for a quality system*

- sampling and inspection procedures;
- packaging specifications;
- miscellaneous, relevant procedures.

Such a quality plan might form part of a detailed operating procedure. A quality plan for part of a contact lens manufacturing process is shown in Figure 5.12.

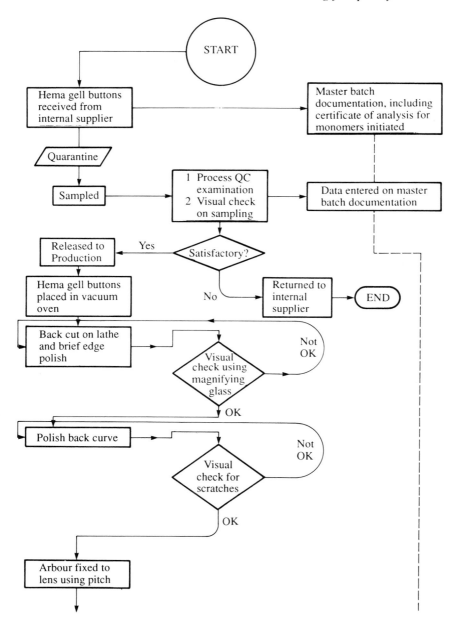

Figure 5.12 *A quality plan for some stages of contact lens manufacture*

For projects relating to new products or services, or to new processes, written quality plans should be prepared to define:

- specific allocation of responsibility and authority during the different stages of the project;
- specific procedures, methods and instructions to be applied throughout the project;
- appropriate inspection, testing, checking, or audit programmes required at various defined stages;
- methods for changes or modifications in the plan as the project proceeds.

Some of the main points in the planning of quality relate very much to the inputs of processes:

Plant	The design, layout, and inspection of plant and equipment, including heating, lighting, storage, disposal of waste, etc.
Processes	The design and monitoring of processes to reduce to a minimum the possibility of malfunction and/or failure.
Workplace	The establishment and maintenance of suitable, clean and orderly places of work.
Facilities	The provision and maintenance of adequate facilities.
Procedures	The preparation of procedures for all operations. These may be in the form of general plans and guides, rather than tremendous detail, but they should include specific operational duties and responsibilities.
Training	The provision of effective training in quality, technology, process and plant operation.
Information	The lifeblood of all quality management systems. All processes should be operated according to the simple rules:

- no data collection without recording;
- no recording without analysis;
- no analysis without action.

The quality plan should focus on providing action to prevent profits leaking away through waste. If the quality management system does not achieve this, then there is something wrong with the plan and the way it has been set up or operated, not with the principle. The whole approach should be methodical, systematic and designed to function irrespective of changes in management or personnel.

The principles and practice of setting up a good quality management system are set out in Chapters 8 and 9. The quality system must be planned and developed to take into account all other functions, such as design, development, production or operations, sub-contraction, installation, maintenance, and so on. The remainder of this chapter and the next are devoted to certain areas of the quality plan which require specific attention.

5.3 Planning for just-in-time (JIT) management

There are so many organizations throughout the world that are looking at, introducing, or practising just-in-time (JIT) management principles that the probability of encountering it is very high. JIT, like many modern management concepts, is credited to the Japanese who developed and began to use it in the late 1950s. It took approximately twenty years for JIT methods to be translated into Western hardgoods industries and a further ten years before businesses realized the generality of the concepts.

Basically JIT is a programme directed towards ensuring that the right quantities are purchased or produced at the right time, and that there is no waste. Anyone who perceives it purely as a material control system, however, is bound to fail with JIT. JIT fits well under the TQM umbrella for many of the ideas and techniques are very similar and, moreover, JIT will not work without TQM in operation. Writing down a definition of JIT for all types of organizations is extremely difficult because the range of products, services and organization structures leads to different impressions of the nature and scope of JIT. It is essentially two things:

1 A series of operating concepts that allow systematic identification of operational problems.
2 A series of technology-based tools for correcting problems following their identification.

An important outcome of JIT is a disciplined programme for improving overall productivity and reducing waste. This leads to cost-effective production or operation and delivery of only the required goods or services, in the correct quantity, at the right time and place. This is achieved with the minimum amount of resources – facilities, equipment, materials, and people. The successful operation of JIT is dependent upon a balance between the suppliers' flexibility and the users' stability and, of course, requires total management and employee involvement and teamwork.

Aims of JIT

The fundamental aims of JIT are to produce or operate:

* to meet exactly the requirements of the customer;

- without waste;
- immediately on demand.

In some manufacturing companies, JIT has been introduced as 'continuous flow production', which describes very well the objective of achieving conversion of purchased material or service receipt to delivery, i.e. from supplier to customer. If this extends into the supplier and customer chains, all operating with JIT, a perfectly continuous flow of material, information or service will be achieved. JIT may be used in non-manufacturing, in administration areas for example, by using external standards as reference points.

The JIT concepts identify operational problems by tracking the following:

- Material movements, when material stops, diverts or turns backwards, these always correlate with an aberration in the 'process'.
- Material accumulations, these are there as a buffer for problems, excessive variability, etc., like water covering up 'rocks'.
- Process flexibility, an absolute necessity for flexible operation and design.
- Value added efforts, much of what is done does not add value and the customer will not pay for it.

The operation of JIT

The tools to carry out the monitoring required are familiar quality and operations management methods, such as:

value analysis and value engineering,
flow charting,
statistical process control,
method study and analysis,
preventive maintenance,
plant layout methods,
standardized design.

But some techniques are more directly associated with the operation of JIT systems:

standardized containers,
kanban or cards with material visibility,
fool-proofing,
batch or lot size reduction,
pull scheduling,
set-up time reduction,
flexible workforce.

In addition, joint development programmes with suppliers and customers will be required to establish long-term relationships and develop single sourcing arrangements which provide frequent deliveries in small quantities. This can only be achieved through close communications and meaningful certified quality.

There is clear evidence that JIT has been an important component of business success in the Far East and that it is used by Japanese companies operating in the West. Many European and American companies which have adopted JIT have made spectacular improvements in performance. These include:

- increased flexibility (particularly of the workforce);
- reduction in stock and work-in-progress, and the space it occupies;
- simplification of products and processes.

These programmes are always characterized by a real commitment to continuous improvement. Organizations have been rewarded, however, by the low-cost, low-risk aspects of implementation, provided a sensible attitude prevails. The major rule is to never remove resources, such as stock, before the organization is ready and able to correct the problems that will be exposed by doing so. Reduction of the water level to reveal the rocks, so that they may be demolished is fine, provided that we can quickly get our hands back on the stock whilst the problem is being corrected.

Successive phases of JIT may well become self-financing by rapid simplification of systems and work flows, but it must never be regarded at the intermediate stage as the 'quick-fix'. Management must contemplate:

- long implementation times – typically 5–7 years;
- a total or company-wide quality and just-in-time management programme;
- never-ending improvement and reduction of waste.

The impact of JIT reflects its title. Materials and/or services are purchased or generated in the exact quantity and just at the time they are needed. The idea was developed into a formal management system by the Toyota company to meet the customer demands for various models and colours of vehicles, with minimum delays in delivery. JIT is one of the major factors contributing to the success of Japanese companies in achieving low production costs with quality.

The primary objective of JIT is the improvement of quality through elimination of waste. It demands that inventory is kept to a minimum, and where inventory costs (insurance, interest, obsolescence, etc.) can be as high as 26 per cent of stock value, significant improvements in costs and quality can be achieved by the elimination of inventory. Defective parts, materials, workmanship is detected promptly and quickly fed back to the producing process, where the problem is identified and corrected on the spot. In addition to quality improvement, there becomes no requirement for a profusion of warehouses, fleets of fork lift trucks, rows of racks, scores of employees, piles of cash to purchase, handle, and move the inventory.

With low inventory in the system, any fluctuation in the final stage of production or operations creates variations in the requirements at preceding stages. This variation becomes larger for processes further away from the final stage. To prevent the variance in earlier stages, a minimum lot or batch size, ideally a lot size of one, should be chosen. Small lot sizes help to reduce nonconformities through the detection of problems and their rapid solution, before large quantities are generated.

In some engineering and process industry applications, the major obstacle in producing small lots is the set-up times of equipment and machines. Long set-up times make the small lot size uneconomical, so clearly cutting set-up times is one of the first tasks. This will also reduce equipment down time, work-in-progress, costs associated with obsolescence, materials handling and control, and quality control. Shorter set-up times also result in shorter lead times which provides greater flexibility for processes to adapt to changes in the market demand and requirements.

The Kanban system

Kanban is a Japanese word meaning visible record, but in the West it is generally taken to mean a card which signals the need to deliver or produce more parts or components. In manufacturing, various types of record cards, e.g. job orders or tickets and route cards, are used for ordering more parts in a *push* type schedule-based system. In a push system, a multi-period master production schedule of future demands is prepared, and a computer explodes this into detailed schedules for producing or purchasing the appropriate parts or materials. The schedules then push the production of the parts or components, out and onward. These systems, when computer based, are usually called material requirements planning (MRP).

The main feature of the Kanban system is that it *pulls* parts and components through the production processes when they are needed. Each material, component, or part has its own special container designed to hold a precise, preferably small, quantity. The number of containers for each part is a carefully considered management decision. Only standard containers are used and are always filled with the prescribed quantity. There are two cards or Kanbans for each container. The production or P-Kanban serves the workcentre producing the part, whereas the conveyance or C-Kanban serves the workcentre using it.

Each container travels between the two workcentres and one Kanban is exchanged for another along the way. No parts may be made at any workcentre unless there is a P-Kanban to authorize it, and workcentres may come to a halt, rather than produce materials or parts not yet requested. The operators will then engage in other activities, such as cleaning, maintenance, improvement or quality circle project work when no P-Kanbans have been submitted. These hold-ups often help to identify and improve bottleneck situations.

A Kanban system provides parts when they are needed but without guesswork and, therefore, without the excess inventory that results from bad guesses. The system will only work well, however, within the context of a JIT system, in general, and the reduction of set-up times and lot sizes in particular. A JIT programme can succeed without a Kanban based operation, but Kanbans will not function effectively independently of JIT.

The implementation of JIT

If it has been decided to embark on JIT, then a pilot scheme should be implemented first. The key features of an appropriate pilot section will be that it is:

- reasonably self-contained;
- concerned with products or services which have established designs and stable markets, for the foreseeable future;
- staffed by people who are keen to try to implement JIT.

Clearly, if the pilot implementation is successful, it is appropriate to proceed to other areas of the business.

The implementation of JIT may be described as a two-stage process:

1 establish foundations;
2 introduce core techniques;

Foundations

The company must be organized and managed to achieve:

- quality;
- low cost;
- minimum lead times;
- high flexibility.

The methods which will be required to reach these goals will include:

- TQM;
- focus on design;

- plant and equipment layout;
- set-up time reduction;
- lot or batch size reduction;
- work-in-progress and/or buffer stock reduction;
- flexible workforce.

Much of this will depend, obviously, on the type of industry and relative position of the company, e.g. many flow production operations will already possess significant focus on standardization of design.

Core techniques

These often provide the most spectacular improvements and savings, but may be more difficult to implement. A satisfactory stage one foundation is essential for the introduction of:

- pull scheduling;
- visibility;
- JIT purchasing;
- buffer stock removal;
- multi-function workforce;
- enforced improvement.

The implementation of JIT requires a planned and coordinated, company-wide JIT organization. This should incorporate three main features: a steering committee, a project manager, and project teams, which is so similar to the organization for TQM that the two may well be run in parallel, at least through stage one.

The steering committee should be a cross-functional group of personnel who meet regularly to direct and monitor the programme. Members of the committee may include people from marketing, design, purchasing, production or operations, quality, personnel, and possibly the workforce. It is beneficial to appoint a project manager to lead the implementation. His/her characteristics and training are vital to the duties of acquiring and organizing resources, facilitating and chairing meetings, internally publicizing results, and training. The project teams are established to implement specific JIT techniques. With help from the project manager, these 'working parties' should establish terms of reference at an early stage. Their membership should be cross-functional, but above all relevant to the JIT technique concerned. The reporting system should be from the teams through the project manager to the steering committee.

The emphasis throughout all stages of JIT or TQM implementation should be on the involvement of all employees, especially those who will be directly involved with changes. This may require some 'enforced' delegation from specialists, such as quality and industrial engineers, to 'shop-floor' personnel. The culture in which JIT will operate successfully will provide support to the project teams' recommendations for change.

6 Planning for quality 2 – purchasing, reliability and maintenance

6.1 Planning the purchasing activity

A company selling wooden products had a very simple purchasing policy, it was that they bought the cheapest wood they could find, anywhere in the world. Down in the workshops, they were scrapping doors and window-frames as if they were going out of fashion – warping, knots in the wood, 'flaking', cracking, splits, etc. When the purchasing manager was informed he visited the workshops and explained to the supervisors how cheap the wood was and instructed them to 'do the best you can – the customer will never notice'. On challenging this policy, the author was told that it would not change until someone proved to the purchasing manager, in a quantitative way, that the policy was wrong. That year the company 'lost' a million pounds worth of wood, in scrap and rework. You can go out of business waiting for such proof.

It is salutary at this point to report the results of some research at Bradford University Management Centre. In an industrial survey the overall position of the factors affecting product competitiveness and purchasing decisions, as ranked by the respondents, are shown in Table 6.1. No association exists between the ranking of these factors with respect to the choice of purchased materials and competitiveness of products. In other words, the managers involved behave as if the two things are not related, yet the bulk of respondents chose quality and reliability first for product competitiveness.

Very few organizations are totally self-contained to the extent that their products and services are all generated at one location, from basic materials. Some materials or services are usually purchased from outside organizations and the primary objective of purchasing is to obtain the correct equipment, materials, supplies and services in the right quantity, of the right quality, from the right origin, at the right time and cost. It also plays a vital role as the organization's 'window-on-the-world', providing information on any new products, processes, materials and services. Purchasing should also advise on probable prices, deliveries, and per-

Table 6.1 Ranking of factors affecting purchasing and product competitiveness ranking by respondents

Factor	Importance to the competitiveness of the company's products	Importance placed by company when purchasing materials used in manufacturing
Price/cost	2	1
Quality/reliability	1	2
Delivery performance	3	4
After-sales/back-up service	5	5
Design/formulation/ technical specification	4	3

formance of products under consideration by the research, design and development functions.

The 'total' cost of bought-in material and/or services usually forms a large proportion of the final selling price of an organization's products or services. Consequently, purchasing is an extremely important, specialized function which should never be underestimated. The value of purchases varies from industry to industry, but it averages 60 per cent of the turnover of all industries, and clearly the effects of good purchasing management on the profitability of a 'typical' manufacturing or service organization can be considerable.

Although purchasing is clearly an important area of managerial activity, it is often neglected by both manufacturing and service industries. The separation of purchasing from selling has, however, been removed in many large retail organizations, which have recognized that the purchaser must be responsible for the whole 'product line' - its selection, quality, specification, delivery, price, acceptability, and reliability. If any part of this chain is wrong, the purchasing function must resolve the problem. This concept is clearly very appropriate in retailing where transformation activities on the product itself, between purchase and sale, are small or zero, but it shows the need to include market information in the buying decision processes in all organizations.

The organization and responsibility for purchasing

The inputs to purchasing appear from various sources, depending on the nature of the operation, but they include:

- design   from the concept to the product or service;

- research and
  development
- production or
  operations

- distribution

- marketing

- finance

- legal services
- general management

of the processes used and the outputs
produced;
detailed requirements of the transformation
process, including data on waste, efficiencies
and conformance with existing or planned
facilities;
either by the supplier or the customer, e.g. in
retailing;
future demands, feed-back on quality, competitors and any other issues which affect
purchasing;
terms of payment, creditors, invoice verification and payment, auditing of procedures,
etc.;
drawing-up and agreeing of contracts;
make or buy decisions.

The purchasing function, like any other in an organization, is ineffective
if it exists in isolation.

Make or buy and supplier selection decisions (see also Chapter 10)

The make or buy decision refers to the problem encountered by an
organization when deciding whether a product or service should be
purchased from outside sources or generated internally. Often make or
buy decisions and the selection of suppliers are based on price, but this is a
dangerous criterion with which to evaluate these strategic decisions. The
lowest price may not necessarily be that which is least costly to the
purchasing organization, since it may attract other costs of correcting,
sorting out, chasing-up, etc. These increase the total cost of the
purchase, and that is a far more useful criterion. Other key points which
must have influence are:

1 quality and how it is controlled;
2 continuity of supply;
3 technological and commercial knowledge and experience required.

The economics of production or operations probably come last in this
list which places operational conditions higher than financial ones.
Moreover, consideration of the 'non-cost' factors encourages longer-
term contracts with suppliers to aid the achievement of production and
quality levels and encourage investment in appropriate resources and
new ideas. This results in excellent, mutually beneficial customer–

supplier relationships developed over long periods, based on trust and the achievement of common objectives. The constant reanalysis of the make or buy decision or re-evaluation of suppliers, in search of short-term advantage, can destroy the relationship needed for long-term supply contracts having mutual profitability as their basic objectives. This does not say that the decisions should be once and for all, for they clearly require some periodic reanalysis to take into account changes in business and environmental conditions, and technology.

Most make or buy decisions are very complex, time consuming and affect many parts of an organization. Senior management involvement is required in a number of the stages of this strategic decision. Problems may well be experienced in calculating accurate costs, and finding information on quality, supply and reliability, and technical know-how requirements, for each side of the equation. Information inputs are required from both inside and outside the purchasing function, which clearly has a vital role to play. Informal and formal involvement of technical, financial (accounts) and production or operations control will always be necessary, together with a systematic approach based on careful weighing of the key factors; it is unlikely that one single factor, such as price, will be so conclusive as to dictate the obvious path to be taken.

The purchasing system

The control of purchasing should be set out in a written 'purchasing manual' which:

1 assigns responsibilities for and within the purchasing function;
2 defines the manner in which suppliers are selected to ensure that they are continually capable of supplying the requirements in terms of material and services (see Section 10.4);
3 indicates the appropriate purchasing documentation – written orders, specifications and certificates of conformity – required in any modern purchasing activity.

The purchase order

The purchase order is a contractual document which may well bind the originating organization to considerable expenditure. It is most important therefore that it should be clear and unambiguous. The following statements

'price to be agreed'
'delivery as soon as possible'

'of good quality'
'of normal commercial quality'
'as previously supplied'
'as discussed with your Mr Jones'

and others of a similar nature should never be used, since they are too loose to be useful, and can cause considerable difficulties later when delivery occurs of a quality or grade other than that required, or at a date later than useful.

The purchase order should carry at least the following information:

1 Name and address of originating organization.
2 Name and address of receiving company.
3 Identifying number.
4 Quantity of product or amount of service required.
5 A full description of the type, style, grade, or other means of precise identification of the product or service.
6 The applicable issue of the product or service specification and any other relevant technical data (a reference to a published, current specification may be used).
7 Reference to any certification of conformity to requirements, which must accompany the delivered product.
8 Price agreed between purchaser and vendor.
9 Delivery agreed between purchaser and vendor.
10 Cost allocation – this for internal use.
11 Delivery instructions.
12 Buyer's signature and standing in the organization.
13 Purchaser's conditions of business.

The authority to sign purchase orders is usually restricted to one or two persons within the organization, and limitations may be imposed as to the amount of expenditure which may be incurred by a signatory: for example, some companies have a rule that orders of value greater than a certain amount must be sanctioned by the board.

Receiving inspection

Inspection on receipt of goods or services may be an essential component of the system of purchasing. The amount and extent of inspection performed on receipt varies, however, with the effectiveness of the supplier's delivery and quality systems. It must be recognized that the conformance quality of supplied material or services can be controlled only at the point of their production. Inspection at receipt for acceptance or rejection is an inefficient and wasteful device to be replaced, as soon as possible, by the use of receiving inspection to check that the necessary systems and procedures, used by the supplier to control quality, are in fact working effectively.

Organizations which have verified their suppliers' quality systems, either by direct audit or by independent third-party assessment (see Chapter 9), often request a 'certificate of conformity', to be delivered with the purchased material. This is a simple statement by the supplier that what is being delivered actually conforms to the requirements, as laid down in a specification. A certificate of conformity should include the following information as a minimum:

1 The supplier's name and address.
2 The serial number and the date of the certificate.
3 The customer's name and address.
4 The customer's purchase order number.
5 A description of the product and the quantity.
6 Where appropriate, the customer's identification marks.
7 The identification of any specification to which the goods are supplied.
8 Any agreed concessions.
9 The following statement, signed by the person nominated by the firm as responsible for quality control or his deputy:

   'Certified that the supplies detailed hereon have been inspected and tested in accordance with the conditions and requirements of the contract or purchase order and, unless otherwise noted below, conform in all respects to the specification(s), drawing(s), relevant thereto.'

There is a difference between a certificate of conformity and a 'certificate of analysis' (C of A). The latter contains particular data resulting from tests, inspections, or measurements carried out on samples taken from the actual material delivered. It is not uncommon for organizations to make a small charge if a C of A is requested, but no charge should be levied for a certificate of conformity.

Just-in-time (JIT) purchasing

Purchasing is an important feature of just-in-time (JIT) methods of inventory control. The development of long-term relationships with a few suppliers, rather than short-term ones with many, leads to the concept of coproducers in networks of trust providing dependable quality and delivery of goods and services. Each organization in the chain of supply is encouraged to extend JIT methods to its suppliers. The requirements of JIT mean that suppliers are usually located near to the purchaser's premises, delivering small quantities, often several times per day, to match the usage rate. Paperwork is kept to a minimum and standard quantities in standard containers are usual. The requirement for suppliers to be located near to the buying organization, which places those at some distance at a competitive disadvantage, causes lead times to be shorter and deliveries to be more reliable.

It can be argued that JIT purchasing and delivery is suitable mainly for assembly line operations, and less so for certain process and service industries, but the reduction in the inventory and transport costs that it brings, should encourage innovations to bring about its widespread adoption. Those committed to open competition and finding the lowest price will find most difficulty, as will those countries which, for geographical reasons, suffer greater transport distances between customer and suppliers. Nevertheless, there must be a recognition of the need to develop closer relationships and to begin the dialogue – the sharing of information and problems – which leads to the product or service of the right quality, being delivered in the right quantity, at the right time. (See also supplier capability in Chapter 10.)

6.2 Quality and time–reliability

Quality is a property which may change with the age of the product or service. Clearly, part of the acceptability of a product will depend on its ability to function satisfactorily over a period of time. This aspect of performance has been given the name *reliability*, which is the ability to continue to be fit for the purpose or meet the customer requirements.

Reliability ranks with quality in importance, since it is a key factor in many purchasing decisions where alternatives are being compared, and many of the general management issues related to achieving quality, are also applicable to reliability.

Clearly, every product will eventually fail, although in some cases the possibility is small enough for the product to be effectively infinitely reliable. With the pressures to reduce cost, and with the need for increasing complexity, the probability of a product or service failing within the user's anticipation of its working life is likely to be finite. As reliability is an exceedingly important aspect of competitiveness, there is a need to plan and design reliability into products and services. Unfortunately, the testing of a design to assess its reliability is difficult, sometimes impossible, and the designer must therefore invest in any insurance which is practicable. Some methods of attempting to assure reliability are:

1 use proven designs;
2 use the simplest possible design – the fewer the components and the simpler their designs, the lower the total probability of failure;

3 use components of known or likely high probability of survival. It is usually easier to carry out reliability tests by over-stressing components than by over-stressing the complete product or service;

4 employ redundant parts where there is a likelihood of failure. It may be that a component or part of a system must be used which has a finite probability of failure (F). Placing two of these parts in parallel will reduce the probability of both failing to F^2. Three in parallel will all fail with a probability of F^3, and so on. Clearly the costs of redundancy must be weighed against the value of reliability;

5 design to 'fail-safe';

6 specify proven production or operational methods.

Failure

In the discussion of reliability, it is important to be clear about what is meant by failure. When a product, system or component no longer performs its required function, it is said to have failed. This definition assumes that the required function is known exactly. A motor car could be described as either working perfectly or broken down completely, but there could be something in between. It may, for example, achieve a lower miles-to-the-gallon than when new. Whether the latter is regarded as failure depends entirely on what is defined as the required function and this in turn may depend on the use of the product or service. To assist in the definition of failure, it may be useful to consider the various types and causes of failure.

Types of failure

Total failure this results in a complete lack of ability of the product or service to perform the required function.

Partial failure the item does not work, or the service is not provided, as well as expected, but it has not completely failed.

Gradual failure this takes place progressively over a period of time and could possibly be anticipated by some sort of examination.

Sudden failure occurs very quickly and is not easily predicted by investigation or examination.

Causes of failure

Clearly there are many causes of product and/or service system failure, but two main general causes are common.

Weakness this is inherent in the product or service itself and, when subjected to the normal stresses of use, results in one of the types of failure described above. Weakness is usually introduced by poor or wrong design, materials, processes, or operation.

Misuse this represents the application of stresses which are outside the usual capability of the product or service system.

Failure mode, effect and criticality analysis (FMECA)

It is possible to analyse products and services to determine possible modes of failure and their effects on the performance of the product or operation of the service system. Failure mode and effect analysis (FMEA) is the study of potential failures to determine their effects. If the results of an FMEA are ranked in order of seriousness, then the word *criticality* is added to give FMECA. The primary objective of a FMECA is to determine the features of product design, production or operation and distribution which are critical to the various modes of failure. It uses all the available experience and expertise from marketing, design, technology, purchasing, production, distribution, service, etc., to identify the importance levels or criticality of potential problems and stimulate action which will reduce these levels. FMECA should be a major consideration at the design stage of a product or service (see Chapter 7).

The elements of a complete analysis are:

1 Failure mode. The anticipated conditions of operation are used as the background to study the most probable failure mode, location and mechanism of the product or system and its components.
2 Failure effect. The potential failures are studied to determine their probable effects on the performance of the whole product or service and the effects of the various components on each other.
3 Failure criticality. The potential failures in the various parts of the product or service system are examined to determine the severity of each failure effect in terms of lowering of performance, safety hazard, total loss of function, etc.

FMECA may be applied at any stage of design, development, production or use, but since its main aim is to prevent failure, it is most suitably applied at the design stage to identify and eliminate causes. With more complex product or service systems, it may be appropriate to consider these as smaller units or subsystems, each one being the subject of a separate FMECA.

Special FMECA proformas are available (for example see Table 6.2) which set out the steps of the analysis as follows:

1 Identify the product or system components, or process function.

Table 6.2   Failure mode, effect and criticality analysis (FMECA)

Part name: emission assembly

Process/ function (1)	Possible failure mode (2)	Effect(s) of failure (3)	Possible cause(s) of failure (4)	P (5)	S	D	C (6)	Corrective action (7)
Inspection of inwards goods	Base material incorrect	Early failure in service	Wrong selection of material by supplier	1	8	9	72	None
	Dimensions incorrect	Loose or tight fit on spigot and in moulding	Extrusion process out of statistical control	8	5	7	280	Supplier to certify and is applying in process controls
	Label incorrect regarding size	Wrong part supplied to customer	Specification incorrect	2	5	7	70	None
	Faulty moulding	Inability to assemble	Incorrect inspection	2	5	5	50	None
		Early failure in service		2	8	6	96	
Washing	Not washed sufficiently	Line marking becomes indistinct and adhesion values reduced	Detergent not added to washer	3	2	6	36	None
			Water not changed	2	6	6	72	None
Air blow	Omitted	Blocked hose	Operator error	2	8	6	96	Positive release system of passed tubing being investigated
		Wet hose could affect sintered disc		2	8	6	96	
Storage	Not stored correctly	Wet hose could affect sintered disc	Incorrect packaging	2	8	6	96	Drying facility under investigation Sept. 1987
	Dirt in component	Incorrect operation	Bad storage	1	8	9	72	None
			Human error operator	2	8	6	96	None

Table 6.2 contd

Part name: emission assembly

Process/ function (1)	Possible failure mode (2)	Effect(s) of failure (3)	Possible cause(s) of failure (4)	(5) P	S	D	(6) C	Corrective action (7)
Stripe application	Wrong colour	Incorrect fitment in assembly	Incorrectly planned	2	8	6	96	None
	Incomplete	Cosmetic rejection	Machine malfunction	8	2	6	96	Co-extruded stripe under investigation Sept. 1987 Target date
Cut to length	Short	Cannot assemble at customer or in plant	Machine capability incorrect	5	9	7	315	New design cutting machine to be evaluated Sept. 1987
	Long	Fouls on fitment, in house difficulty to perform next operation		4	3	7	84	
Storage awaiting assembly	Mixed parts	Incorrect length supplied to assembler	Parts mixed during transit	2	5	7	70	None
	Incorrect labelling	Incorrect length supplied to assembler	Operator error	2	8	6	96	Assembly boards and attribute charts to be introduced
Subassembly of mouldings	Incorrect units assembled	Customer cannot fit unit	Incorrect selection	2	8	6	96	None
	Bonding	Leaks. Failing vacuum requirement affects driveability	Incorrect bonding agent preparation, overage material	2	8	7	112	Improved adhesive application under evaluation

Part name: emission assembly

Process/ function (1)	Possible failure mode (2)	Effect(s) of failure (3)	Possible cause(s) of failure (4)	P	S	D	C	Corrective action (7)
				(5)			(6)	
	Fit incorrect length of tubing	Long and short lengths can result in customer being unable to assemble	Incorrect selection	2	8	6	96	Increased use of inspection
				2	3	6	36	boards as per sampling plan
Assembly	Assembly fitted circuit broken	Short length unable to join components		2	8	7	112	
	Missed parts	Failure of unit to function on vehicle	Operator error	6	6	6	216	Increased use of inspection boards in hand
	Valve orientation incorrect	Failure of unit to function on vehicle	Operator error	2	7	6	84	Increased use of inspection boards in hand
	Fuel trap orientation incorrect	Failure of unit to function on vehicle	Operator error	2	8	6	96	Increased use of inspection boards in hand
	Rubber elbow orientation incorrect	Will not fit on vehicle	Operator error	2	6	6	72	Increased use of inspection boards in hand
Packaging	Label omitted	Wrong part supplied	Operator error	2	8	6	96	Increased use of inspection boards in hand
	Incorrect label	Part sent to wrong destination	Human error, incorrect data	5	7	9	315	Improved labelling system is being introduced
	Incorrect container	Rejected at customer	Human error, incorrect data	2	5	6	60	None

satisfactory maintenance policy. As in all other areas of management, this 'most satisfactory' policy is unlikely to occur by chance. Data must be systematically gathered and analysed. The costs associated with failure and the costs of corrective action are compared and a maintenance plan prepared, which offers a satisfactory match of costs and equipment availability. In this sense, all maintenance work should be planned.

Historically, the term 'planned maintenance' has been misguidedly restricted to the overhaul work; this is better described as preventive. There are many cases where the best policy is to allow the equipment to fail before carrying out maintenance work. Such work is undoubtedly 'planned' even though the timing of the work is uncertain.

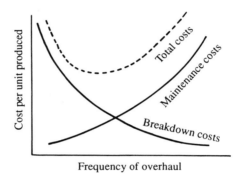

Figure 6.5 *Derivation of the total cost of maintenance policy*

There are then broadly two types of maintenance policy:

1 Repair or replacement due to failure.
2 Preventive maintenance.

The first type is an emergency-based policy, in which the plant or equipment is operated until it fails and then it is maintained. Formal preventive maintenance may take four different forms:

(a) Time based, means doing maintenance at regular intervals – say every 2 months. It is easy to monitor time and this form is used when deterioration is likely to be time rather than usage dependent, or when usage cannot easily be measured.
(b) Work based, i.e. maintenance after a set number of operating hours of volume of work produced, e.g. every 40 000 photocopies. Usage can be more difficult than time to monitor and some form of 'auto-counting' of output should be used, if possible.
(c) Opportunity based, where repair or replacement takes place when

the equipment or system is available, e.g. during a holiday closure. This can extend the interval between maintenance to an unacceptable level, but it may be suitable for equipment which has intermittently heavy use.

(d) Condition based, which often relies on planned inspection to reveal when maintenance is prudent, e.g. replace a brake pad when it has worn to 2 mm thickness. This is dependent on monitoring equipment condition which can be difficult, and out of the question if a time-consuming strip-down precedes any examination or inspection.

These various types of policy often operate together, overlap or coincide. For example, time-based and work-based maintenance will coincide if the rate of work is constant, condition-based replacement may occur during a time-, work- or opportunity-based maintenance activity.

The need for data

Choice between the various policies needs to be made on objective grounds if possible and this underlines the need for good data collection and analysis. It is not easy to try to discover the actual time taken and the work involved when carrying out a maintenance task, particularly when the plant is large and/or complex and the maintenance work carried out far from simple. Rational policies, however, need to be based on data and the need for the collection and analysis of reliability and maintenance information cannot be overemphasized. Furthermore, it is invaluable to feed particular problems and difficulties back to the designer or supplier of equipment since it may be possible to reduce downtimes and overhaul times on new equipment.

The collection of costs over the life of a piece of equipment, and the use of these costs to project costs over the life of new equipment, is known as life cycle costing. Basically the question to be asked is, 'How does the cost of maintaining compare with the cost of not maintaining?' This is not always an easy question to answer, and some policies, particularly preventive maintenance policies, are often taken 'on trust'.

Preventive maintenance

Well designed, preventive maintenance plans can reduce the incidence of emergency maintenance. In the production of standardized product design along flow lines, where there is little if any work-in-progress between adjacent operations, an equipment breakdown at one operation will quickly cause all other down-stream operations to come to a standstill. This situation can arise just as easily in the supply of cheeseburgers in a 'burger-bar' and the preparation of letters of credit in a bank, as in the assembly of motor cars. An extensive preventive maintenance programme is essential to reduce the frequency and severity of work flow interruption in these situations.

In automated production environments, again not restricted to manufacturing, preventive maintenance programmes must be part of the operating quality policy. Where automated equipment operates continuously, without the need for operatives, human intervention will be required in the form of a maintenance unit to keep the equipment lubricated, adjusted and generally operating in good condition. As automation increases throughout various types of operation, we will see a need to move to smaller production workforces and larger maintenance crews. Hence, some of the production operatives replaced by robotics and computer-aided production systems will require retraining to provide the necessary increase in maintenance staff.

As we see the increasing introduction of just-in-time (JIT) methods, in which in-process stocks and batch sizes are reduced to very low levels, the near absence of work-in-progress will focus attention on equipment and system failure. JIT demands perfect equipment maintenance, since breakdowns cannot be tolerated. It is not sufficient to speed up repairs to minimize down-time, breakdowns must be eliminated through an effective prevention strategy.

Where operatives are employed in production, this strategy requires their total involvement. They must be given the responsibility for preventing equipment failure by conducting checks, inspecting, lubricating and adjusting their own equipment with meticulous attention to detail. Just as in the achievement of quality of conformance, operators must be given the tools to do this, and this means providing the appropriate training to be able to detect, find and eliminate potential causes of trouble before they manifest themselves in a system failure.

Aspects of modern maintenance

Technology is increasingly more complex with electronics, robotics and computer control now influencing every walk of life. These have clearly led to many changes in maintenance activities. Special and continuous training programmes are required to provide the necessary knowledge, understanding and skills to service the increasingly specialized equipment, and to keep up with the developments in the field.

Specialist organizations have developed to provide maintenance services on a sub-contract basis and transport vehicles, computers, office equipment and medical support systems are often serviced by outside companies. The specialized technical knowledge and skills are frequently more economical to acquire on a call-in fee basis than an in-house team.

The advances in technology have enabled the development of systems which reduce the cost of maintenance, whilst improving operational performance. These are usually computer-based devices which enable the detection of faults before severe difficulties, and even damage, occur. For example, sensing devices may be installed to monitor factors such as vibration, local temperatures, pressures, consumption of lubricants, changes in electrical resistance, composition of products from a chemical plant, etc. Changes in such factors often indicate changes in the condition of equipment, or the operation of a process, and can give timely warning of approaching failure. This approach has been called *predictive maintenance* and can usefully be coupled to a preventive maintenance policy. Computers can, of course, be used in the actual maintenance for:

planning maintenance;
financial control of maintenance;
spare part inventory control;
reliability and failure data collection and analysis;
operational research models applied to maintenance, e.g. queuing theory and simulation.

Modern maintenance management is far more than repairing and servicing equipment. The perspectives of maintenance planning must be broadened to the long-range performance aspects of the complete customer service system. Failure of any component in that system can cause total disaster and the viability of the whole organization is dependent on effective maintenance policies, plans and operations.

7 Design for quality

7.1 Design and the requirements

Quality of design concerns far more than the product or service design and its ability to meet the customer requirements. It is also about the activity of design itself. The appropriateness of the actual design process has a profound influence on the quality performance of any organization, and much can be learned by examining successful organizations and how their strategies for research, design, and development are linked to the efforts of marketing and operations.

The terms design and R and D need some clarification if their management is to be effective. The following working definitions may avoid confusion:

> *Research* is the discovery of novel techniques, ideas, information or systems. Market research is clearly part of research.
> *Development* is the improvement of existing techniques, ideas or systems.
> *Design* is the translation of the 'customer' requirements into a form suitable for operation, production, or use. It may include redesign to cater for ease of operation or changes in specification.

Design may encompass both research and development and all of these are creative activities.

All businesses competing on the basis of quality need to update periodically their products and services. In markets such as electronics, audio and visual goods, and office automation, new variants of products are offered frequently, almost like fashion goods. Whilst in other markets, the pace of innovation may not be as fast and furious, there is no doubt that the rate of change for product and service design has accelerated on a broad front. In the face of aggressive innovation, an established organization has four main choices. It can:

- stick to its old services and products and try to fight off new products;
- search for unexploited market niches to safeguard its sales volume;
- update its services and products to stay abreast of the competition;
- develop completely new products or services.

The latter is the most 'exciting' as it changes the competitive rules, but it requires sufficient intellectual and material resources.

Innovation then entails both the invention and design of radically new products and services, embodying novel ideas, discoveries and advanced technologies, and the continuous development and improvement of existing products, services, and processes to enhance their performance and quality. It may also be directed at reducing costs of production or operations throughout the life cycle of the product or service system.

In many organizations, innovation is predominantly either technology-led (in some chemical and engineering industries, for example) or marketing-led (in some food companies, for example). What is always striking about leading product innovators – many of those in the electronics industry, for example – is that their product developments are market-led. Market-led is different from marketing-led. The latter means that the marketing function takes the lead in product and service developments. But most leading innovators identify and set out to meet profitably the existing and potential demand; therefore, they are market-led, constantly striving to meet the requirements even better through appropriate experimentation.

Commitment to quality in the most senior management helps to build in quality throughout the design process and to ensure good relationships and communication between various groups and functional areas. Designing customer satisfaction into products and services contributes greatly to competitive success. Clearly, it does not guarantee it because the conformance aspect of quality must be present and the designed process must be capable of producing to the design. As in the marketing/operations interfaces, it is never acceptable to design a product, service, system or process which is what the customer wants but which the organization is incapable of achieving.

As explained, the design process often concerns technological innovation in response to, or in anticipation of, changing market requirements and trends in technology. Those companies with impressive records of product-led growth have demonstrated a state-of-the-art approach to innovation based on three principles:

1 *Strategic balance* to ensure that both old and new product developments are important. Updating old products and services ensures continuing cash generation from which completely new products may be funded.
2 *Top management approach* to design to set the tone and ensure that commitment is the common objective by visibly supporting the design effort. Direct control should be concentrated on critical decision points, since over-meddling by very senior people in day-to-day project management can delay and demotivate staff.

3 *Teamwork* to ensure that, once projects are underway, specialist inputs, e.g. from marketing and technical experts, are fused and problems are tackled simultaneously. The teamwork should be urgent yet informal, for too much formality will stifle initiative, flair and the fun of design.

The extent of the design activity should not be underestimated, but it often is. Many people associate design with styling of products, and this is certainly an important aspect. But for certain products and many service operations, the secondary design considerations are vital. Anyone who has bought an 'assemble-it-yourself' kitchen unit will know the importance of the design of the assembly instructions, for example. Aspects of design which affect quality in this way are: packaging, customer-service arrangements, maintenance routines, warranty details and their fulfilment, spare-part availability, etc. An industry which has learned much about the secondary design features of its products is home computers. Many of the problems of customer dissatisfaction experienced in this market were not product design features but problems with user manuals, availability and loading of software, and applications. For technically complex products or service systems, the design and marketing of after-sales arrangements are an essential component of the design activity. The design of production equipment and its layout to allow ease of access for repair and essential maintenance, or simple use as intended, widens the management of design quality into suppliers and contractors and requires their total commitment and involvement.

Proper design of plant and equipment plays a major role in the elimination of errors, defectives, and waste. Correct initial design also obviates the need for costly and wasteful modifications to be carried out after the plant or equipment has been constructed. It is at the plant design stage that such important matters as variability, reproducibility, ease of use in operation, maintainability, etc. should receive detailed consideration.

Designing

If quality design is taking care of all aspects of the customer requirements, including cost, production, safe and easy use, and maintainability of products and services, then designing must take place in all aspects of:

- identifying the need (including need for change);
- developing that which satisfies the need;
- checking the conformance to the need;
- ensuring that the need is satisfied.

Designing covers the work involved from the identification of a problem to be solved, usually a market need, through the development of design concepts and prototypes to the generation of detailed specifications or instructions required to produce the artefact or provide the service. It is the process of presenting needs in some physical form, initially as a solution, and then as a specific configuration or arrangement of materials, resources, equipment, and people.

The activities in designing include:

- basic research;
- invention;
- concept design;
- prototype development;
- prototype testing;
- final product or service testing;
- after-sales service and trouble-shooting.

These are performed by people with different skills, the composition of which depend on many factors including the products or services being developed and the size of the operation. In many consumer industries, such as cars, video equipment, electronics, and computers, 'engineering' designers are seen to be heavily involved in designing. But in other industries and service operations, designing is carried out by people who do not carry the word 'designer' in their job title. The failure to recognize the design inputs they make, and to provide appropriate training, will limit the success of the design activities and result in some offering which does not generate satisfaction of the customer. This is particularly true of internal customers.

Responsibility for design

Usually the design function sits between the marketing and the operations functions. Its purpose is essentially to take the needs of the market, as determined by the marketing department, and translate them into such a form that they can be satisfied within the operating unit. It is clear that the decisions taken during the design stage can have significant and very long-term effects on the whole organization. A badly designed piece of furniture, for example, will never sell however well it is made; a poorly designed menu which offers the wrong choices will not attract customers, however well it is presented and advertised.

The importance of the design function cannot be overestimated, and its organizational location is not easily defined. Three locations are commonly found:

1 Within the marketing department, on the basis that the marketing department is the only source of detailed knowledge about the needs of

a customer. This is true both for products which involve high technology and for services which are dependent on an extremely variable market. It is particularly true for products and services designed to a customer's specification, since the marketing department are, effectively, the customer's representative within the organization.

2 Within the operations department, on the basis that, providing an accurate and comprehensive specification has been laid down by the marketing department, it is essential that it should be executed as rapidly and economically as possible. The organizational links between design and operations need to be as tight as possible and this sort of organization function will be satisfactory where the products or services are standardized, requiring only minimum modification to make them acceptable to the customer.

3 As an independent unit, directly responsible to the top management. The advantages of independence are clear: the designers are not inhibited either by marketing or operations and can, therefore, produce the most effective design. This situation probably holds best where products or services are genuinely in advance of the market. This sort of design function may very well provide the stimulus for the marketing department to 'create a market'.

As with all organizational problems, the design of the structure of the organization must be made on the basis of the detailed requirements of each organization. One thing, however, is clear – close liaison must be maintained at all times between the design, marketing and operational functions.

7.2 Specifications and standards

There is a strong relationship between standardization and specification. To ensure that a product or a service is standardized and may be repeated a large number of times in exactly the manner required, specifications must be written so that they are open to only one interpretation. The requirements and, therefore, the quality must be built into the design specification. National and international standards exist which, if used, help to ensure that specifications will meet certain accepted criteria of technical or managerial performance, safety, etc.

Standardization does not guarantee that the best design or specification is selected. It may be argued that the whole process of standardization slows down the rate and direction of technological development and affects what is produced. If standards are used correctly, however, the process of drawing up specifications should provide opportunities to learn more about particular innovations and to change the standards accordingly.

It is possible to strike a balance between innovation and standardization. Clearly, it is desirable for designers to adhere where possible to past-proven materials and methods, in the interests of reliability, maintainability and variety control. Hindering designers from using recently developed materials, components, or techniques, however, can cause the design process to stagnate technologically. A balance must be achieved by analysis of materials, products and processes proposed in the design, against the background of their known reproducibility and reliability. If breakthrough innovations are proposed, then analysis or testing should be directed objectively, justifying their adoption in preference to the established alternatives.

One aspect of the design specification which is often debated is the setting of realistic tolerances and the selection of appropriate standards. This is required for, and at, all stages of the design and development process and is an important step in translating a design brief into specifications that can be used by production personnel or in the operation of the service system. The aim should be to reflect the tolerances that are the true requirements of the product or service function and are capable of being achieved. It is indicative of the lack of communication in many organizations that some production people claim that their colleagues in design set unnecessarily tight tolerances to make life in production more difficult. Designers, on the other hand, have been known to set tighter limits than necessary in order to encourage production to concentrate on 'controlling' the process and thereby achieve the true requirements. This conflict, which is explained quantitatively in Chapter 10, leads only to increased variability of processes and greater mismatch between the specifications and the capability of the process.

The specification is the principal document in respect of attaining and maintaining quality, irrespective of the product or service. Without it, there is no basis for the control of quality and we cannot be sure that a pair of shoes of a certain size bought in the UK will be the same size as a pair bought in the USA, France, or Australia. We could never be confident that, by quoting a number, we may obtain a replacement part for a motor car that will fit perfectly.

It is useful to define a specification. The International Standards Organization (ISO) define it in ISO 8402 (1986) as 'the document that prescribes the requirements with which the product or service has to conform'. A document which does not give a detailed statement or description of the requirements to which the product or service must comply cannot be regarded as a specification, and this is true of much sales literature.

The specification conveys the customer requirements to the supplier to allow the product or service to be designed, engineered, produced, or operated using conventional or stipulated equipment, techniques, and technology. The basic requirements of a specification are that it gives the:

- performance requirements of the product or service;
- parameters, such as dimensions, concentration, turn-round-time, which describe the product or service adequately (these should be quantified and include the units of measurement);
- materials to be used by stipulating properties or referring to other specifications;
- method of production or operations;
- inspection/testing/checking requirements;
- references to other applicable specifications or documents.

To fulfil its purpose the specification must be written in terminology which is readily understood, and in a manner which is unambiguous and so cannot be subject to differing interpretation. This is not an easy task and is one which requires all the expertise and knowledge available. Good specifications are usually the product of much discussion, deliberation and sifting of information and data.

7.3 'Seven new tools' for quality design

Success at continual quality improvement requires an integrated 'company-wide' approach, and all parts of an organization must cooperate to produce economically services and products which fully satisfy the customer's needs. Much emphasis has been placed on the use of quality control systems to improve existing processes and products, but many businesses have very dynamic service or product portfolios. The design and development of new products and services are essential, therefore, to success.

To improve the design of a product or service 'seven new tools', collectively known as quality function deployment (QFD), may be used to address various aspects of the design process. These do not replace the seven basic SPC tools described in Chapter 10 and neither are they extensions of these. The new tools are systems and documentation methods used to achieve success in design by identifying objectives and intermediate steps in the finest detail. The 'seven new tools' are the:

1 affinity diagram;
2 interrelationship digraph;
3 tree diagram;

4 matrix diagrams or charts;
5 matrix data analysis;
6 process decision program chart (PDPC);
7 arrow diagram.

The tools are inter-related, as shown in Figure 7.1. The promotion and use of the tools, which are summarized below, should obtain better designs in less time.

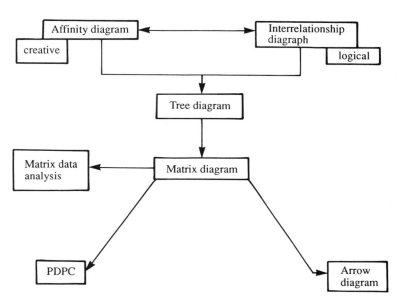

Figure 7.1 *The 'seven new tools' of quality design*

1 Affinity diagram

This is used to gather large amounts of language data (ideas, issues, opinions) and organize it into groupings based on the natural relationship between the items. In other words, it is a form of brainstorming. One of the obstacles often encountered in the quest for improvement is past success or failure. It is assumed that what worked or failed in the past will continue to do so in the future. Although the lessons of the past should not be ignored, unvarying patterns of thought which can limit progress should not be enforced. This is especially true in the area of design where new logical patterns should always be explored.

The affinity diagram, like other brainstorming methods, is part of the creative process. It can be used to generate ideas and categories that can be used later with more strict, logic-based tools. This tool should be used to 'map the geography' of an issue when:

- facts or thoughts are in chaos and the issues are too large or complex to define easily;
- breakthroughs in traditional concepts are needed to replace old solutions and to expand a team's thinking;
- support for a solution is essential for successful implementation.

The affinity diagram is not recommended when a problem is simple or requires a very quick solution.

   The steps for generating an affinity diagram are as follows:

(a) Assemble a group of people familiar with the problem of interest. 6–8 members in the group works best.
(b) Phrase the issue to be considered. It should be vaguely stated so as not to prejudice the responses in a predetermined direction. For example, if brainstorming on why issues are not followed up in an organization, it would be better to state the question as, 'why do issues remain unresolved?' rather than 'why don't people take the responsibility to complete their assignments?'

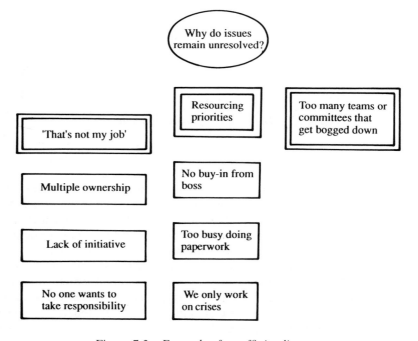

Figure 7.2   *Example of an affinity diagram*

(c) Give each member of the group a stack of cards and allow 5–10 minutes for everyone in the group to record ideas on the cards, one per card. During this time, the objective is to write down as many ideas as possible, as concisely as possible. There should be no communication between members of the group during the 5–10 minutes.

(d) At the end of the 5–10 minutes, each member of the group, in turn, reads out one of his/her ideas and places it on the table for everyone to see. There should be no criticism or justification of ideas and it is allowable to write new ideas during this time, if fresh thoughts are generated.

(e) When all ideas are presented, members of the group place together all cards with related ideas. This process is repeated until the ideas are in approximately ten groups.

(f) Look for one card in each group that captures the meaning of that group.

The output of this exercise is a compilation of a maximum number of ideas under a limited number of major headings (see for example Figure 7.2). This data can then be used with other tools to logically define areas for attack. One of these tools is the interrelationship digraph.

2 Inter-relationship digraph

This tool is designed to take a central idea, issue or problem and map out the logical or sequential links among related factors. While this still requires a very creative process, the inter-relationship digraph begins to draw the logical connections that surface in the affinity diagram.

In designing, planning, and problem solving, it is obviously not enough to just create an explosion of ideas. The affinity diagram method allows some organized creative patterns to emerge but the inter-relationship digraph lets *logical* patterns become apparent. This is based on a principle that the Japanese frequently apply regarding the natural emergence of ideas. This tool starts, therefore, from a central concept, leads to the generation of large quantities of ideas and finally the delineation of observed patterns. To some this may appear to be like reading tea leaves, but it works incredibly well. Like the affinity diagram, the inter-relationship digraph allows those unanticipated ideas and connections to rise to the surface.

The inter-relationship digraph is adaptable to both specific operational issues as well as general organizational questions. For example, a classic use of this tool at Toyota focused on all of the factors involved in the establishment of a 'billboard system' as part of their JIT program. On the other hand, it has also been used to deal with issues underlying the problem of getting top management support for TQM.

In summary, the inter-relationship digraph should be used when:

(a) An issue is sufficiently complex that the inter-relationship between ideas is difficult to determine.
(b) The correct sequencing of management actions is critical.
(c) There is a feeling or suspicion that the problem under discussion is only a symptom.
(d) There is ample time to complete the required iterative process and define cause and effect.

The inter-relationship digraph can be used by itself, or it can be used after the affinity diagram, using data from the previous effort as input. The steps for using this tool are:

(a) Clearly define one statement that describes the key issue to be discussed. Record this statement on a card and place it on the wall or a table, in the centre of a large sheet of paper. Mark this card in some way so that it can be easily identified as the central idea, for example, use a double circle around the text.
(b) Generate related issues or problems. This may be done in wide open brainstorming, or may be taken directly from an affinity diagram. (Note, due to the volume of material being dealt with, it is advisable to look at only one major category of the affinity diagram at a time.) Place each of the ideas on a card and place the cards around the central idea card.
(c) Use arrows to indicate which items are related and what leads to what. Look for possible relationships between all items.
(d) Look for patterns of arrows to determine key factors or causes. For example, if one card has seven arrows coming from it to other issues, the idea on that card is a key factor or cause. Mark these key ideas in some way, for example using a double box.
(e) Use the key factors in a tree diagram for further analysis.

Figure 7.3 gives an example of a simple inter-relationship digraph.

3 Systems flow/tree diagram

The systems flow/tree diagram (usually referred to as tree diagram) is used to systematically map out the full range of activities that must be accomplished in order to reach a desired goal. It may also be used to identify all of the factors contributing to a problem under consideration. As mentioned above, major factors identified using an inter-relationship digraph can be used as inputs for the tree diagram. One of the strengths of this method is that it forces the user to examine the logical and chronological link between tasks. This assists in avoiding a natural tendency to

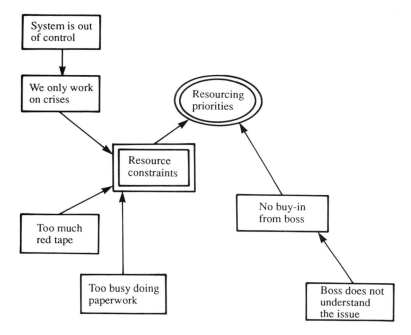

Figure 7.3 *Example of the inter-relationship digraph*

jump directly from goal or problem statement to solution (ready –
. . . fire . . . aim!).

The tree diagram is indispensable when a thorough understanding of
what needs to be accomplished is required, together with how it is to be
achieved, and the relationships between these goals and methodologies.
It has been found to be most helpful in situations when:

(a) very ill-defined needs must be translated into operational characteristics, and to identify which characteristics can presently be controlled;
(b) all the possible causes of a problem need to be explored. This use is
closest to the cause-and-effect diagram or fishbone chart;
(c) identifying the first task that must be accomplished when aiming for a
broad organizational goal;
(d) the issue under question has sufficient complexity and time available
for solution.

Depending on the type of issue being addressed, the tree diagram will
be similar to either a cause-and-effect diagram or a flow chart (see
Chapters 5 and 10), although it may be easier to interpret because of its

clear linear layout. If a problem is being considered, each branch of the tree diagram will be similar to a cause-and-effect diagram. If a general objective is being considered, each branch may represent chronological activities, in which case the diagram will be similar to a flow chart. Although this tool is similar to other tools, suggestions on the stepwise procedure are included below. The procedure is based on trying to accomplish a goal, but it can be easily modified for use in problem solving:

(a) Start with one statement that clearly and simply states the overall issue or goal. Write the idea on a card and place it on the left side of a flip chart or table.
(b) Ask the question 'what method or task is needed to accomplish this goal or purpose?' Use the inter-relationship digraph to find ideas that are most closely related to that statement, and place them directly to the right of the overall statement card.
(c) Look at each of these 'second tier' ideas and ask the same question. Place these ideas to the right of the ones that they relate to. Continue this process until all of the ideas are gone. Note, if none of the existing ideas on the inter-relationship digraph can adequately answer the question, new ideas may be developed so as not to leave holes in the tree diagram.

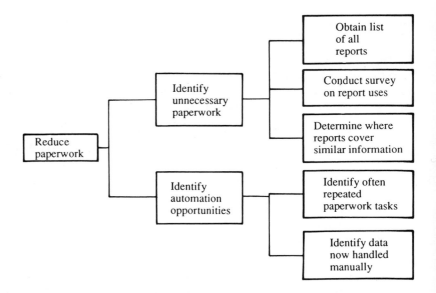

Figure 7.4   *An example of the tree diagram*

(d) Review the entire tree diagram by starting on the right, and asking the question 'if this is done, will it lead to the accomplishment of the next idea or task?' The diagram produced will be similar to an organization chart.

An example is shown in Figure 7.4.

4 Matrix diagram

The matrix diagram is the heart of the seven new tools. The purpose of the matrix diagram is to outline the inter-relationships and correlations between tasks, functions or characteristics and to show their relative importance. There are many versions of the matrix diagram, but the most widely used is a simple L-shaped matrix known as the *quality table*.

L-shaped matrix diagram

This is the most basic form of matrix diagram. In the L-shape two interrelated groups of items are presented in line and row format. It is a simple two-dimensional representation that shows the intersection of related pairs of items as shown in Figure 7.5. It can be used to display relationships between items in all operational areas, including administration, manufacturing, personnel, R and D etc., to identify all the organizational tasks that need to be accomplished and how they should be allocated to individuals. In teamwork it is even more interesting if each person completes the matrix individually and then compares the coding with everyone in the work group.

In a quality table, customer demands are analysed with respect to substitute quality characteristics (Figure 7.6). Correlations between the two are categorized as strong, moderate and possible. The customer demands shown on the left of the matrix are determined in cooperation with the customer. This effort requires a kind of verbal 'ping-pong' with the customer to be truly effective: ask the customer what he wants, write it down, show it to him and ask him if that is what he meant, then revise and repeat the process as necessary. This should be done in a joint meeting with the customer, if at all possible. It is often of value to use a tree diagram to give structure to this effort.

The right side of the chart is often used to compare current performance to competitors' performance, company plan and potential sales points with reference to the customer demands. Weights are given to these items to obtain a 'relative quality weight'. This can be used to identify the key customer demands. The relative quality weight is then used with the correlations identified on the matrix to determine the key quality characteristics.

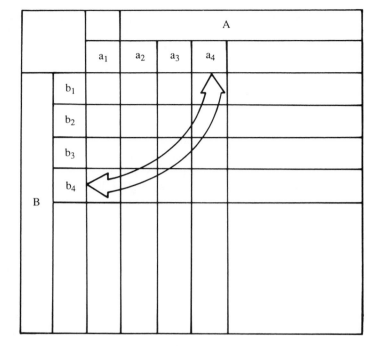

Figure 7.5 *L-shape matrix*

One modification that is often added to the quality table is a second matrix that explores the correlations between the quality characteristics. This is done so that errors caused by the manipulation of variables in a one-at-a-time fashion can be avoided. This also gives indications of where designed experiments would be of use in the design process. In the training required for use of this technique, several hours should be dedicated to a detailed explanation of the steps in the construction of a quality table, and the system to be used to compare numerically the various items.

T-shaped matrix diagram

The T-shaped matrix is nothing more than the combination of two L-shaped matrix diagrams. As can be seen in Figure 7.7 it is based on the premise that two separate sets of items are both related to a third set. Therefore, A items are somehow related to both B and C items.

Figure 7.8 shows one application. In this case, it shows the relationship between a set of courses in a curriculum and two important

Substitute quality characteristics

	MFR	Ash	Importance	Current	Best competitor	Plan	IR	SP	RQW
No film breaks	○ 17	◀ 6	4	4	4	4	1	○	5.6
High rates	◉ 23		3	3	4	4	1.3		4.6
Low gauge variability	◉ 37	◀ 7	4	3	4	4	1.3	○	7.3

Customer demands

◉ Strong correlation
○ Some correlation
◀ Possible correlation
IR Improvement ratio
SP Sales point
RQW Relative quality weight

Figure 7.6   *An example of the matrix diagram (Quality Table)*

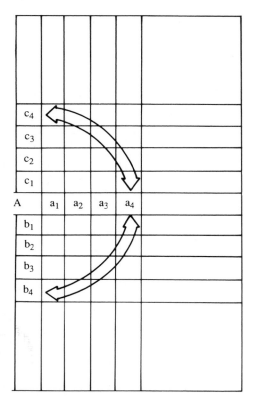

Figure 7.7   *T-shape matrix*

sets of considerations: who should give the training for each course, and which would be the most appropriate functions to attend each of the courses?

It has also been widely used to develop new materials by simultaneously relating different alternative materials to two sets of desirable properties.

There are other matrices that deal with ideas such as product or service function, costs, failure modes, capabilities, etc., and there are at least 40 different types of matrix diagrams available.

5 Matrix data analysis

Matrix data analysis is used to take data displayed in a matrix diagram and arrange it so that it can be more easily viewed and show the strength of the relationship between variables. It is used most often in marketing and

Who trains?

- Human resource dept.
- Managers
- Operators*
- Consultants
- Production operator
- Craft foreman
- GLSPC coordinator
- Plant SPC coordinator
- University
- Technology specialists
- Engineers

*Need to tailor to groups

X = Full
O = Overview

Courses

SQC · 7 Old tools · 7 New tools · Reliability · Design review · QC basics · QCC facilitator · Diagnostic tools · Problem solving · Communication skills · Organize for quality · Design of experiments · Company mission · Quality planning · Just in time · New superv. training · Company TQM system · Group dynamics skills · SQC course/execs.

Who attends?

- Executives
- Top management
- Middle management
- Production supervisors
- Supervisor functional
- Staff
- Marketing
- Sales
- Engineers
- Clerical
- Production worker
- Quality professional
- Project team
- Employee involvement
- Suppliers
- Maintenance

Figure 7.8   T-matrix diagram on company-wide training

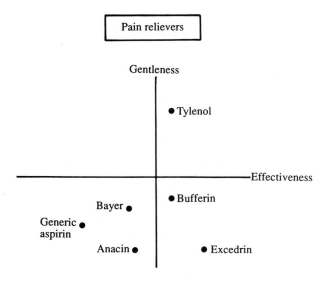

Figure 7.9   *An example of matrix data analysis*

product research. The concept behind matrix data analysis is fairly simple, but its execution (including data gathering) is complex.

A good idea of the uses and value of the construction of a chart for matrix data analysis may be shown in a simple example in which types of pain relievers are compared based on gentleness and effectiveness (Figure 7.9). This information could be used together with some type of demographic analysis to develop a marketing plan. Based on the information, advertising and product introduction could be effectively tailored for specific areas. New product development could also be carried out to attack specific niches in markets that would be profitable.

6 Process decision program chart

A process decision program chart (PDPC) is used to map out each event and contingency that can occur when progressing from a problem statement to its solution. The PDPC is used to anticipate the unexpected and plan for it. It includes plans for counter-measures on deviations. The PDPC is related to a failure mode and effect analysis (see Chapter 6) and its structure is similar to that of a tree diagram. An example of the PDPC is shown in Figure 7.10. Suggested steps for constructing a PDPC are as follows:

(a) Construct a tree diagram as described previously.

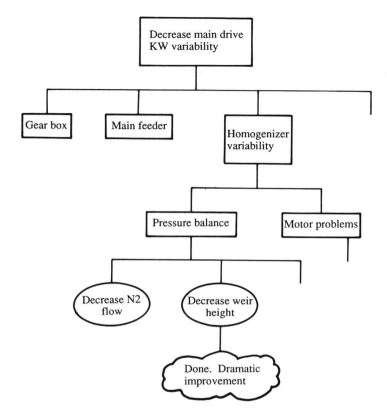

Figure 7.10 *Process decision program chart*

(b) Take one major branch of the tree diagram (an item just to the right of the main goal or purpose). Ask the question 'what could go wrong at this step?' or 'what other path could this step take?'
(c) Answer the questions by branching off the original path in 'organization chart' manner.
(d) Off to the side of each step, list actions or counter measures that could be taken.
(e) Continue the process until the branch is exhausted.
(f) Repeat with other main branches.

The PDPC is very simply an attempt to be proactive in the analysis of failure and to construct, on paper, a 'dry' run of the process so that the 'check' part of the cycle can be defined in advance. PDPC is likely to enjoy widespread use because of increasing attention to product liability.

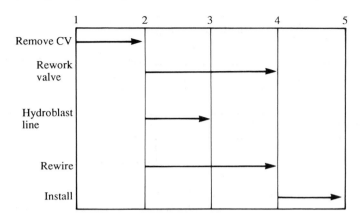

Figure 7.11 *Gantt chart*

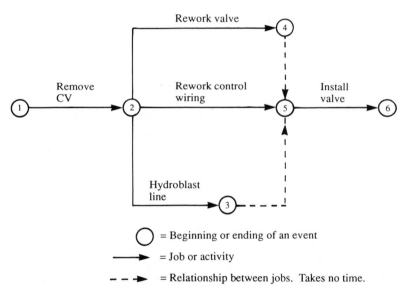

Figure 7.12 *The arrow diagram*

7 Arrow diagram

The arrow diagram is used to plan or schedule a task. To use it, the subtask sequence and duration must be known. This tool is essentially the same as the standard 'Gantt chart' shown in Figure 7.11. Figure 7.12 is the same sequence shown as an arrow diagram. Although it is a simple and well-known tool for planning work, it is surprising how often it is ignored. The arrow diagram is useful in understanding a repetitive job in order to make it more efficient. Some suggestions on constructing arrow diagrams are:

(a) Use a team of people involved in a job or project to list all the tasks necessary to complete the job and write them on individual cards. On the bottom half of the card, write the time required to complete the task.
(b) Place related tasks together. Place them in chronological order.
(c) Summarize the cards on a chart similar to Figure 7.12.

There are refinements and modifications that can be applied to make the arrow diagram more detailed or to account for contingency. The technique is used widely in project planning, where it is known as critical path analysis (CPA). It is easily computerized and has led to further developments, such as programme evaluation and review technique (PERT).

Summary

What has been described in this section is a system for improving the design of products and services involving the use of 'seven new tools', sometimes called quality function deployment. For the most part, the seven tools are neither new nor revolutionary, but rather a compilation and modification of some tools that have been around for a long time. The tools do not replace statistical methods but they are meant to be used together with SPC as part of the design process (see also Chapter 10).

The tools work best when representatives from all parts of an organization are involved in their use and execution of the results. Besides the structure that the tools provide, the cooperation between departments that is required will help break down barriers within the organizations. While product designers and marketing personnel will see the most direct applications for these tools, proper use of the 'philosophy' behind them requires participation from all parts of an organization. In addition, some of the seven new tools can be used in problem-solving activities not directly related to design.

7.4 Design control and management

Design, like any other activity, must be carefully managed. A flow chart of the various stages and activities involved in the design and development process appears in Figure 7.13. By structuring the design process in this way, it is possible to:

● control the various stages;

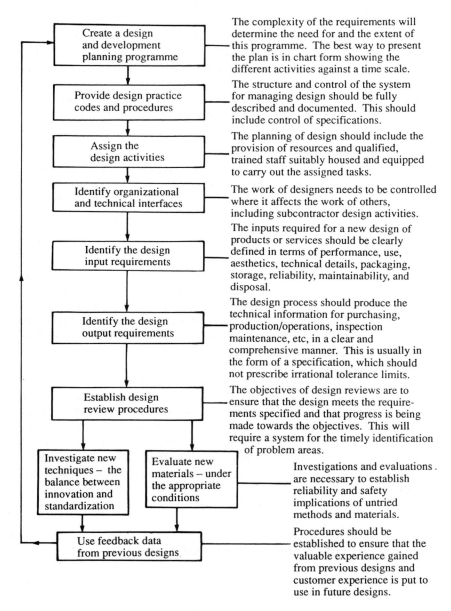

Figure 7.13 *The design control process*

- check whether they have been completed;
- decide which management functions need to be involved and at what stage;
- estimate the level of resources needed.

The design control must be carefully handled to avoid stifling the creativity of the designer(s) which is crucial in making design solutions a reality.

It is clear that the design process requires a range of specialized skills, and the way in which these skills are managed, the way they interact, and the amount of effort devoted to the different stages of the design and development process is fundamental to the quality, producibility, and price of the service or final product. A team approach to the management of design can play a major role in the success of a project.

It is never possible to exert the same tight control on the design effort as on other operational efforts, yet the cost involved and the time used are often substantial and both must appear somewhere within the organization's budget.

There are certain features which make control of design difficult:

1 No design will ever be 'complete' in the sense that, with effort, some modification or improvement can always be made.
2 Few designs are entirely novel. An examination of most 'new' products or services will show that they employ existing techniques, components or systems to which has been added a comparatively small novel element.
3 The longer the time which is spent on a design, the less the increase in the value of the design unless a technological breakthrough is achieved. This diminishing return from the design effort must be carefully managed.
4 External and/or internal customers will impose limitations on design time and cost. It is as difficult to imagine a design project whose completion date is not implicitly fixed, either by a promise to a customer, the opening of a trade show or exhibition, a seasonal 'deadline', a production schedule or some other constraint, as it is to imagine an organization whose funds are unlimited, or a product whose price has no ceiling.

Five stages of a design project

In every project the design programme will pass through the following stages:

1 *Conception*, when a draft specification is laid down incorporating the requirements. This first stage is most important in providing the basis for control of all subsequent design activity. A specification must be

drawn up in as much detail as possible by marketing in discussion with design personnel. In effect, this is a translation of a marketing requirement into terms intelligible to the designer. Time spent here will not only indicate to the designers exactly what is required, it will enable marketing to discuss the project with actual or potential customers, and it will enable some measure of the cost of changes in requirement upon the design effort to be made.

2 *Acceptance*, where the specification is shown to be achievable by mathematical calculation, preliminary drawings, trials, models, or laboratory-scale processes. It is here that the trade-offs between requirements and achievability are made explicit and must be resolved. This is a function carried out in the design department by designers and their associates. It is usually the first stage where costs for the design work will be assigned directly to the project, and is normally initiated by a formal instruction embodying the draft specification laid down at conception. The draft specification is tested, being subjected to trials, calculation, model-making or such other activity as is appropriate, and is then accepted, rejected as impracticable, or modified in conjunction with marketing. Sometimes, particularly in simple projects, this stage will coincide with the previous one, and may consist of only a meeting between all interested parties. At this stage it is particularly important for the designer to know the capability of the operating unit which will carry out the final design. Formal and frequent consultation between design and operations here and in all later stages can save much trouble and cost during operations.

3 *Execution*, where a number of trials are carried out, models are prepared, or pilot-plants are constructed, following the laboratory-scale experiments. These are based on the ideas generated at stage 2, and on general design considerations, both theoretical and practical. The 'models' should, as far as possible, conform to the specification and, where this is not possible, the differences should be known and their effects considered. The differences usually arise either from the scale of the project (for example, the design of an oil refinery) or from the need for special aspects or parts, the costs of which cannot be justified until the design is finalized. Whilst cost considerations must not be overlooked, the requirements are most important at this stage, and the trials or models made should indicate clearly the feasibility of the proposed design meeting the specification at all points. The cost of the final product or service is a matter which must be accepted by the design department as a factor as important as any other, although subsequent technical development can often produce significant reductions in cost.

4 *Translation*, where the process is put into a form in which it can be

operated within the organization, and to the specification laid down at stage 2. At this stage the appropriate operations and after sales service departments must be involved in the design work. It is quite common practice for the teams responsible for the original work and for the 'model' to hand over their task to a development team which, while appreciating the originality of the design, can also appreciate the problems involved in its application. The development team should discuss at all stages the operating problems with the appropriate departments. Detailed estimates will begin to be formed, and it should be possible to assign maximum acceptable costs to the various stages or components. Lack of cooperation at this stage between marketing, designers and the operating departments will prove very costly; the design eventually placed upon the operating units will be difficult to reproduce, and emergency redesigns carried out during operations will result in a debasing of the service or product. Work should be proceeding on preparing the final operating information which summarizes all the design and development effort. Control of the amount of work put into drawing up this information is both important and difficult, and it must be remembered that the information is intended to aid operation, and not be an end in itself.

5 *Preoperational*, where products are produced or a service provided in quantities sufficient to check the design, equipment and specification under normal operating conditions. It is not until this stage that the specifications can be considered to be final and not liable to change without authorization. This task should be done at some time before the start of 'delivery' in order that any faults or weaknesses which are shown up can be corrected. Such a preoperation run will check:

(a) operational information;
(b) operational resources;
(c) operational techniques and estimates;
(d) specifications;

and only after such a run should the operational information be considered to be final.

The above outline of the processes of designing for satisfying the customer's requirements is an attempt to separate out the various stages of a creative act. These five steps are always present in some form, although in small organizations they may be telescoped. In one-off or small quantity product or service situations, the execution stage may generate the first and only product. Hence, in projects where large articles, such as hovercraft or power plants, are being designed, the last three stages effectively coalesce with the actual production stage. It must be remembered that the decisions taken at each stage are never taken in isolation. They all affect, in some degree, previous and succeeding stages and the activities of the marketing and operations functions. Once a design is complete, steps must be taken to maintain it, or to amend it formally.

Design review

Design review is a method to ensure that the process of designing progresses towards the objectives of the programme. It does this by studying the process and identifying problem areas systematically and in time for them to be solved. The aims of design reviews are to establish that:

- the design of the service or product will meet *all* the specified performance criteria;
- the product or service being designed can be produced, inspected tested or checked, installed, operated, and maintained to provide satisfaction to the 'customer';
- all viable design alternatives have been considered;
- any statutory requirements will be met;
- adequate documentation exists to define the design and how the service or product is to be used and maintained.

Design reviews should cover all the quality-related factors and check lists of these should be drawn up for each review. These are usually carried out at the preliminary, intermediate, and final stages of the design process, by people who represent the relevant disciplines. The extent of the design review, the membership of the review team, and the methods used will depend on many factors including the

- service or product application;
- 'state-of-the-art';
- complexity of the design;
- competence of the designers or originators;
- similarity with previous, proven designs;
- degree of standardization.

The design review methods to be used should be identified and recorded, together with the results of the review. Techniques of value analysis, reliability engineering, and service or product testing may be incorporated.[1] The main theme of the review must be objectivity. This

[1] See *Production and Operations Management* Keith Lockyer, Alan Muhleman and John Oakland, Pitman 1988.

often requires the involvement of experienced specialists who take the formal design review meetings very seriously with agendas, minutes, and action-plans for follow-up.

The use of computer-aided design (CAD) in quality

The tremendous speed and vast storage capacity of a computer aid the designer in a number of ways:

1 Quantities of data can be held in the computer's store and withdrawn with such ease that it becomes possible to refer readily to previous designs, experience, data, and respond very quickly to the customer requirements.
2 Computer graphics may well permit a visual display of a design under various conditions, so that various ideas and changes can be immediately observed.
3 The computer can store the results of the design process and issue them in a useful form, often obviating the need for the preparation of drawings.
4 A library of 'ready-made' designs can be easily stored in and retrieved from a computer.
5 Frequently-repeated, and long, tedious calculations can be carried out rapidly. Without a computer, a designer will reduce the need for calculations by using tables or graphs of 'established standards' or 'good practice'. These, to become manageable, are the abbreviated results either of a few calculations or of a series of trials, and in either case contain ample 'safety' factors which usually over-compensate for the inadequacies of the calculations. As a result, the design produced may not meet the requirements or be unnecessarily costly in some way. The computer enables these calculations to be carried out as and when needed, reducing wasted effort. Some calculations are so lengthy that they cannot be carried out by hand. A computer may perform these if appropriate software is available.
6 The computer's abilities may be used to check the effect of modification(s). The manual effort of examining the effect of changing one or other of the constituent parameters may be so great that no such examination is made. This may result in accepting a result which could be modified.

Computer-aided design is so common in some industries that organizations which intend to compete successfully for market share cannot avoid it as a way of life in the future. In industries where it is less used, breakthroughs will continually update the need for companies to adopt CAD in the most unlikely situations.

8 System for quality 1 – design and contents

8.1 Why a documented system?

In earlier chapters we have seen how the keystone of quality management is the concept of customer and supplier working together to their mutual advantage. For any particular organization, this becomes 'total' quality management if the supplier/customer interfaces extend beyond the immediate customers, back inside the organization, and beyond the immediate suppliers. In order to achieve this, a company must organize itself in such a way that the human, administrative and technical factors affecting quality will be under control. This leads to the requirement for the development and implementation of a quality management system which enables the objectives set out in the quality policy to be accomplished. Clearly, for maximum effectiveness and to meet individual customer requirements, the quality management system in use must be appropriate to the type of activity and product or service being offered.

It may be useful to reflect on why such a device is necessary to achieve control of processes. The author remembers being at a table in a restaurant with eight people who all ordered the 'chef's special individual soufflé'. All eight soufflés arrived together at the table magnificent in their appearance and consistency, each one exhibiting an almost identical size and shape – a truly remarkable demonstration of culinary skill. How had this been achieved? The chef had *managed* such consistency by making sure that, for each soufflé, he used the same ingredients (materials), the same equipment (plant), the same method (procedure) in exactly the same way every time. The process was under control. This is the aim of a good quality management system, to provide the 'operator' with consistency and satisfaction in terms of methods, materials, and equipment (Figure 8.1).

The soufflés were not British Standard, ANSI Standard, Canadian Standard, or ISO Standard soufflés – they were the chef's special soufflés. It is not conceivable that the chef sat down with a blank piece of paper to invent a soufflé recipe, why re-invent wheels? He probably used a standard formula and changed it slightly to meet his own requirements and make it his own. This is exactly the way in which organizations must use the international standards on quality systems which are available. The 'wheel' has been invented but it must be built in a way which meets the specific organizational and product or service requirements. The International Standards Organization (ISO) Standard 9000 Series sets out the methods by which a management system, incorporating all the activities associated with quality, can be implemented in an organization to ensure that all the specified performance requirements and needs of the customer are fully met.

Let us return to the chef in the restaurant and propose that his success leads to a desire to open eight restaurants in which are served his special soufflés. Clearly he cannot rush from each one of these establishments

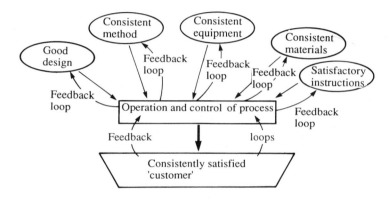

Figure 8.1   *The systematic approach to quality management*

to another every evening making soufflés. The only course open to him to ensure consistency of output, in all eight restaurants, is for him to write down in some detail the system he uses, and then make sure that it is used on all sites, every time a soufflé is produced. Moreover, he must periodically visit the different sites to ensure that:

1 the people involved are operating according to the documented system (a system audit);
2 the soufflé system still meets the requirements (a system review).

If in his system audits and reviews he discovers that an even better product or less waste can be achieved by changing the method or one of the materials, then he may wish to effect a change. To maintain consistency, he must ensure that the appropriate changes are made to the documented system and that everyone concerned is issued with the revision and begins to operate accordingly.

A fully documented quality management system will ensure that two major requirements are met:

1 The customer's requirements – for confidence in the ability of the organization to deliver consistently the desired product or service.
2 The organization's requirements – both internally and externally, and at an optimum cost, with efficient utilization of the resources available, material, human, and technological.

These requirements can be truly met only if objective evidence is provided in the form of information and data, which supports the system activities, from the ultimate supplier through to the ultimate customer.

A *quality system* may be defined then as an assembly of components, such as the organizational structure, responsibilities, procedures, processes and resources for implementing quality management. These components interact together and are affected by being in the system, so the isolation and study of each one in detail will not necessarily lead to an understanding of the system as a whole. Often the interactions between the components, such as materials and processes, procedures and responsibilities, are just as important as the components themselves, and problems can arise from these interactions as much as from the components. Clearly if one of the components is removed from the system, the whole thing will change.

8.2 Quality system design

The quality system should apply to and interact with all activities of the organization. This begins with the identification of the requirements and ends with their satisfaction, at every transaction interface. The activities involved may be classified in several ways; generally as processing, communicating, and controlling, but more usefully and specifically as:

1 marketing;
2 market research;
3 design;
4 specifying;
5 development;
6 procurement;
7 process planning;
8 process development and assessment;
9 process operation and control;
10 product or service testing or checking;
11 packaging (if required);
12 storage (if required);

13 sales;
14 distribution or installation/operation;
15 technical service;
16 maintenance.

These may be regarded as slats on a rotating drum (Figure 8.2), the driving force of which is the centralized quality system. The drum will not operate until the system is in place and working. The first step in getting the drum rolling is to prepare the necessary documentation. This means, in very basic terms, that procedures should be written down, preferably in

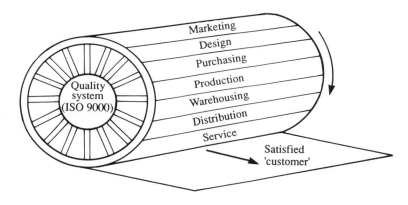

Figure 8.2   *The quality system power unit to 'customer' satisfaction*

such a way that the system conforms to one of the national or international standards. This is probably best done in the form of a quality manual (see Chapter 9).

In most organizations, established methods of working already exist and all that is required is the writing down of what is currently done. In some instances, companies may not have procedures to satisfy the requirements of a good standard and they may have to begin to devise them. Alternatively, it may be found that two people, supposedly performing the same task, are working in different ways and there is a need to standardize the procedure.

One of the best-documented quality systems the author has even seen was in a small hand-tool manufacturing company. It possessed an excellent quality manual, beautifully laid out in sections covering each paragraph heading of ISO 9002. Each procedure described exactly how compliance with the standard was achieved, identified the responsibilities and authorities of the individuals concerned, but it was a work of fiction!

It did not bear any relation to what actually happened. There were two main reasons for this:

1 The quality manager had written the manual to describe how he would have wished things to happen or how he thought they happened, without discovering the reality before documenting the system.
2 The other people involved in certain procedures had not been involved, had not been asked simply to write down how they operated.

One person alone cannot document a quality system, the task must involve all personnel who have responsibility for any part of it. The quality manual must be a practical working document, that way it ensures that consistency of operation is maintained and it may be used as a training aid.

8.3 Quality system requirements

The special methods and procedures which need to be documented and implemented will be determined by the nature of the process or processes carried out. Certain fundamental principles are applicable, however, throughout industry, commerce, and the services. These fall into generally well-defined categories, as follows:

1 Quality policy (see Chapter 2)

The organization should define and publish its quality policy. Full commitment is required from the most senior management to ensure that the policy is understood, implemented, and maintained at all levels in the organization.

2 Organization (see Chapter 3)

Organizations should have an organization chart, and define the responsibilities of those shown in the chart, which should include all functions that affect quality. One manager with the necessary authority, resources, support, and ability should be given the responsibility to coordinate, implement, and monitor the quality system, resolve any problems and ensure prompt and effective corrective action. Those who control processing, warehousing, delivery, and reworking of nonconforming product or service must also be identified.

3 Quality system

The organization should prepare a quality plan and a quality manual which is appropriate for the 'level' of quality system required:

- A level 1 system relates to design, production or operation and installation, which applies when the customer specifies the goods or services in terms of how they are to perform, rather than in established technical terms.
- A level 2 system is relevant when an organization is producing goods or services to a customer's or published specification.
- A level 3 system applies only to final production or service inspection, check, or test procedures.

The reader is referred to the International Standard, ISO 9000 series as follows:

Quality systems ISO 9000 Series 1987

Standard no.	Title
9000	Quality management and quality assurance standards – guidelines for selection and use.
9001–3	Quality system models
9001	Design/development, production, installation and servicing
9002	Production and installation
9003	Final inspection and test
9004	Quality management and quality system elements – guidelines

Detailed recommendations for the development of a quality manual are given in Chapter 9, but briefly it should set out the general quality policies, procedures, and practices of the organization. In the quality manual for large organizations, it may be convenient to indicate simply the existence and contents of other manuals, which contain the details of procedures and practices in operation in specific areas of the system.

Before an organization can agree to supply to a specification, it must ensure that:

(a) the plant and processes involved (including any which are sub-contracted) are capable of meeting the requirements;
(b) the operators have the necessary skills;

(c) the operating procedures are written down and not simply passed on verbally;

(d) the plant and equipment instrumentation are capable of measuring the process variables with the appropriate accuracy and precision (see Chapter 10);

(e) the quality control procedures and any inspection, check, or test methods available, provide results to the required accuracy and precision, and are documented (see Chapter 11);

(f) any subjective phrases in the specification, such as 'finely ground', 'low moisture content' are understood and procedures exist to establish the exact customer requirements.

4 Contract review

Each accepted customer order should be regarded as a contract, and 'order entry procedures' should be developed and documented. These should ensure that:

(a) the customer requirements are absolutely clear and in writing, although verbal call-offs from a written master order are acceptable;

(b) differences between the order and any original enquiry and/or quotation are agreed or resolved;

(c) the terms of the order (contract) can be met.

Clearly, a procedural dialogue should be established between customer and supplier with regard to the specification, interfaces and the communication of changes. The system must ensure that everyone in the organization understands the commitments, skills, and resources required to meet any particular contract and that these have been scheduled.

5 Design control (see Chapter 7)

Where a level 1 system is required, there must be procedures which control and verify design of products or services to ensure that the customer requirements will be met. The translation of the information derived from market research into practical designs, which are achievable by the operating units, should be the core of the documented design control system. This will include the following activities which were dealt with in more detail in Chapter 7:

(a) planning of research, design and development;

(b) assignment of design activities to qualified staff;

(c) identification of the organizational and technical interfaces between different groups;

(d) preparation of a design brief relating to the requirements of the product or service (inputs);
(e) production of clear and comprehensive technical data to enable complete operation of the service or production and delivery of the product, according to the requirements (outputs);
(f) verification that the design outputs meet the requirements of the inputs;
(g) identification and control of all design changes and modifications and the associated documentation.

Attention, in detail, to the above areas will form the basis of a research, design and development programme. With correct implementation it will maintain a balance between innovation and standardization, which encourages the use of new techniques whilst retaining reliable, proven designs, materials and methods.

6 Document control

All documents relating to quality, including the following:

(a) quality manual and supplementary manuals;
(b) departmental operating manuals;
(c) written procedures;
(d) purchasing specifications;
(e) lists of approved suppliers;
(f) product or service formulations and specifications;
(g) intermediate, part, or component formulations and specifications;

should be 'controlled' to ensure that only the most up-to-date issues are used and referred to at the various locations. Clearly, this will require records of who holds the documents, and a written procedure for the issue of amendments and for reissues, together with some form of acknowledgement of receipt. Computerized techniques may be very helpful here. If additional copies of 'controlled' documents are produced for temporary purposes, procedures should exist to prevent their misuse. Sales literature is not usually regarded as controlled documentation, unless it forms the basis of a contract. In industries where continuous innovation, redesign and/or improvements are a major feature, good document change control is vital.

7 Purchasing (see Chapter 6)

The objective of the purchasing system is very simple – to ensure that purchased products and services conform to the requirements of the organization. The means of achieving this should be concentrated on assessments of the suppliers' own quality systems, rather than by an elaborate scheme of checking, testing and inspection on receipt.

Suppliers should be selected on the basis of their ability to meet the requirements, and objective documentary evidence will be required to show that the supplier:

(a) has the capability to do so (see Chapter 10);
(b) will do so reliably and consistently.

When deciding the extent of *vendor appraisal* necessary, the following factors should be taken into consideration:

(a) feasibility of appraisal;
(b) historical evidence from records;
(c) any independent third party quality system assessment, certification, or registration;
(d) objective evidence, e.g. information from other customers of the supplier (not 'reputation' which is subjective).

Vendor appraisal of any product or service sub-contractors is often necessary to ensure that their quality system matches the standard of the purchasing organization, and appraisal visits may form part of the corrective action following unsatisfactory performance.

Purchasing documents have been referred to in some detail in Chapter 6, but the basic requirements are that they:

(a) are written;
(b) include the specification or reference to it;
(c) are made available to the supplier.

Call-offs can be made by telephone or computer means, but must refer to the appropriate purchasing document. The system should allow customers to impose quality system requirements on their suppliers' suppliers, and so on, if specified in the contract. This may include independent third party certification, assessment of products, services or records.

8 Customer-supplied product or services

Where a customer supplies material or services, on which further transformation work is required, it is necessary to have systems which ensure its suitability for use and which enable traceability of the material or service through all processes and storage. Any such material which is damaged, lost, or not suitable for use should be reported to the customer. Special considerations may be necessary when the customer supplies material which is used in a continuous process with other purchased material.

9 Identification and traceability

Identification and traceability from raw materials to finished products and services are essential if effective methods of process control are to be applied and quality problems are to be related to cause. Material in process or bulk storage should be identified, if necessary by virtue of its location and time, and the design of procedures and record keeping should allow for this. Traceability requirements are an optional part of an agreed specification or contract.

10 Process control (see Chapters 10 and 11)

To control the operation of any process clearly requires some planning activity, that is careful consideration of the inputs to the process so that they become suitable for the purpose. It may be difficult to imagine, but the author has seen too often the operation of processes, about which too little is known in terms of the ability to meet the requirements.

To operate processes under controlled conditions, documented work instructions must be available to staff. These do not need to repeat the basic skills of the operator's profession, but they must contain sufficient detail to enable the process to be carried out under the specified conditions. A fully documented 'process manual' should contain, where appropriate:

(a) a description of the process with appropriate technological information, this may be in the form of a process flow chart;
(b) a description of the plant or equipment required;
(c) any special process 'set-up' or 'start-up' procedures;
(d) reference to any instrumentation and calibration procedures, related to control of the process;
(e) simplified operator instructions or a summary which includes the quantity of materials required and the order in which the process is carried out.

For certain special processes, such as welding, plastic moulding, heat treatment, application of protective treatments, and cooking, where deficiencies may become apparent only after the product is in use, continuous monitoring of adherence to the documented procedures is the only effective method of process control.

11 Checking, measuring, inspecting and testing

Incoming materials and services

All need to be either inspected or otherwise verified. The amount of inspection is clearly a function of the situation, and might consist simply of:

(a) checking a product label or delivery note against a **purchase order**;
(b) visual examination for damage in transit;
(c) checking the evidence from a Certificate of Conformity or of Analysis.

(These are valid only if an adequate assessment of the supplier's quality system has been carried out.)

Whatever the system, it must be operated in accordance with the written procedures. If bought-in materials have to be released into production before adequate verification or checking can take place, the system should ensure that it is possible to identify the material and recall it if problems arise. This may prevent the acceptance of certain bulk materials without the appropriate receiving inspection.

In process

This answers the 'are we doing the job OK?' question which involves some form of process monitoring and control. Ideally it is the actual process parameters, such as temperature, cutting speed, feedrate, pressure, typing speed, flow rate, which should be monitored to ensure feedforward control of the process. The work instructions should also indicate the action to be taken in the event of process parameters being found to be incorrect, or 'out of control'.

Finished product and/or service

Whatever final checking, inspecting or testing activities have been set out in the quality plan should be documented, including any delaying of despatch until the checks have been carried out.

Records must be kept of all the checks, tests, measurements, etc., carried out at inwards goods or services receipt, during operation of the process, or at the final product or service stage which are required to demonstrate conformance to the requirements or specifications. These may include Certificates of Conformity or Analysis, and evidence on plant records or in a computer, that process control parameters were actually monitored.

12 Measuring, inspection and test equipment

All measuring and test equipment, which is relevant to the quality system, must be controlled, calibrated and maintained. This includes equipment used for in-process parameter measurement and control, such as temperature and pressure gauges, as well as that used in laboratories or test/measurement rooms. Where equipment is used only for observation, safety, or fault diagnosis reasons it may be excluded from the fully documented inspection equipment calibration system.

The system for the instrumentation should:

(a) refer to the measurements to be made, their accuracy and precision, and the equipment to be used to ensure the necessary capability;
(b) identify the equipment and ensure its calibration against the appropriate standard(s) with suitable procedures, and its correct handling, preservation, storage, etc.;
(c) maintain calibration records for all inspection, measuring and test equipment.

13 Inspection and test status

There are essentially three statuses for all materials and services – incoming, intermediate or in-process, and finished:

(a) Awaiting inspection, check or test.
(b) Passed requirements of inspection, check or test.
(c) Failed requirements of inspection, check or test.

The test status of material is identified by any suitable means: labels, stamps, markings, position in the process, records (including computer), etc. These should be used to ensure that only material or services which conform to the requirements are passed on to the next stage, or despatched. The test or check carried out may, of course, refer to a process control parameter.

14 Nonconforming products or services

To prevent inadvertent use or delivery of materials and services which do not conform to the specified requirements, a documented system should exist which clearly identifies and, if possible, segregates them. The procedures should also show how the nonconforming output will be reworked, disposed of, accepted with concession, or regraded, and what corrective action will take place.

15 Corrective action

This is a very important part of the system in any organization, since it provides the means to never-ending improvement of process operation. Systematic planning is a basic requirement for effective corrective action programmes. The procedures for major corrective action should be in the form of general guidance and should define the duties of the managers, supervisors and key personnel. The detailed action to be taken will be dependent upon the circumstances prevailing at the time and it is not, therefore, appropriate for the written procedures to be too detailed. All employees must be involved and made fully aware of the general corrective action procedures appertaining to their own processes and activities. The written procedures for corrective action should be implemented when there are:

(a) failures in *any* part of the quality system;
(b) complaints from customers (internal or external);
(c) complaints to suppliers (internal or external) and to sub-contractors.

The underlying purpose of this part of the system is to eliminate the causes of nonconformance by initiation of investigations, analyses, and preventive actions. Controls must be built in to make sure that the corrective actions are taken and effective, and that any necessary changes in procedures are recorded and implemented. The provision of *corrective action teams*, with regular training and updating, enables people to become used to working together to solve problems.

16 Protection of product or service quality

The sight of a warehouseman, in dirty wellington boots, climbing over clean sacks of finished product to count them, still remains in the author's memory. A great deal of damage can be done to products and services between their 'production' and their transfer to the customer. This highlights the need for the quality system to cover such things as handling, storage, packaging, transport, and delivery of final product or services. The written procedures should be aimed at preventing damage or deterioration. The use of the correct type of packaging and labelling may invoke national or international regulations and/or codes of practice. Where contract hauliers or outside transport are employed, their ability to meet the requirements of cleanliness, schedules, etc., should be established and appropriate procedures documented.

17 Servicing

If servicing is an important part of the customer requirement, e.g. the provision of a burglar alarm service, procedures should be documented for its operation and to verify that it satisfies the needs. The servicing system may well include some or all of the contents of the overall quality system; design, documentation control, process control, training, review, etc. In particular it must ensure that:

(a) the servicing procedures are effectively carried out;

(b) adequate resources are made available, in terms of people, time, equipment, materials, information, etc.;
(c) good interfaces exist for dealing with the customer, in terms of regular service contracts, items returned, customer complaints or call outs.

18 Quality records

The records which are retained provide objective evidence that work is being carried out in accordance with the documented procedures. Attention should be paid to identifying which records need to be retained and to their easy retrieval. On one occasion, one of the author's colleagues was performing a vertical audit for traceability purposes in a garment manufacturers. He selected some items from stock and, on attempting to trace back to purchased materials, discovered that final inspection records on certain items were missing. It transpired that one of the final inspectors spent three months in hospital, and the chief inspector, who insisted that she had stood in and carried out the necessary inspection, was too busy to write down the results. This represents a failure of the system to demonstrate compliance with its own requirements, and can be as serious as an ineffective procedure.

Records will have been established if the documented quality system has been set up as described above, but there must be procedures for the collection, indexing, filing or storage, retrieval, and disposition of records. Serious thought should be given to the retention time of records, which should then be stated in the documented system.

19 Training (see Chapter 13)

For all staff, written procedures should be established and maintained for:

- identifying training needs;
- carrying out the training;
- keeping records of training.

It should be possible to go to the training records and establish from them whether an individual has been instructed to carry out the various tasks associated with his/her job. This has implications, of course, for task analysis.

20 Use of statistical techniques (see Chapters 10 and 11)

Statistics is simply the handling and use of data. Certain techniques exist which enable meaningful analyses to be carried out, and procedures for using them should be established where appropriate. The use of statistical process control (SPC) methods is essential in many instances where knowledge of the process, with respect to its state of control and capability, is a requirement.

21 Quality system audits and reviews

An internal audit sets out to establish whether the quality management system is being operated according to the written procedures. A review addresses the much wider issue of whether the quality system actually meets the requirements and aims to determine the system's effectiveness. Clearly the results of quality audits will be used in the reviews, for if procedures are not being operated according to plan, it may be that improvements in the system are required, rather than enforcing adherence to unsuitable methods. Organizations should plan to self-police the quality system by carrying out both internal audits and reviews, and the person responsible for organizing these is the manager with responsibility for coordinating and monitoring the whole quality system (see also Chapter 9, section 2).

8.4 The quality system rings of confidence

The activities which must be addressed in the design and implementation of a good quality management system may be considered to be attached to a 'ring of confidence', which starts and ends with the customer (Figure 8.3). It is possible to group these into two spheres of activities:

- those involving direct interaction with the customer;
- those concerning primarily the internal activities of the supplier.

The overlap necessary between customer and supplier is clearly illustrated by this model. Equally obvious is that separation will lead to dysfunction and disaster.

It cannot be stated too often that the customer–supplier interactions, which generate satisfaction of needs, are just as necessary internally. The principles of quality system design, documentation and implementation set out in this and the next chapter must apply to every single person, every department, every process transaction, and every type of organization. The vocabulary in the engineering factory system may be different to that used in the hotel; the hospital system will be set out differently to that of the drug manufacturer, but the underlying concepts will be the same.

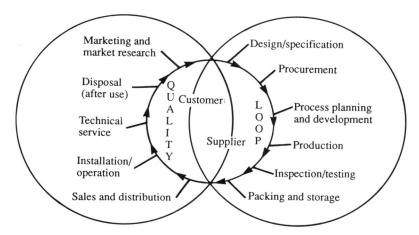

Figure 8.3 *The quality system rings of confidence*

It is not acceptable for the managers in industries, or parts of organizations, less often associated with standards on quality systems to find 'technological' reasons for avoiding the requirement to manage quality. The author and his colleagues have heard the excuse that 'our industry (or organization) is different to any other industry (or organization)', in almost every industry or organization with which they have been involved. Clearly, there are technological differences between all industries and nearly all organizations, but in terms of managing total quality there are hardly any at all.

Senior managers in every type and size of organization must take the responsibility for the adoption of the appropriate documented quality system. If this requires translation from 'engineering language', so be it – get someone from inside or outside the organizaton to do it. Do not wait for the message to be translated into different forms – inefficiencies, waste, high costs, crippling competition, loss of market.

9 System for quality 2 – documentation and implementation

9.1 The quality manual

The quality manual is the document in which it is explained how the organization carries out the quality policy. The author has visited many companies which, when asked to produce the quality manual, have required three people to carry it in, or pointed to a bank of filing cabinets. That volume of material is not a quality manual, it is usually a test and inspection procedures manual, a calibration and measurement system, a plant operating procedures manual, and sometimes a purchasing system.

A good quality manual should be no longer than 25 to 30 pages. It is perhaps misnamed, it should be called the management manual, for it explains how the organization's management systems operate to achieve the general policies, the explanation being in the form of a series of simple statements of what is actually done, and it refers to where detailed procedures may be found, if necessary. There will be a section – a page – on how the purchasing system operates, one on what happens if customers complain, another on the organizational structure with allocation of responsibility for the management of the quality system clearly stated, and so on. The quality manual then sets out the general policies, procedures, and practices of the organization, in a well-organized, comprehensive, and succinct manner.

Planning a quality manual

There is no standard form for writing a quality manual since each one must describe the particular policies and system to which it refers, and this must be the system which is actually operated, not the one the quality manager would like to see operating. Every organization produces and serves, and is organized in a unique way, and it is this that must be reflected in the documented system. All this means, of course, that organizations must write their own quality manuals.

If an international standard, such as the ISO 9000 series is being used as the framework for the organization's quality system, it is necessary at this stage to decide which level or part of the standard will best suit the activities. It is not possible to move on to the detailed planning of the manual until this has been decided. The chosen standard and level should be mentioned in the quality manual at an early stage.

It is important to appreciate that there are various types of quality system and that the quality manual will reflect this. The ISO 9000 series specifies requirements for quality systems designed to generate products and services which meet the agreed specifications. Hence, it addresses a limited number of activities, and differs from a system whose purpose is to achieve total quality management. For a TQM system, *every* activity in the organization must be included. Of course, ISO 9000 series systems may be applied to every activity but, as pointed out at the end of Chapter 8, a conscious effort must be made to interpret the standard in this way, and for it to be applied at every transformation interface. For example, it is not necessary to include the personnel or accounts department in an ISO 9000 series quality manual, but they must be included if the aim of the organization's quality policy is TQM.

The organization of the quality manual may reflect the standard which is chosen as the template, or it may be grouped under the managerial functions and activities. For example, one chemical company had arranged its manual according to the latter, which generated the headings listed on the left hand side of Table 9.1. These related to the requirements of ISO 9001 (1987) (also BS 5750, Part 1) according to the right-hand side of the table. Clearly, each organization will differ in some of these aspects, but the main requirement is to ensure that all the listed activities are covered by the documentation. These then provide headings under which more detailed statements are made. For the special operations undertaken by some organizations, other categories may be created. Some of the standard requirements appear in two or more of the functional areas; this is often necessary to ensure that the system operates effectively at functional or departmental interfaces.

Writing a quality manual

Once the organization has been classified into groups of activities, and the requirements of any standard being used have been allocated to one or more groups, the construction of the quality manual may begin with the format. This should facilitate the incorporation of alterations or modifications as the organization, products, services, and processes change. A loose-leaf system obviously provides good flexibility, as does a computerized system, if the ability to make changes is incorporated in the software.

The author has found a systematic questioning technique useful in

Table 9.1   Arrangement of a quality manual by functional area

Section	Functional area	ISO 9000 requirement	Clause number
1	Quality management	Management responsibility	4.1
		Quality system	4.2
		Document control	4.5
		Quality records	4.16
		Internal quality system audits and reviews	4.17
		Training	4.18
		Corrective action	4.14
2	Marketing and sales	Contract review	4.3
		Servicing	4.19
3	Product research and development	Design control	4.4
4	Purchasing and sub-contracting	Purchasing	4.6
		Purchaser supplied product	4.7
		Corrective action	4.14
		Document control	4.5
		Packaging	4.15.4
		Delivery	4.15.5
5	Production	Product identification, traceability	4.8
		Process control	4.9
		In-process inspection and testing	4.10.2
		Inspection, measuring and test equipment	4.11
		Inspection and test status	4.12
		Control of nonconforming product	4.13
		Corrective action	4.14
		Statistical techniques	4.20
6	Quality control	Inspection and testing	4.10
		Inspection, measuring and test equipment	4.11
		Inspection and test status	4.12
		Control of nonconforming product	4.13
		Quality records	4.16
		Statistical techniques	4.20
		Corrective action	4.14
7	Stock control (including warehousing despatch, delivery and transport)	Product identification, traceability	4.8
		Inspection and test status	4.12
		Control of nonconforming product	4.13
		Handling, storage, packaging and delivery	4.15
		Corrective action	4.14

setting out to help organizations to write a quality manual (see Chapter 5). The following questions should be asked with regard to each requirement being met:

- What is done? (to meet the requirement).
- Why is it done? (or why is it done that way?)
- Where is the requirement met?
- When is the requirement met?
- Who is responsible for ensuring that it is done?
- How is it done?

The sequence of these questions is important if an organization wishes to review its working practices at the same time as writing the quality manual. If the second question receives the response 'because it has always been done that way', then the third question may lead to better methods by developing into 'how else might it be done?'

The question relating to who is responsible should be answered by job titles not names, to avoid changes to the manual being required after every change of personnel. For the responsibilities to be clarified, the organizational structure must be set down. This is then amplified by listing, under the various divisions, the responsibilities and activities which may affect quality. Chapter 3 of this book may prove helpful in this task. At this point it is worth mentioning that job descriptions or specifications should not appear in the quality manual, but may form part of the general documentation referred to in the manual.

Cross-references to detailed written procedures such as test methods, plant operation, and warehousing will answer the 'how is it done?' question. It is not necessary for these to appear again in the quality manual. This applies also to commercially sensitive material or technical data, approved suppliers, details of processes, etc. These have no place in the manual, which needs to refer only to where the information is kept, who is responsible for it, when it must be referred to, and how it is used and updated. A test of a good quality manual with adequate cross-referencing is that it may be shown to a customer, potential customer, supplier or competitor, without revealing anything of a sensitive nature. It is usual somewhere at the front of the manual to define, again with cross-references, the terms common to the organization's industry, products, services, processes, etc.

Large organizations

Organizations with several thousand employees and/or many different sites will probably require a quality manual with several layers. Those organized into business groups may find it convenient to write a manual for each business, although in some very large companies even these will require further segregation, possibly on a site or unit basis. A multi-layer quality manual may take the following form:

Layer 1 overall quality policy manual
Usually very brief and extending the quality policy statement, it may be issued by 'headquarters'.

Layer 2 business group quality manual
Brief summary of one of the organization's multi-site business groups, it will probably address the issues related to managerial responsibilities.

Layer 3 site quality manual
Detailed description of how the standard requirements are actually met on the site generally, it will cross-reference any departmental manuals and procedures as necessary.

Layer 4 departmental or functional group quality manual
Detailed description of how the standard requirements are met at the local level, it will cross-reference test methods, product or service specifications, technical and operational procedures, and any commercially sensitive material.

Layer 5 detailed operational procedures
Details of how all methods pertaining to the business of the organization are performed, it will be the base point from which the documentation in support of the complete quality system is assembled.

In each layer the documentation must reflect what is actually done, and thereby it serves the system, it does not master it.

The system and the standard

The questioning does not stop with the written manual, for it is necessary at this stage to ask if the system, accurately described in the written word, actually meets the requirements of the chosen standard. If the answer is no, in one or more areas, then it must be ascertained whether the misalignment can be remedied by a minor change requiring minimum paperwork. It is far too easy to create 'additional forms' for every slight deviation and create a bureaucracy in which the dynamic quality system becomes completely bogged down. The act of writing a quality manual often proves a valuable means of exposing root causes of problems. It is necessary then, of course, to correct or remove those causes, rather than merely document them.

A Level 2 quality manual for one site of a large manufacturing group may have the following contents list:

Confidentiality of quality manual
Distribution list

Quality policy
Responsibility of manual hoiders to update/record changes
Terms and definitions
Organization chart
Block diagram of processes
Section 1   Management responsibility
Section 2   Quality system
Section 3   Contract review
Section 4   Purchasing
Section 5   Purchaser supplied product
Section 6   Product identification and traceability
Section 7   Process control
Section 8   Inspection and testing
Section 9   Inspection, measuring and test equipment
Section 10   Inspection and test status
Section 11   Control of nonconforming product
Section 12   Corrective action
Section 13   Handling, storage, packaging and delivery
Section 14   Quality records
Section 15   Internal quality audits
Section 16   Training
Section 17   Statistical techniques

9.2 Securing error/defect prevention in the system

Error or defect prevention is the process of removing or controlling error/defect causes in the system. There are two major elements of this:

- Checking the system.
- Error/defect investigation and follow-up.

These have the same objectives – to find, record and report *possible* error causes, and to recommend future corrective action.

Checking the system

There are basically six methods in general use:

1 *Quality audits and reviews* which subject each area of an organization's activity to a systematic critical examination. Every component of the total system is included, e.g. quality policy, attitudes, training, process, design features, plant construction and layout, operating procedures, documentation. Audits and reviews, as in the field of accountancy, aim

to disclose the strengths and weaknesses and the main areas of vulnerability or risk.

2 *Quality survey* which is a detailed, in-depth examination of a narrower field of activity, e.g. major key areas revealed by quality audits, individual plants, procedures or specific problems common to an organization as a whole.

3 *Quality inspection* which takes the form of a routine scheduled inspection of a unit or department. The inspection should check standards, employee involvement, working practices, and that work is carried out in accordance with the procedures, etc.

4 *Quality tour* which is an unscheduled examination of a work area to ensure that, for example, the standards of operation are acceptable, obvious causes of errors are removed, and in general quality standards are maintained.

5 *Quality sampling* which measures by random sampling, similar to activity sampling, the error potential. Trained observers perform short tours of specific locations by prescribed routes and record the number of potential errors or defects seen. The results may be used to portray trends in the general quality situation.

6 *Quality scrutinies* which are the application of a formal, critical examination of the process and technological intentions for new or existing facilities, or to assess the potential for maloperation or malfunction of equipment and the consequential effects on quality. There are similarities between quality scrutinies and FMCEA studies (see Chapter 6).

The design of an error-prevention programme, combining all these elements, is represented below:

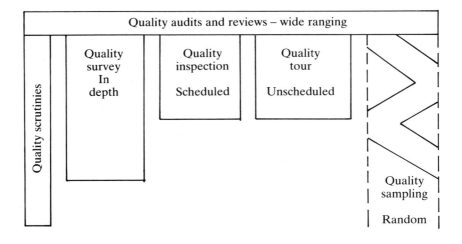

Error or defect investigations and follow-up

The investigation of errors and defects can provide valuable error-prevention information. The method is based on:

collecting	data and information relating to the error or defect;
checking	the validity of the evidence;
selecting	evidence relevant to the investigation aims; and
analysing	the evidence without making assumptions or jumping to conclusions.

The results of the analysis are then used to:

decide	the most likely cause(s) of the errors or defects;
notify	immediately the person(s) able to take corrective action;
record	the findings and outcomes; and
report	them to everyone concerned, to prevent a recurrence.

The investigation should not become an inquisition to apportion blame, but focus on the positive preventive aspects. The types of follow-up to errors and their effects are shown below:

System type	Overall aim	General effects
Investigation	To prevent a similar error or defect	Positive: identification notification correction
Inquisition	To identify responsibility	Negative: blame claims defence

It is hoped that errors or defects are not normally investigated so frequently that the required skills are developed by experience, nor are these skills easily learned in a classroom. One suggested way to overcome this problem is the development of a programmed sequence of questions which form the skeleton of an error or defect investigation questionnaire. This can be set out with the following structure:

Plant/equipment	description, condition, controls, maintenance, suitability, etc.
Environment	climatic, space, humidity, noise, etc.
People	duties, information, supervision, instruction, training, attitudes, etc.

| Systems | procedures, instructions, monitoring, control methods, etc. |

Internal and external quality system audits and reviews

A good quality system will not function without adequate audits and reviews. The system reviews, which need to be carried out periodically and systematically, are conducted to ensure that the system achieves the required effect, whilst audits are carried out to make sure that actual methods are adhering to the documented procedures. The reviews should use the findings of the audits, for failure to operate according to the plan often signifies difficulties in doing so. A re-examination of the procedures actually being used may lead to system improvements unobtainable by other means.

A schedule for carrying out the audits should be drawn up, different activities perhaps requiring different frequencies. All procedures and systems should be audited at least once during a specified cycle, but not necessarily all at the same audit. For example, every three months a selected random sample of work instructions and methods could be audited, with the selection designed so that each procedure is audited at least once per year. There must be, however, facility to adjust this on the basis of the audit results.

A quality system review should be instituted, perhaps every six months, with the aims of:

- ensuring that the system is achieving the desired results;
- revealing defects or irregularities in the system;
- indicating any necessary improvements and/or corrective actions to eliminate waste or loss;
- checking on all levels of management;
- uncovering potential danger areas;
- verifying that improvements or corrective action procedures are effective.

Clearly, the procedures for carrying out the audits and reviews and the results from them should be documented, and themselves be subject to review.

The assessment of a quality system against a particular standard or set of requirements by internal audit and review is known as a first party assessment or approval scheme. If an external customer makes the assessment of a supplier against either its own or a national or international standard, a second party scheme is in operaton. The external assessment by an independent organization, not involved in any contract between customer and supplier, but acceptable to them both, is known as an independent third party assessment scheme. The latter usually involves some form of certification or registration by the assessment body.

One advantage of the third party schemes is that they obviate the need for customers to make their own detailed checks, saving both suppliers and customers time and money, and avoiding issues of commercial confidentiality. Just one knowledgeable organization has to be satisfied, rather than a multitude with varying levels of competence. This often qualifies suppliers for quality assurance based contracts without further checking.

Each certification body usually has its own recognized mark, which may be used by registered organizations of assessed capability in their literature, letter headings, and marketing activities. There are also publications containing lists of organizations whose quality systems and/ or products and services have been assessed. To be of value, the certification body must itself be recognized and, usually, assessed and registered with a national or international accreditation scheme.

Many organizations have found that the effort of designing and implementing a written quality management system, good enough to stand up to external independent third party assessment, has been extremely rewarding in:

- involving staff and improving morale;
- better process control;
- reduced wastage;
- reduced customer service costs.

This is also true of those organizations that have obtained third party registration and supply companies which still insist on their own second party assessment. The reason for this is that most of the standards on quality systems, whether national, international, or company specific, are now very similar indeed. A system which meets the requirements of the ISO 9000 series will meet the requirements of all other standards, with only the slight modifications and small emphases here and there required for specific customers. It is the author's experience, and that of his immediate colleagues, that an assessment carried out by one of the independent certified assessment bodies is at least as rigorous and delving as any carried out by a second party representative.

Internal system audits and reviews must be positive and conducted as part of the preventive strategy and not as a matter of expediency resulting from quality problems. They should not be carried out only prior to external audits, nor should they be left to the external auditor, whether second or third party. An external auditor, discovering discrepancies between actual and documented systems, will be inclined to ask why the internal review methods did not discover and correct them. This type of behaviour in financial control and auditing is commonplace, why should things be different in the control of quality?

Managements which are anxious to display that they are serious about quality must become fully committed to operating an effective quality system which involves all personnel within the organization, not just the staff in the quality department. The system must be planned to be effective and achieve its objectives in an uncomplicated way. Having established and documented the procedures it is necessary to ensure that they are working and that everyone is operating in accordance with them. The system once established is not static, it should be flexible to enable the constant seeking of improvements or streamlining.

9.3 Computers in quality information systems

In order to be sure of meeting customer requirements, and continuing to meet them, it is clearly necessary to create a quality information system. Digital computers may be used in such systems since the tasks of collection, recording, and analysis of data and information are easily automated. This can save large amounts of human time otherwise expended in merely collecting and recording numbers and words. A microprocessor can form the basis of a small quality information system, particularly if 'dedicated' use is required for a particular line of production or service.

Whatever the size and type of the computer system employed, it must:

1 provide 'real-time' computing;
2 be able to handle, or be linked into, a sufficiently large database.

For rapid response and maximum availability, part of the computer system should be dedicated to quality information and data handling. A real-time mini computer which enables data to be collected in this way across the whole work base – the shop floor, or office – allows relatively easy implementation of statistical process control (SPC).

Application software packages are now available which have been purpose-designed for quality information systems. The basic requirements of any such package is for it to 'drive' the preventive model of quality management (Figure 9.1). It should include all the SPC techniques necessary to implement the process-control strategy and when problems occur operate a stepwise procedure to:

1 identify the problem;
2 identify the causes of the problem;
3 eliminate the causes of the problem;
4 continuously monitor the process for recurrence of the problem.

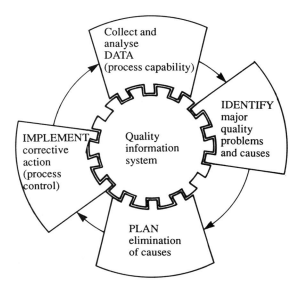

Figure 9.1   *The quality information system 'drives' preventive quality management*

Clearly, human managerial decisions must interface with the package in this procedure, particularly during the elimination stage, but the efficient use of this type of data/information crunching power is invaluable in many complex process situations.

System requirements

The information system should permit process and product information to be entered into a database. Ideally, the user should then be able to employ a high-level report generator to extract data, with various search criteria, analyse and report it, preferably in graphic fashion. The functions of a good quality information system are visualized in Figure 9.2, the details of which are:

The database

The structure of the database should be fixed and completely clear to the end user. A standard database software subsystem, which does not require optimization for different applications and allows the advanced user to access the database with self-written programs, should be used. The system should be capable of storing simultaneously onto magnetic tape, all data and information introduced into the database. If the

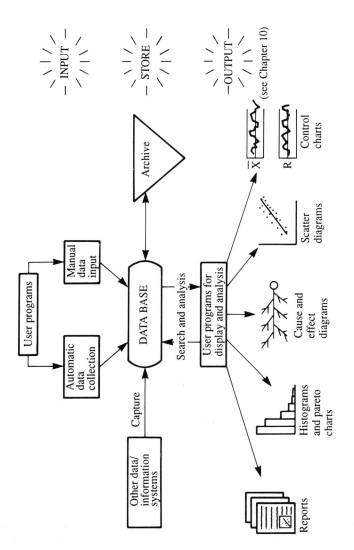

Figure 9.2 *Quality information system requirements*

database should become corrupt or damaged, this will enable the entire database to be re-established. This important requirement for database integrity should not be neglected.

Data input

It should be possible to input data in two different ways – automatically or manually. For automatic transmission into the database, no user intervention is necessary. Data may be provided by process control systems, data collectors and concentrators, measurement or test devices with local intelligence, or by a program running on the same computer. In applications where rapid evaluation of measured or counted data is required for control of the process to take place, the measurement or test control may be handled by a microprocessor-based desk-top computer, which transmits the results automatically to the database, via the automatic input route.

In the case of manual input, the end-user enters data using appropriately designed terminals. The system should be capable of validating data and sending error messages. Bar-code input devices may ease the manual entry of data in applications, such as inwards goods receipt, sample test data input, and so on.

Report/graph output

Normally the output generator will consist of two parts: a configurator and an interpreter. The former provides the user with the means to build or adjust output reports and graphs, through screen instructions and menus, whilst the latter actually generates the desired output. Reports, tables, figures, graphs, etc., should be obtainable on a regular basis or by simple demand. The graphical reports most likely to be required include pie charts, histograms, Pareto charts, cause-and-effect diagrams, scatter diagrams, and various types of control charts (mean and range, proportion defective, cusum, etc. – see Chapter 10). The choice of colour graphics may be desirable for presentation purposes.

Computer-integrated operations

Computers are used increasingly in all parts of all types of organizations. The advantages to be gained from linking computerized quality information to the rest of the computer network are substantial. Free movement of data around the whole system offers enormous flexibility and efficiency in the overall operational process. Considerable savings in staff time can be realized just in information transfer. Databases can be shared by networks and data entered into the system on one occasion instead of several. The time released may be put to more productive, higher-level activities.

9.4 Implementation of the system

Even the most meticulous quality system design will not eliminate the need to consider the involvement of people. Instructions to them must be clear, concise and precise. Those involved in supervision must ensure that the instructions are followed and that the processes and plant are properly used and maintained, according to the system. The quality management system should be a living thing, not a bureaucracy or a paperwork model, and to make it come to life requires the involvement of every person in the organization. This can only be achieved by effective communications about what the system is, how it operates, and what role each individual plays in it.

When organizations begin to document their quality systems, it is often necessary to ask people to change the habits of a lifetime. The author recalls some advisory work on a hand-tool manufacturer's premises in which all components and parts were identified with classification numbers and grade of material, until the very last process where all identification mysteriously disappeared leaving box after box of apparently identical products. When this was brought to the attention of the shop foreman, Jim, he pointed out that he had worked for the company for nearly 30 years and knew every product and grade by 'sight and sound'. Upon being asked what would happen if he was struck down by lightning whilst walking his dog one evening, he observed that his colleague Harry had worked in the same workshop for 25 years and knew almost as much as Jim. These people are conscientious people – worth their weight in gold – but they need to be persuaded or to learn that part, component and product identification can be reliable, transferable, and verifiable only if a properly documented system exists. When people have been working in a certain way for very long periods, it can be difficult for them to accept and adopt new procedures.

Quality systems and small organizations

The increasing demands for fully documented quality systems are bound to have a marked effect on those organizations employing less than 100 people, which are less likely to have a formal system than larger organizations. The small organization may be:

- unaware of the implications of a quality management system, and how to meet the requirements of, say, ISO 9000;

- unable to fend off or pass on pressure from customers;
- subjected to increasing demands for vendor assessment, use of SPC, certification, etc.;
- subject to demands for verification of their quality system, the costs of which are out of proportion to the contract value;
- unable to afford a specialist full-time quality manager;
- inspection oriented with respect to quality, with little feedback of information gathered.

Many small organizations, which maintain a commendable flexibility in their operations and produce excellent service or quality products, are frequently unable to demonstrate that they have maintained adequate process control throughout their operations. The reasons for the lack of documentation often lie in the belief that verbal communications will suffice. This is particularly true of tiny companies which have grown with many employees continuing to carry out the same tasks on the same or similar product or service range. In such organizations, formalized documentation is often seen as unnecessary or costly, with new employees being instructed verbally or by example.

Meeting the requirements of an international standard on quality management can be a formidable obstacle to small organizations, requiring from the management an appreciation of the standard(s), motivation, technical competence, and resources to achieve and implement the necessary changes. The motivation may arise from an overall philosophy of raising standards of quality management, but it is more likely to arise when the companies encounter new types of activity and behaviour from customers, competitors, and suppliers that change the requirements. This can lead to anxiety and panic if certain customers or contracts may be retained only by compliance or registration.

The inability of the management of many small organizations to achieve the necessary standards may well be exposed by this type of pressure. Many will have little if any experience outside their own organization, and their multi-functional roles exacerbate the difficulties of setting aside time to contemplate, initiate, and implement the improvements. The mere clerical effort required to draw up manuals and operating procedures may be beyond their resources.

Where subsidized or grant-aided provision of outside help in the form of consultancy is available, perhaps through government schemes, this should be utilized to obtain a professional objective view. Considerable help towards manual preparation and recommendations for system design and practice should then be forthcoming, but it may leave the residual problem of implementation and maintenance largely unsolved. One solution to this problem is for a group of small organizations to share a professional quality manager, who operates on an internal/external consultancy basis. This person reports to the chief executives of each of the collaborating partners in which he/she plays a functional role. Manuals can be prepared, changes implemented, audits and reviews carried out, and on a longer time scale a continuous quality-monitoring process established.

Whether the organization is large or small, the expertise comes from within or without, or is shared, there will be a requirement for some initial advisory work. This is best carried out in the form of a project.

A quality system advisory project

In giving advice concerning a quality management system it is seldom useful to do so in isolation. The services offered for such advisory projects should, therefore, be built round the specific requirements of a standard or recognized quality system. These include the British BS 5750 series, the American ANSI/ASQC Q90 series, and the equivalent International ISO 9000 series, as well as individual company requirements such as Ford's Q 101.

Organizations should select a consultant who does not offer a standard package around which a company is asked to build or rebuild its quality systems. The systems must reflect the established practices of the company, modified if necessary to bring them into line with the requirements of the defined standard. The advice given during a project, therefore, begins with the current practices of the company. Where modifications are required, the company employees should be involved to the maximum, consistent with the availability of in-house facilities. A standard set of procedures detailed by a third party consultant is not embraced as the property of a company and seldom becomes so – it is either a work of fiction or an alien and unwanted dictate.

A good advisory project covers one, or several, of a series of distinct phases:

Phase one

The initial phase, which should include a preliminary visit, is concerned with a clear, agreed and accepted definition of the work to be carried out. This should become the subject of written *terms of reference* which include:

- an introduction including the background to the enquiry for an advisory project;
- the objectives of the project;
- a brief description of the quality systems in use within the company;

- the programme of work to be carried out, including details of the areas where systems will need to be modified or expanded in order to meet the requirements of the quality systems standard chosen;
- a detailed estimate of the time required by the consultant in order to complete his part of the work;
- the general conditions and total costs for carrying out the following phases of the work.

Phase two

Once the terms of reference have been agreed and accepted by the company, the consultant should prepare an *interim report*. This report results from a more detailed interrogation of the company's actual systems and procedures, and includes sufficient detail to allow an *action plan* to be drawn up. The action plan shows the work to be undertaken both by the consultant and the company for each of the quality systems' individual requirements and the overall time likely to pass before a satisfactory, operational system will exist. Guidance should be given on the revisions that will be required to the quality systems.

Phase three

This phase covers the consultant's work as outlined in the terms of reference and detailed in the interim report. A full written *final report* of the consultant's findings and recommendations should be presented to the company, along with a *draft quality manual* which includes as much of the quality systems as have been clearly defined at the time of presentation. This phase may also include arranging and holding a tripartite meeting with an assessment body, if some sort of independent third party assessment will be sought.

Phase four

When the consultant and the company have both finished their work, it is often useful to invite the consultant to *audit* the systems during a short visit, and to report on any remaining deficiencies found. A similar use of consultants may be made by a company which considers that its systems are ready for assessment, without the advisory work.

Estimated times

Experience has demonstrated that a total input from the consultant of approximately 15 man-days is sufficient, in nearly all cases, to establish what has to be done, to participate in the vital elements of the work, to detail the remainder and to make a preliminary assessment of a site. The project must seek to involve company employees as much as possible in the detailed work of completing the quality systems, their documentation and implementation. There is seldom a requirement which exceeds 100 man-days of employees' time in order to complete the company's part of the work. The work of bringing quality systems into line with modern practices and standards will often encompass a period of at least six months but seldom requires more than twelve months in total.

10 Capability for quality

10.1 Statistical process control (SPC)

The responsibility for quality in any transformation process must lie with the operators of that process – the producers. To fulfil this responsibility, however, people must be provided with the tools necessary to:

- know whether the process is capable of meeting the requirements;
- know whether the process is meeting the requirements at any point in time;
- make correct adjustments to the process or its inputs when it is not meeting the requirements.

To begin to monitor and analyse any process, it is necessary to first of all identify what the process is, and what the inputs and outputs are. Many processes are easily understood and relate to known procedures, e.g. drilling a hole, compressing tablets, filling cans with paint, polymerizing a chemical using catalysts. Others are less easily identified, e.g. servicing a customer, delivering a lecture, storing a product in a warehouse, inputting to a computer. In many situations it can be extremely difficult to define the process. For example, if the process is inputting data into a computer terminal, it is vital to know if the scope of the process includes obtaining and refining the data, as well as inputting. Process definition is so important because the inputs and outputs change with the scope of the process.

Once the process is specified, the inputs and suppliers, outputs and customers can also be defined, together with the requirements at each of the interfaces. The most difficult areas in which to do this are in non-manufacturing organizations or parts of organizations, but careful use of the questioning method, introduced in Chapter 1, should release the necessary information. Examples of outputs in non-manufacturing include: training courses or programmes, typed letters, statements of intent (following a decision process), invoices, share certificates, deliveries of consignments, reports, serviced motor cars, purchase orders, wage slips, forecasts, material requirements plans, legal contracts, design change documents, clean offices, recruited trainees, and advertisements. The list is endless. Some processes may produce primary and secondary outputs, such as a telephone call answered and a message delivered.

If the requirements are not clarified or quantified, they are often assumed or estimated. Even if this does not lead to direct complaints, it will lead to waste – lost time, confusion – and perhaps lost customers. It is salutory for some suppliers of internal customers to realize that the latter can sometimes find new suppliers if their true requirements are not properly identified and/or repeatedly not met.

Inputs to processes include the:

- equipment, tools, or plant required;
- materials, including paper;
- information, including the specification for the outputs;
- methods or procedures, including instructions;
- people (and the inputs they provide, such as skills, training, knowledge, etc.);
- records.

Again this is not an exhaustive list.

Prevention of failure in any transformation is possible only if the process definition, inputs, and outputs are properly documented and agreed. The documentation of procedures will allow reliable data about the process itself to be collected, analysis to be performed, and action to be taken to improve the process and prevent failure or nonconformance with the requirements. The target in the operation of any process is the total avoidance of failure. If the idea of no-failures or error-free work is not adopted, at least as a target, then it certainly will never be achieved.

All processes can be monitored and brought 'under control' by gathering and using data. This refers to measurement of the performance of the process and the feedback required for corrective action, where necessary. Statistical process control (SPC) methods, backed by management commitment and good organization, provide objective means of controlling quality in any transformation process, whether used in the manufacture of artefacts, the provision of services, or the transfer of information.

SPC is not only a tool kit. It is a strategy for reducing variability, the cause of most quality problems: variation in products, in times of deliveries, in ways of doing things, in materials, in people's attitudes, in equipment and its use, in maintenance practices, in everything. Control by itself is not sufficient. Total quality management requires that the process should be improved continually by reducing its variability. This is brought about by studying all aspects of the process using the basic question 'could we do this job more consistently and on target?' the answering of which drives the search for improvements. This significant feature of SPC means that it is not constrained to measuring conformance, and that it is intended to lead to action on processes which are operating within the 'specification' to minimize variability.

Process control is essential and SPC forms a vital part of the overall TQM strategy. Incapable and inconsistent processes render the best design impotent and make supplier quality assurance irrelevant. Whatever process is being operated, it must be reliable and consistent. SPC can be used to achieve this objective.

In the application of SPC there is often an emphasis on techniques rather than on the implied wider managerial strategies. It is worth repeating that SPC is not only about plotting charts on the walls of a plant or office, it must become part of the company-wide adoption of TQM and act as the focal point of never-ending improvement. Changing an organization's environment into one in which SPC can operate properly may take several years rather than months. For many companies SPC will bring a new approach, a new 'philosophy', but the importance of the statistical techniques should not be disguised. Simple presentation of data using diagrams, graphs, and charts should become the means of communication concerning the state of control of processes.

10.2 A systematic approach

In process control and capability analysis, numbers and information will form the basis for decisions and actions, and a thorough data recording system is essential. There is a difference between data and numbers. Data is information, including numerical, that is useful in solving problems, or that provides knowledge about the state of a process. Numbers alone often represent meaningless measurements or counts which tend to confuse rather than to enlighten. Numerical data on quality will arise either from:

1 counting; or
2 measurement.

Data which arises from counting can only occur at definite points or in 'discrete' jumps. There can only be 0, 1, 2, etc. errors in an invoice page, there cannot be 2.46 errors. The number of bubbles on a windscreen, the number of absentees, the number of pens which fail to write properly give rise to discrete data which are called attributes. As there is only a two-way classification to consider right or wrong, present or not present, attributes give rise to counted data, which necessarily varies in jumps.

Data which arises from measurement can occur anywhere at all on a continuous scale and is called variable data. The weight of a capsule, the diameter of a piston, the tensile strength of a piece of rod, the time taken to process an insurance claim, are all variables, the measurement of which produces continuous data.

In addition to the basic elements of a quality system, which will provide a framework for recording, there exists a set of 'tools' which the Japanese quality guru Ishikawa has called the seven basic tools. These should be used to interpret fully and derive maximum use of data. The simple methods listed below will offer any organization means of collecting, presenting, and analysing most of its data:

- Process flow charting — what is done.
- Check sheets/tally charts — how often it is done.
- Histograms — what overall variations look like.
- Pareto analysis — which are the big problems.
- Cause-and-effect analysis and brainstorming — what causes the problems.
- Scatter diagrams — what are the relationships between factors.
- Control charts — which variations to control and how.

It is only rarely that more sophisticated techniques, such as analysis of variance, regression analysis, and design of experiments, need to be employed. What follows is a brief description of each technique, but a full description and further examples may be found in *Statistical Process Control* by the author.

Process flow charting

The use of this technique, which is described fully in Chapter 5, ensures a full understanding of the inputs and flow of the process. Without that understanding, it is not possible to draw the correct flow chart of the process.

Check sheets or tally charts

Check sheets are a tool for data gathering and a logical point to start in most process control or problem-solving efforts. They are particularly useful for recording direct observations and helping to gather in facts rather than opinions about the process.

Check sheets are prepared by following five steps:

1 Select and agree on the exact event to be observed.
2 Decide on the data collection time period. This includes both how often the data is to be obtained (frequency) and for how long it will be collected (duration).

Observer F. Oldsman	Computer No. 148		Date 26 June	
Number of observations 95			Total	Percentage
Computer in use		ШТ ШТ ШТ ШТ ШТ ШТ ШТ ШТ ШТ ШТ ШТ	55	57·9
Computer idle	Repairs	ШТ	5	5·3
	No work	ШТ ШТ II	12	12·6
	Operator absent	ШТ ШТ	10	10·5
	System failure	ШТ ШТ III	13	13·7

Figure 10.1 *Activity sampling record in an office*

3 Design a form that is simple, easy to use and large enough to record the information. Each column must be clearly labelled.
4 Collect the data and fill in the check sheet. Be honest in recording the information and allow enough time for it to be collected and recorded.
5 Follow up the recording by some analysis or presentation of the data.

The use of simple check sheets or tally charts aids the collection of data of the right type, in the right form, at the right time. The objectives of the data collection will determine the design of the record sheet used. Two examples of tally charts for different purposes are shown in Figures 10.1 and 10.2. These give rise to frequency distributions.

Histograms

Histograms show, in a very clear pictorial way, the frequency with which a certain value or group of values occurs. They can be used to display both attribute and variables data, and are an effective means of communicating directly to the people who operate the process, the results of their efforts. The data gathered on the tally chart of Figure 10.2 is drawn as a histogram in Figure 10.3.

Pareto analysis

If the symptoms or causes of defective output are identified and recorded, it will be possible to determine what percentage can be attributed to any

Truck turn round time (minutes – rounded to nearest 5)	Tally	Number of trucks (frequency)
10	l	1
15	lll	3
20	ЈЖГ l	6
25	ЈЖГ llll	9
30	ЈЖГ ЈЖГ ЈЖГ ЈЖГ ЈЖГ ЈЖГ ЈЖГ ЈЖГ ll	42
35	ЈЖГ ll	107
40	ЈЖГ ЈЖГ	170
45	ЈЖГ ЈЖГ ЈЖГ ЈЖГ ЈЖГ ЈЖГ ЈЖГ ЈЖГ ЈЖГ ЈЖГ ЈЖГ ЈЖГ ЈЖГ ЈЖГ ЈЖГ ЈЖГ ЈЖГ ЈЖГ ЈЖГ ЈЖГ	100
50	ЈЖГ ЈЖГ ЈЖГ ЈЖГ ЈЖГ ЈЖГ ЈЖГ lll	38
55	ЈЖГ ЈЖГ ЈЖГ l	16
60	ЈЖГ	5
65	ll	2
70	l	1
	Total	500

Figure 10.2   *Tally chart and frequency distribution for truck turnround times*

cause, and the probable result will be that the bulk (typically 80 per cent) of the errors, waste, or rejections derive from a few of the causes (typically 20 per cent). For example, Figure 10.4 shows a ranked frequency distribution of incidents in the distribution of a certain product. To improve the performance of the distribution process, therefore, the major incidents (broken bags/drums, truck scheduling, temperature

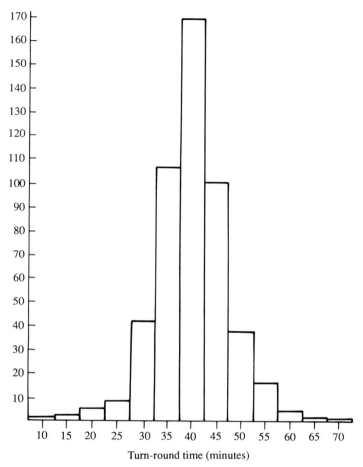

Figure 10.3   *Frequency distribution for truck turnround times (histogram)*

problems) should be tackled first. An analysis of data to identify the major problems is known as Pareto Analysis, after the Italian economist who realized that approximately 90 per cent of the wealth in his country was owned by approximately 10 per cent of the people. Without an analysis of this sort, it is far too easy to devote resources to addressing one symptom only because its cause seems immediately apparent.

Cause-and-effect analysis and brainstorming

A useful way of mapping the inputs which affect quality is the cause-and-effect diagram, also known as the Ishikawa diagram (after its originator)

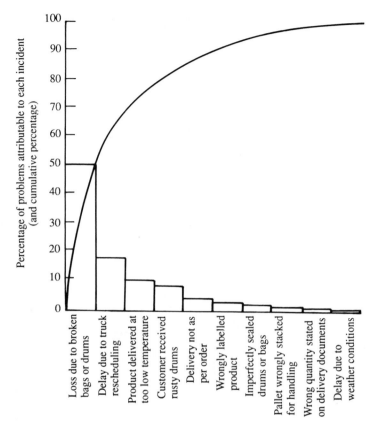

Figure 10.4 *Incidents in the distribution of a chemical product*

or the fishbone diagram (after its appearance, see Figure 10.5). The effect or incident being investigated is shown at the end of a horizontal arrow. Potential causes are then shown as labelled arrows entering the main cause arrow. Each arrow may have other arrows entering it as the principal factors or causes are reduced to their sub-causes, and sub-sub-causes by brainstorming.

Brainstorming is a technique which is used to bring ideas out into the open and may be used in a variety of situations. Each member of a group, in turn, may be invited to put forward ideas concerning a problem under consideration. Wild ideas are safe to offer, as criticism or ridicule is not permitted during a brainstorming session. The main objective is to create an atmosphere of enthusiasm and originality. All ideas offered are recorded for subsequent analysis. The process is continued until all the conceivable causes have been included. The proportion of nonconform-

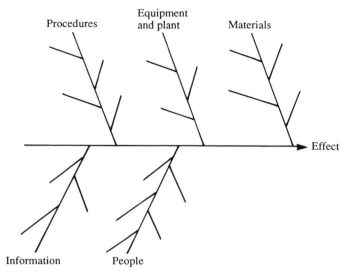

Figure 10.5   *The cause and effect, Ishikawa or fishbone diagram*

ing output attributable to each cause is then measured or estimated, and a simple Pareto analysis identifies the major causes which are most worth investigating.

Brainstorming, cause-effect, and Pareto analyses together provide a most effective means of tackling problems and presenting quality improvement plans or the results of quality improvement projects. A typical project cycle is shown in Figure 10.6.

Scatter diagrams

Depending on the technology, it is frequently useful to establish the association, if any, between two parameters or factors. A technique to begin such an analysis is a simple X–Y plot of the two sets of data. The resulting grouping of points on scatter diagrams (e.g. Figure 10.7) will reveal whether or not a strong or weak, positive or negative correlation exists between the parameters. The diagrams are simple to construct and easy to interpret, and the absence of correlation can be as revealing as finding that a relationship exists. A note of caution – association does not equal causation.

Control charts

A control chart is a form of traffic signal, the operation of which is based on evidence from the small samples taken at random during a process. A

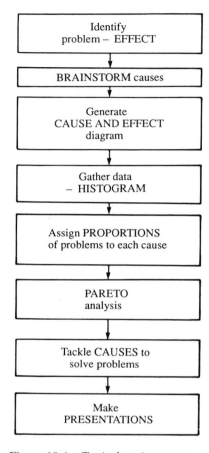

Figure 10.6   *Typical project sequence*

green light is given when the process should be allowed to run. All too often, processes are 'adjusted' on the basis of a single measurement, check or inspection, a practice which can make a process much more variable than it is already. The equivalent of an amber light appears when trouble is possibly imminent. The red light shows that there is practically no doubt that the process has changed in some way and that it must be investigated and corrected to prevent production of defective material or information. Clearly, such a scheme can be introduced only when the process is 'in control'. Since the samples taken are usually small, there are risks of errors, but these are small, calculated risks and not blind ones. The risk calculations are based on various frequency distributions.

These charts should be made easy to understand and interpret and they can become, with experience, sensitive diagnostic tools which can be used by staff and first-line supervision to prevent errors or defective output being produced. Time and effort spent to explain the working of the charts to all concerned is never wasted.

There are different types of control charts for variables and attribute data. The most frequently used charts for variables are mean and range charts which are used together. Number defective or np charts and proportion defective or p charts are the most common ones in use for

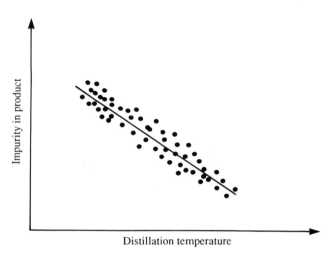

Figure 10.7 *Scatter diagram showing a negative correlation between two variables*

Table 10.1 *Control charts*

Variables	
Centring	*Spread*
Mean	Standard deviation
Moving average	Range
Median	Moving range
Mid-range	
Attributes	
Defectives	Defects/errors
np number	c number
p proportion	u per unit/area
Cusum	

attributes. Other charts found in use are moving average and range charts, number of defects (c and u) charts, and cumulative sum (Cusum) charts. The latter offer very powerful management tools for the detection of trends or changes in attributes and variable data. The range of type and use of control charts is now very wide and within the present text it is not possible to indicate more than the basic principles underlying such charts. This is done in Chapter 11, but the book *Statistical Process Control*, by the author provides a comprehensive text on the subject. Table 10.1 provides a summary of the major control chart techniques.

10.3 Process variability and capability

A systematic study of a process through answering the questions:

> Are we capable of doing the job correctly?
> Do we continue to do the job correctly?
> Have we done the job correctly?
> Could we do the job more consistently and on target?[1]

provides knowledge of the process capability and the sources of nonconforming outputs. This information can then be fed back quickly to marketing, design, and the 'technology' functions. Knowledge of the current state of a process also enables a more balanced judgement of equipment, both with regard to the tasks within its capability and its rational utilization.

Statistical process control procedures exist because there is variation in the characteristics of all material, articles, services, and people. The inherent variability in every transformation process causes the output from it to vary over a period of time. If this variability is considerable, it is impossible to predict the value of a characteristic of any single item or at any point in time. Using statistical methods, however, it is possible to take meagre knowledge of the output and turn it into meaningful statements which may then be used to describe the process itself. Hence, statistically based process control procedures are designed to divert

---

[1] This system for process capability and control is based on Frank Price's very practical framework for thinking about quality in manufacturing:

> Can we make it OK?
> Are we making it OK?
> Have we made it OK?
> Could we make it better?

which he presented in his excellent book, *Right First Time*.

attention from individual pieces of data and focus it on the process as a whole. SPC techniques may be used to measure and control the degree of variation of any purchased materials, services, processes, and products and to compare this, if required, to previously agreed specifications. In essence, SPC techniques select a representative, simple, random sample from the 'population', which can be an input to or an output from a process. From an analysis of the sample it is possible to make decisions regarding the current performance of the process.

Causes of process variability

At the basis of the theory of process control is a differentiation of the causes of variation in quality during operation of the process. Certain variations belong to the category of chance or random variations, about which little may be done, other than to revise the process. This type of variation is the sum of the effects of a complex interaction of 'random' or 'common' causes, each of which is slight. When random variation alone exists, it may not be possible to trace the major part of it to a single cause. The set of random causes which produces variation in the quality of products may include: draughts, atmospheric pressure or temperature changes, passing traffic or equipment vibrations, electrical or humidity fluctuations, and changes in operator physical and emotional conditions. This is analogous to the set of forces which cause a coin to turn up heads or tails when tossed. When only random variations are present in a process, the process is considered to be 'in statistical control'. There is also variation in test equipment, and inspection and checking procedures, whether used to measure a physical dimension, an electronic or a chemical characteristic, or a property of an information system. The inherent variation in checking and testing contributes to the overall process variability and may be an important factor. In a similar way, processes whose output is not an artefact will be subject to random causes of variation: traffic problems, electricity supply, operator performance, the weather, will affect the time taken to complete an insurance estimate, the efficiency with which a claim is handled, etc.

Causes of variation which are relatively large in magnitude, and readily identified, are classified as 'assignable' or 'special' causes. For the most part, these consist of differences among plant, equipment, processes, operators, information, materials, and other miscellaneous factors. When an assignable cause of variation is present, process variability will be excessive and the process is classified as 'out of control' or beyond the expected random variations.

In Chapter 1 it was suggested that the first question which must be asked of any process is 'are we capable of doing this job correctly?'

Following our understanding of random and assignable causes of variation, this must now be divided into two questions:

1 'Is the process stable, or in-control?' In other words, are there present any assignable causes of variation, or is the process variability due to random causes only?
2 'What is the extent of the process variability?' or what is the natural capability of the process when only the random causes of variation are present?

This approach may be applied to both variables and attribute data, and provides a systematic methodology for the process examination, control and investigation.

Variables

When dealing with process inputs and parameters, products or services having properties which are measured on a continuous scale, it is important to realize that no two measurements made will be exactly alike. The variation may be quite large and easily noticeable, such as in the weights of men or women. When variations are very small, it may appear that each element of the output is identical. This is in fact due to the limitations of measurement and 'instruments' with greater precision will show differences.

In sampling a continuous variable, e.g. the length of a piece of steel, or the time of arrival of delivery, the main assumption on which the statistical analysis is based is that the variable – the length or time – will be 'normally distributed', i.e. it will be bell shaped. For example, on measuring the 'turn-round times' of delivery vehicles, it was found that they gave the frequency distribution shown in Figure 10.2 and the histogram of Figure 10.3. The shape and general symmetry of the distribution indicate that a normal or Gaussian distribution (Figure 10.8) conveniently describes the variation in the turn-round times.

The measure of 'central tendency' most frequently used is the mean or average (μ) of the process data, obtained by summing all the measured values and dividing the result by the total number of observations (N). The measure of spread of values from the process is given by the standard deviation (σ) which is calculated by adding together all the squares of the differences between the measured values and the mean value, dividing the resultant sum by N, and then taking the square root of the result. A simpler method of estimating σ, based on the mean range of samples, is usually used in SPC.

A process whose average is equal to a 'nominal' or 'target' value is said to be 'accurate'. One which has a relatively small spread is said to be 'precise'; the smaller the value of σ, the higher the precision. A specification related to variables, therefore, requires a statement on both accuracy and precision. Often 'high quality' is associated with high precision, whereas the true requirements may be for a correctly 'centred' process, with a stated measure of precision.

Suppose the target concentration of a chemical process was 600 mg/l and that the process was being operated with a mean value, μ= 600 mg/l, and a standard deviation, σ = 5 mg/l, then from a knowledge of the

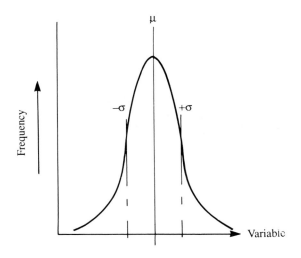

Figure 10.8   *The normal distribution of a continuous variable*

bell shape curve and the properties of the normal distribution, the following facts would emerge:

68.3 per cent (about two-thirds) of the product produced is within ±5 mg/l of the average ($\mu \pm \sigma$)

95.4 per cent of the product is within average ±10 mg/l ($\mu \pm 2\sigma$)

99.7 per cent (nearly all the product) is within average ±15 mg/l ($\mu \pm 3\sigma$)

(Figure 10.9)

Since almost all the output is contained within the values corresponding to $\mu \pm 3\sigma$, this is often known as the 'natural process capability'. It will be observed that it is not necessary to quote a specification in terms of a tolerance around the target value to be able to measure and quote the capability of the process in this way.

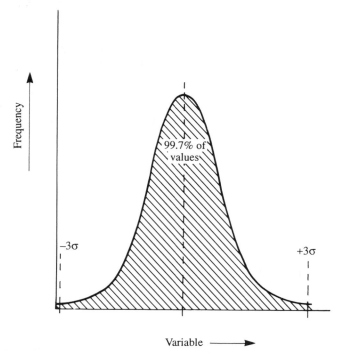

Figure 10.9 *The proportion of output contained in (μ ± 3σ)*

The usual aim in any operation is not to achieve everything with the same value, the same length, or the same turn-round time, but to meet the requirements in the form of specified limits or tolerances. Ensuring that the tolerance zone exceeds the spread of the distribution is thus an essential prerequisite to avoiding nonconformance to requirements. If we require that all the chemical product has a concentration which lies between 580 and 620 mg/l, then using the above process, very little product will fall outside this range (Figure 10.10a). Conversely, if the requirement was to tighten to 600 ± 10 mg/l, then the process spread exceeds this (Figure 10.10b) and there will be inevitably some dissatisfaction.

In manufacturing, there are many variables – dimensions, physical and chemical properties – which are normally distributed. It is possible in these cases to analyse the process variability and make comments with respect to its ability to meet the requirements of the specification. Similarly in non-manufacturing situations, the variability of 'processes' may be measured and compared with the ideal requirements.

The relationship between process capability and specified tolerances

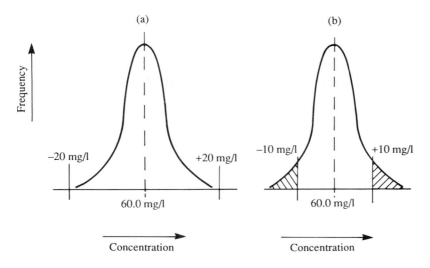

Figure 10.10   *Relationship between tolerance and process variability*

may be formalized using the standard deviation σ of the process. In order to produce within the specified requirements, the distance between the upper specification limit (USL) and the lower specification limit (LSL), i.e. USL − LSL must be equal to or greater than the width of the base of the process, i.e. 6σ. When a process is in-statistical-control, i.e. only random causes of variation are present, a process capability index may be calculated to relate the actual performance of the process to its specified requirements. The simplest index is Cp, which quantifies the spread of the process relative to the specification limits:

$$Cp = \frac{USL - LSL}{6\sigma}$$

A second index, Cpk quantifies both the spread and the setting or centring of the process:

$$Cpk = \text{minimum of } \frac{USL - \bar{X}}{3\sigma} \text{ or } \frac{\bar{X} - LSL}{3\sigma}$$

where $\bar{X}$ = the measured mean of the process in-control.

Values for Cp and Cpk greater than 1 indicate that three process standard deviations (3σ) either side of the mean are contained within the specification or tolerance band. To operate a process safely inside the required limits, the values of Cp and Cpk must approach 2. Clearly, when

Cp or Cpk is less than 1, the process is incapable of achieving the requirements. If that is found to be the case, then the process capability must be improved by a thorough examination and elimination of the major causes of variation. This is difficult work since the causes are, by definition, random and not easily identified. Nevertheless, a study of equipment and its maintenance, variation in materials and methods of operation, differences between operators, etc. will usually lead to a gradual reduction in variability. The use of control charts as a 'map' of the process is vital here.

Attributes

When a process is in-statistical-control and no assignable causes of variation are present, the remaining level of errors, defects, late deliveries, or whatever is being counted, will represent the capability of the process. As with variables, to improve process capability for attributes requires a systematic investigation of the whole process system. It is often difficult to make progress in process improvement when only attribute data is being used. Some form of variable data may be available to improve the analysis, but the only course of action for process improvement is to find out more about the process and, using Pareto and cause-and-effect analysis, and the resulting greater understanding of the process, eliminate the reasons for the holes in the socks, the errors in the invoices, the late deliveries, etc.

The quality system in improving capability

The impact of an efficient quality management system is that of gradually reducing process variability to achieve continuous or never-ending improvement. The requirement to set down defined procedures for all aspects of an organization's operations, and to stick to them, will reduce the variations introduced by the numerous different ways often employed in doing things. Go into any factory without a well-defined and managed quality system in operation and ask to see the operators' 'black-book' of plant operation and settings. Of course, each shift has a different black book, each with slightly different settings and ways of operating the process. Is it any different in office work or for salespeople in the field? Do not be fooled by the perceived simplicity of a process into believing that there is only one way of operating it. There are an infinite variety of ways of carrying out the simplest of tasks – the author recalls seeing various course participants finding fourteen different methods for converting A4 size paper into A5 size (half A4) in a simulation of a production task. The ingenuity of human beings needs to be controlled if these causes of variation are not to multiply together to render processes completely incapable of consistency or repeatability.

The role of the quality system here is to define and control process procedures and methods. Continual system audit and review will ensure that procedures are either followed or corrected, thus eliminating assignable or special causes of variation in materials, methods, equipment, information, etc. to ensure a 'could we do this job with more consistency?' approach.

10.4 Supplier capability

Four suppliers are being considered for a purchasing contract for a particular material. Investigations have shown that the capability of their processes is as shown in Figure 10.11. Which supplier will be chosen? It does not require much thought to realize that supplier A will cause endless problems. The process capability is such that defective material is being produced which must be inspected out. By whom? Whether the supplier or the buyer carries out the sorting, it is time consuming, expensive, and unreliable. It will never be cheaper overall to use supplier A.

Supplier B is capable of meeting the requirements – just. Any slight deviation in the centring of the process, any increase in spread will generate defective output. To deal with this supplier is to live on the edge of disaster. This could turn out to be even more costly than receiving material from A, some of which it is known is defective, and where routine screening inspection is carried out.

Supplier C has the inherent process capability ($Cp > 2$) to easily meet the requirements, but lacks the control to centre the process ($Cpk \simeq 1$). These results may reflect an attitude 'if everything is within the specified limits, what is the problem?' The automotive manufacturers have discovered the problem – take two suppliers X and Y, delivering different components x and y respectively. Component x must fit snugly inside component y. If both processes are capable of producing components within the specifications but x is being produced with diameters towards the lower specification limit and the distribution of y diameters lies at the top end of the specified range, then some assemblies of x and y will cause oil leaks as a small diameter x is inserted into a large diameter y.

Supplier D has a desirable process capability and is running the process centred on the target value. If suppliers X and Y were to produce their respective components with precision and accuracy, rather than simply within the specification limits, then the largest y being produced can meet with the smallest x and oil leaking assemblies will not result.

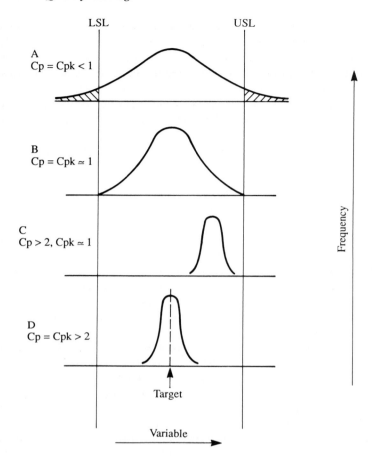

Figure 10.11   *Supplier capability*

So, what does an organization require from its suppliers? The answer is easy to state, but less easy to obtain:

- Consistency – low variability.
- Centring – on target.
- Process evolution and development to continually reduce variation.
- A systematic quality management approach to achieve the first three.

Historically many organizations, particularly in the manufacturing industries, operated an inspection-oriented quality system for bought-in parts and materials. Such an approach has many disadvantages. It is expensive, imprecise, and impossible to apply evenly across all material and parts, which all lead to variability in the degree of appraisal. Many organizations, such as Ford and Jaguar, found that survival and future growth in both volume and variety demanded that changes be made to this approach.

The prohibitive cost of holding large stocks of components and raw materials also pushed forward the 'just-in-time' (JIT) concept (see Chapter 5). This requires that suppliers make frequent, on time, deliveries of small quantities of material, parts, components, etc., often straight to the point of use, in order that stocks can be kept to a minimum. Clearly, the approach requires an effective supplier network which can produce goods and services which consistently conform to the real requirements, with a high degree of confidence.

Confidence and certificates

In a company operating TQM, materials may need to be received accompanied by a 'certificate of conformance or compliance'. The difference between such a document and a 'certificate of analysis' is that the latter contains test data from the material actually delivered, while conformance or compliance means that the delivery is certified to comply with all the agreed specification(s). This should not be regarded, however, as a blank cheque, and to achieve the confidence required to accept this type of certification from a supplier, may require a logical progression taking several years. Here, acceptance sampling (see Chapter 11) may play a role to ensure that requirements for the use by suppliers of good quality systems and SPC, manifest themselves in the quality of the product delivered. Such a progression, starting with a standard acceptable sampling scheme, may pass from tightened inspection through normal to reduced inspection, and eventually to various degrees of skip-lot sampling. As sampling is decreased, work should be taking place with the supplier to match specifications, test methods, and procedures.

One company, purchasing rubber sheeting for use in the manufacture of seals, moved in four years from opening every carton delivered and taking measurements on three rolls of rubber, every metre of a ten-metre roll, to receiving material straight to stock. This followed the development at the suppliers of an internal process control system based on mean and range charts, and a quality system of assessed capability. The documented savings were 40 man hours per week in a department with five hourly paid workers. Jobs were not lost, however, as the company used the 'extra' resource to audit and further improve their own production processes.

Commitment and involvement

The process of improving suppliers' performance is complex and clearly relies very heavily on securing real commitment from the senior management of the supplier organizations. This may be aided by presentations made to groups of directors of the suppliers, brought together to share the realization of the importance of their organizations' performance in the quality chains. The synergy derived from different suppliers meeting together, being educated, and discussing mutual problems will be tremendous. If this can be achieved, within the constraints of business and technical confidentiality, it is always a better approach than separate meetings and presentations on the suppliers' premises. The author recalls the benefits which accrued from bringing together suppliers of a photocopier, paper, and ring binders to explain to them the way their inputs were used to generate training course materials and how they in turn were used during the courses themselves. The suppliers were able to understand the business in which their customers were engaged, and became involved in the whole process.

A supplier of goods or services which has received such attention, education and training, and understands the role its inputs play is less likely to knowingly offer nonconforming materials and services, and more likely to alert customers to potential problems.

Policy

One of the first things to communicate to any external supplier is the purchasing organization's policy on quality of incoming goods and services. This can include such statements as:

- It is the policy of this company to ensure that the quality of all purchased materials and services meets its requirements.
- Suppliers will be selected who incorporate a quality management system into their operations. This system should be designed, implemented, and operated according to the International Standards Organization (ISO) 9000 series.
- Suppliers will be selected who incorporate statistical process control (SPC) methods into their operations.
- Routine inspection, checking, measurement, and testing of incoming goods and services will not be carried out by this company on receipt.
- Suppliers will be audited and their operating procedures, systems, and SPC methods will be reviewed periodically to ensure a never-ending-improvement approach.
- It is the policy of this company to pursue uniformity of supply, and to

encourage suppliers to strive for continual reduction in variability. (This may well lead to the narrowing of specification ranges.)

Many customers examine their suppliers' quality management systems themselves, operating a second party assessment scheme (see Chapter 9). Inevitably this involves high costs and duplication of activity, for both the customer and supplier. If a qualified, independent third party is used instead to carry out the assessment, attention may be focused by the customer on any special needs and in developing closer partnerships with suppliers. Visits and dialogue across the customer/supplier interface are a necessity if the true requirements are to be met and for future growth of the whole business chain. These should be concentrated, however, on improving understanding and capability, rather than on close scrutiny of operating procedures which is best left to experts, including those within the supplier organizations charged with carrying out internal system audits and reviews.

Supplier approval and single sourcing

Most organizations have as an objective to obtain at least two 'approved' suppliers for each material or service purchased on a regular basis. It may be argued, however, that single sourcing – the development of an extremely close relationship with just one supplier for each item or service – encourages greater commitment and a true partnership to be created. This clearly needs careful management, but it is a sound policy based on the premise that it is better to work together with a supplier to remove problems, improve capability, and generate a mutual understanding of the real requirements, than to hop from one supplier to another and thereby experience a different set of problems each time.

To become an 'approved supplier' it is usually necessary to pass through a number of stages:

Technical approval

Largely to determine if the product/service meets the technical requirements. This stage should be directed at agreeing a specification, which is set about the 'mean' of the supplier's process and describes the process capability about this point.

Conditional approval

At which stage it is known that the product/service meets the requirements, following customer in-process trials and there is a good commercial reason for purchase.

Full approval

When all the requirements are being met, including those concerning the operation of the appropriate management systems, SPC, etc.

Supplier capability audits and reviews

It is normal for organizations to carry out audits of their suppliers and to review their systems and process capabilities. This may take many forms. A questionnaire, visits to sites and premises, interviews with personnel, and simple calculations of indices are just a few of the many methods employed. The planning of the audit and review system is vital to successful cooperation with suppliers. And they must be aware, involved, and contribute to it so that it is viewed as a desirable part of the collaboration between two organizations.

Often an organization which understands that it cannot inspect quality into its products or services, tries to inspect quality into its suppliers' systems. This manifests itself as a 'policeman' approach by the auditor who arrives unannounced and determined to 'nail' the supplier with a few system discrepancies. The aim should be to help the supplier identify problems, by acting as a fresh pair of outside eyes, and to offer advice in their solution. The penalty-issuing auditor will create a desire to cover up rather than expose difficulties. If exposure results in help and advice being offered, rather than business being withdrawn, then clearly the partnership will foster and develop to a strength which resists all attempts by men, materials and machines to interfere. The principles behind this are not new, but they are often not practised. Being rude to, irritating, or simply bullying your suppliers, whether internal or external ones, will achieve one thing – conflict, and where is the evidence that this breeds anything other than defeat and frustration? A firm hand is required, but it must be used to lead and support rather than beat into submission.

Any supplier quality audit and review system should be designed to assess the quality and reliability of suppliers through a complete survey of the producing system. The objectives should be to improve the four Cs: communication, capability, confidence, and control. This will develop respect for each party and make sure that the frequency and organization of the audits is appropriate.

In the search for new suppliers the following questions are useful to see if there is even the chance of a partnership developing:

- Do you have a quality system which meets the requirements of ISO 9000?
- Do you have quality assured purchased materials and services?

- Do you have a system for traceability?
- Do you use statistical process control?
- What are your process capabilities?
- Have you set up quality improvement teams?
- Do you operate total quality management?

A lack of understanding by potential suppliers of the meaning of any of these questions suggests much work will be required to bring them to the required standard. Once potential suppliers have been identified, the questions may become more insistent for the partnership to develop further:

- You must operate a quality system which meets the requirements of ISO 9000 (this could become: You must have certification of assessed capability against ISO 9000).
- You must send a certificate of conformity (of analysis) with each consignment.
- We want to see your quality policy.
- We want to see your quality manual.
- We want to see your process control charts or their equivalent.
- We want to know your process capability indices (Cp and Cpk).
- We want to carry out quality audits and system reviews with you.

As with so much in quality management, data will provide the objective evidence of supplier capability. But the records must be used with skill and sensitivity to forge long-term associations, built with trust and collaboration for continuity and mutual success.

10.5 Taguchi methods

Genichi Taguchi is a noted Japanese engineering specialist who has advanced 'quality engineering' as a technology to simultaneously reduce costs and improve quality. The popularity of 'Taguchi methods' today testifies to the merit of his philosophies on quality. The basic elements of Taguchi's ideas, which have been extended here to all aspects of product, service and process quality, may be considered under four main headings:

1 Total loss function

An important aspect of the quality of a product or service is the total loss to society that it generates. Taguchi's definition of product quality as, 'the loss imparted to society from the time a product is shipped', is rather strange since the word 'loss' denotes the very opposite of what is normally conveyed by using the word 'quality'. The essence of his definition is that the smaller the loss generated by a product or service from the time it is transferred to the customer, the more desirable it is.

There are two particular problems with this idea:

(a) it does not include losses to society during manufacture of the product or operation of the service;
(b) it is rather profound and requires much thought, data collection, and analysis to be useful in the detailed business of quality management.

Its main advantage is that it encourages a new way of thinking about investment in quality improvement projects, which become attractive when the resulting savings to customers are greater than the cost of improvements.

Taguchi claims, with some justification, that any variation about a target value for a product or process parameter causes loss to the customer. The loss may be some simple inconvenience, but it can represent actual cash losses due to rework or badly fitting parts, and it may well appear as loss of customer goodwill and eventually market share. The loss (or cost) increases exponentially as the parameter value moves away from the target, and is at a minimum when the product or service is at the target value.

Taguchi calculates an average loss to customers by a statistically based averaging process which involves a quadratic approximation of loss associated with the values of the parameter being measured. This concept is also used to characterize process capability, independently from specification limits, which Taguchi sees as no more than tentative cut-off points. These ideas emphasize the importance of continuously reducing process variability.

2 Design of products, services and processes

In any product or service development, three stages may be identified: product or service design, process design, and production or operations. Each of these overlapping stages has many steps, the output of which is often the input to others. The output/input transfer points between steps clearly affect the quality and cost of the final product or service. The complexity of many modern products and services demands that the crucial role of design be recognized. Indeed the performance of the quality products from the automotive, banking, camera, and machine tool industries can be traced to the robustness of their product and process designs.

The prevention of problems in using products or services under varying operating and environmental conditions must be built in at the design stage. Equally, the costs during production or operation are determined very much by the actual manufacturing or operating process. Controls, including SPC methods, added to processes to reduce imperfections at the operational stage are expensive, and the need for controls and the production of nonconformance can be reduced by correct initial design of the process itself.

Taguchi distinguishes between 'off-line' and 'on-line' quality control methods, 'quality control' being used here in the very broad sense to include quality planning, analysis, and improvement. Off-line QC uses technical aids in the design of products and processes, whereas on-line methods are technical aids for controlling quality and costs in the production of products or services. Too often the off-line QC methods focus on evaluation rather than improvement. The belief by some people (often based on experience!) that it is unwise to purchase a new model of a motor car 'until the problems have been sorted out' testifies to the fact that insufficient attention is given to improvement at the product and process design stages. In other words, the bugs should be removed before, not after, product launch. This may be achieved in some organizations by replacing detailed quality and reliability evaluation methods with approximate estimates and using the liberated resources to make improvements.

3 Reduction in variation

The objective of a continuous quality improvement programme is to reduce the variation of key product performance characteristics about their target values. The widespread practice of setting specifications in terms of simple upper and lower limits conveys the wrong idea that the customer is satisfied with all values inside the specification band, but is suddenly not satisfied when a value slips outside one of the limits. The practice of stating specifications as tolerance intervals only can lead manufacturers to produce and despatch goods whose parameters are just inside the specification band. Owing to the interdependence of many parameters of component parts and assemblies, this is likely to lead to quality problems.

The target value should be stated and specified as the ideal, with known variability about that mean. For those performance characteristics which cannot be measured on a continuous scale, the next best thing is an ordered categorical scale such as: excellent, very good, good, fair, unsatisfactory, very poor; rather than the binary classification of 'good' or 'bad' that provides meagre information with which the variation reduction process can operate.

Taguchi has introduced a three-step approach to assigning nominal values and tolerances for product and process parameters:

System design

The application of scientific, engineering and technical knowledge to produce a basic functional prototype design. This requires a fundamental understanding of the needs of the customer and the production environment.

Parameter design

The identification of the settings of product or process parameters that reduce the sensitivity of the designs to sources of variation. This requires a study of the whole process system design to achieve the most robust operational settings, in terms of tolerance to ranges of the input variables. This is similar to the experiments needed to identify the plant varieties which can tolerate variations in weather conditions, soil, and handling. Manual processes which can tolerate the ranges of dimensions of the human body provide another example.

Tolerance design

The determination of tolerances around the nominal settings identified by parameter design. This requires a trade-off between the customer's loss due to performance variation and the increase in production or operational costs.

4 Statistically planned experiments

Taguchi has pointed out that statistically planned experiments should be used to identify the settings of product and process parameters that will reduce variation in performance. He classifies the variables that affect the performance into two categories: design parameters and sources of 'noise'. As we have seen earlier, the nominal settings of the design parameters define the specification for the product or process. The sources of noise are all the variables that cause the performance characteristics to deviate from the target values. The key noise factors are those that represent the major sources of variability and these should be identified and included in the experiments to design the parameters. The object of the experiments is to identify the settings of the design parameters at which the effect of the noise factors on the performance is minimum. This is done by systematically varying the design parameter settings and comparing the effect of the noise factors for each experimental run.

Statistically planned experiments may be used to identify:

(a) the design parameters which have a large influence on the product or performance characteristic;
(b) the design parameters which have no influence on the performance characteristics (the tolerances of these parameters may be relaxed);
(c) the settings of design parameters at which the effect of sources of noise on the performance characteristic is minimal;
(d) the settings of design parameters that will reduce cost without adversely affecting quality.

Taguchi methods have stimulated a great deal of interest in the application of statistically planned experiments to product and process designs. The use of 'design of experiments' to improve industrial products and processes is not new; Tippett used these techniques in the textile industry more than fifty years ago. What Taguchi has done, however, is to acquaint us with the scope of these techniques in off-line quality control.

Taguchi's methods, like all others, should not be used in isolation, but be an integral part of total quality management.

11 Control of quality

11.1 Inspection, checking, measurement and test

The task of inspection or checking is taken by many to be the passive one of sorting out the good from the bad, when it should be an active device to prevent errors, defects, or nonconformance. When human inspection is used to sift out the result of quality problems, it is frequently found that every item, every word, every number, or every element of a service is examined in an attempt to stop errors or defects reaching or being seen by the customer. In this type of monotonous, repetitive inspection procedure, '100 per cent inspection' generally turns out to be something less than 100 per cent. Monotonous tasks cause people to behave in a certain manner and to stop thinking about the job in hand. Research has shown that, typically, 15 per cent of the defectives present are missed during so-called 100 per cent inspection, and that examination of a sample provides a higher, more consistent detection rate.

Any control system based on detection of poor quality by post-production inspection is unreliable, costly, wasteful, and uneconomical. It must be replaced by the strategy of prevention, and the inspection must be used to check the system of transformation, not the product. This leads to a 'how-am-I-doing' type of control of the process, which should be carried out by the operatives, not by a separate 'QC police force' dedicated to detection and rejection.

The measurement of inputs, outputs, and processes themselves is a vital component of TQM. It monitors quality and may be used to determine the extent of improvements and deterioration in quality. Measurement may take the form of simple counting to produce attribute data, or it may involve more sophisticated methods to generate variable data, which appears on a continuous scale, such as height, current, speed, length, concentration, and time.

Processes operated without measurement are processes about which very little can be known. Conversely, if inputs and outputs can be measured and expressed in numbers, then something is known about the process, and control is possible. The first stage in using measurement as part of process control is to identify precisely the activities, materials, equipment, etc., which will be measured. This enables everyone concerned with the process to be able to relate to the target values and the focus provided will encourage improvements.

The size of the measurement task must be managed so that a reasonable parameter can be obtained. Some companies, for example, attempt to 'measure' supplier performance using schemes which distil down every aspect of all the relevant interfaces to one number. This is the equivalent of describing the building of a house in one sentence, and does not do justice to the detailed individual tasks involved.

Measurement should only be carried out if some action on the inputs or process will result, otherwise it is a dreadful and often expensive waste of time. This rule usually leads to asking:

- what should be measured? and
- how should the results be presented?

The answers to these questions depend very much on the requirements of the customer of the measurement process. If, for example, the senior management of an organization are interested in measuring quality, the costs of failure, probably in bar chart form, would be far more appropriate than a table of data detailing defect rates at each production stage. The latter would be very useful, however, for a production supervisor who wished to deploy resources in the most effective way to reduce overall defects. The criteria which are most helpful in these decisions are:

- what will be most helpful to the recipient of the information? and
- will it direct him/her to the action required?

Decisions regarding the actual measurement process and the people who will carry out the measurement must be made consciously if the activity is to lead to improvements in quality. The growth in specialist metrology has been partly responsible for the removal of responsibility of quality from the people actually performing the task. Constant revision and refining of measurement to remove it from the point of production will serve to measure with greater and greater precision the inability of processes to meet the requirements. Frequently an 'operator' is bound up with a process in such a way that he/she is the most suitable person to perform the measurement, and this has implications for the method to be employed. The forfeit of ultra-precise test results to bring under control the process being measured is usually worthwhile, and organizations would derive much benefit from devoting resources to providing simpler and simpler methods of measurement, which can be used by the process operator. It is clearly nonsense to commit resources to sophisticated external devices to find every typing error when the 'measurement' and correction is best done by the typists themselves.

For measurements to be used for quality improvement, they must be accepted by the people involved with the process being measured. The simple self-measurement and plotting, or the 'how-am-I-doing' chart, will gain far more ground in this respect than a policing type of observation and reporting system which is imposed on the process and those who operate it. Similarly, results should not be used to illustrate how bad one operator or group is, unless their performance is 100 per cent under their own control. The emphasis in measuring and displaying data must always be on the assistance that can be given to correct a problem or remove obstacles preventing the process from meeting its requirements first time, every time.

Measurement is an important part of the TQM control process, being used to plan, evaluate and correct, but it is only a part and must not become an end in itself. The measurement of failure to an infinite degree of precision by itself does nothing to prevent that failure, and the enthusiasm of analytical chemists, precision test engineers, and even industrial engineers, may need to be carefully controlled. One of the author's favourite quotations is the statement made by Gauss:

> Lack of mathematical culture is revealed nowhere so conspicuously as in meaningless precision in numerical calculation.

The same is true of measurement.

Standards and metrology

It is clear that defined standards of measurement of dimensions, temperature, pressure, weight, electric current and voltage, etc. are vital to a world in which a motor car designed in Japan may be assembled in the UK using parts from all over the world. For this to be possible, all devices used for measurement must be calibrated and traced back through a chain to some form of standard which is accepted internationally.

Measurement, like any other process, is variable. If exactly the same measurement (e.g. weight, length, concentration, viscosity, time) of exactly the same item, batch, or service, is taken on several occasions, exactly the same result will not be obtained each time. The variation between the readings may arise from random or assignable causes, as with any process. The variation due to the measurement process will tend to give rise to a normal distribution (Figure 10.8) with a mean μ_m and standard deviation σ_m. The accuracy of the measurement process then is a function of how closely the mean μ_m agrees with the 'true' value and is controlled by the calibration system. The precision of the measurement is a function of σ_m.

Components of process variation and its analysis

The standard deviation σ is the most commonly used description of variation. However, the square of the standard deviation, the variance σ^2, is of particular importance, especially when variation arises from a number of contributory sources. For example, in determining the quantity of shampoo in bottles, the apparent variation may comprise the real bottle-to-bottle variation in net quantities, the variation in tare weights of containers, and variation in the measurement system. It is frequently possible to measure these contributions separately by means of variance components.

The breaking down of variations, which is necessary to understand the impact on a process, of measurement variations, is the principle of the science known as analysis of variance. By use of the addition of independent contributing variations, it may be possible, with the correct recording of data, to isolate and identify the magnitude of the precision of the measurement. Going one step further, it is possible to examine the components of variation within the measurement itself, those due to:

- the human element, the skill and repeatability of the measurement operator;
- the inherent precision of the measurement equipment itself;
- the variations in the sample preparation;
- the variations in any materials used in the test or measurement.

Turning attention to the process itself, the variation can be broken down into various input elements; materials, equipment, operators, etc.

Analysis of variance, especially in industrial research and experimentation, can become a very complex subject and the reader is referred to more specialist texts for a complete treatment. Unlike control charts, histograms, Pareto and cause-and-effect analysis, analysis of variance is not normally used routinely at the point of production or operation. It is a technique for disentangling the components of overall process variation, in which a great deal of thought must be given to the collection, analysis and interpretation of data. The average manager need not be familiar with the complexity of analysis of variance, but should be aware of the approach and the type of information it can provide. Special assistance can usually be found, either inside or outside an organization, for the design of the data collection and analysis programme.

11.2 Process control of variables (or measuring things)

In Chapter 10 the concept of variability was examined. For successful total quality management, it is essential that everyone understands variation and how and why it arises. The absence of such knowledge will lead to action being taken to adjust or interfere with processes which, if left alone, would be quite capable of achieving the requirements. Many processes are found to be out-of-statistical-control when first examined using control chart techniques. It is frequently observed that this is due to an excessive number of adjustments being made to the process based on individual tests or measurements. This behaviour, commonly known as

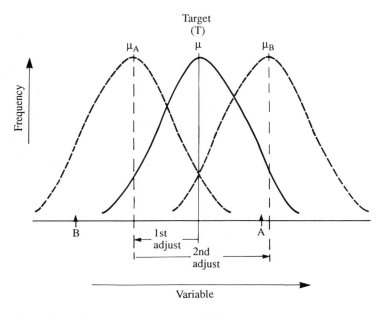

Figure 11.1   *Increase in process variability due to frequent adjustment*

hunting, causes an overall increase in variability of results from the process, as shown in Figure 11.1

The process is initially set at the target value $\mu = T$, but a single measurement at A results in the process being adjusted to a new mean μ_A. Subsequently, another single measurement at B results in a second adjustment of the process to a new mean μ_B. Clearly if this behaviour continues throughout the process operation, its variability will be greatly increased with a detrimental effect on the ability of the process to meet the specified requirements. Indeed it is not uncommon for such behaviour to lead to a call for even tighter tolerances and for the process to be 'controlled' very carefully. This in turn leads to even more adjustment, further increases in variability, and more failure to meet the requirements.

The standard deviation σ of a process distribution is one measure of variation. As the sample size in statistical process control is usually less than or equal to ten, a more convenient measure of spread is the sample range – the difference between the largest and smallest values in the sample. To control a process it is necessary to check the centring and the spread of the distribution and this may be achieved with the aid of mean and range charts.

If the length of a single piece of metal is measured, it is clear that occasionally a length will be found which is towards one end of the tail of the process normal distribution. This, if examined on its own, may lead to the wrong conclusion that a cutting process requires adjustment. If, however, a sample of five pieces is taken, it is extremely unlikely that all five lengths will lie towards one extreme end of the distribution. The average or mean length of five pieces will, therefore, provide a much more reliable indicator of the setting of the process. Moreover, the range of the sample will give an indication of the spread of the results from the process.

A capability study

1 Is the process in-control?

A series of measurements is taken from the process over a period of time, hopefully when no adjustments to the process have been made. The results are then grouped into samples of size four to ten (n = 4 to 10). A total of 50 individual results, taken over a 'recognized' period of stability, is the minimum requirement for a capability study. The mean and range of each group of five results are calculated and the grand mean of means (process mean $\overline{X}$) is determined, together with the mean of the sample ranges $\overline{R}$.

Mean charts

The means of samples taken from a stable process will vary with each sample taken, but the variation will not be as great as for the individual results. Comparison of the two frequency diagrams of Figure 11.2 shows that the spread of the sample means is much less than the spread of the individual measurements.

In setting up a mean chart, where samples of a given size *n* are taken from the process over a period when it is thought to be under control, the sample mean is recorded on a control chart. Providing that the sample size is *n* = 4 or more then, the mean values will be normally distributed even if the original population itself is not truly normal. The standard deviation of the sample means, called the standard error to avoid

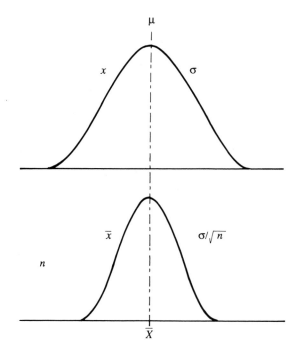

Figure 11.2   *What happens when we take samples of size* n *and plot the means?*

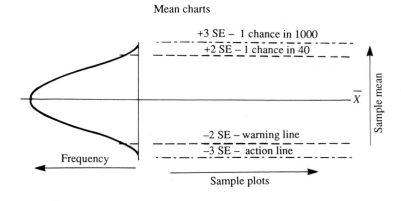

Figure 11.3   *The principle of the mean chart*

confusion with the standard deviation of the parent population, is smaller than the parent standard deviation:

$$\text{standard error of the sample means} = \sigma \sqrt{n}$$

where σ is the standard deviation of the parent population.

Figure 11.3 shows the principle of the control chart for sample mean. If the process is running in-control, we expect almost all the means of successive samples to lie between the lines marked upper action and lower action. These are set at a distance equal to $3\sigma/\sqrt{n}$ either side of the process mean. The chance of a mean falling outside either of these lines is about 1 in 1000, unless the process has altered. If a point does fall outside, this indicates the presence of an assignable cause and the process should be investigated or the setting appropriately adjusted.

Figure 11.3 also shows warning limits which have been set at $2\sigma/\sqrt{n}$ either side of the process mean. The chance of a sample mean plotting outside either of these limits is about 1 in 40, i.e. it is expected to happen once in every 40 samples. When it does happen, however, there are grounds for suspicion and the usual procedure is to take another sample immediately, before making a definite decision about the setting of the process. Two successive sample means outside one of the warning lines indicate that action to adjust the process should be taken immediately.

In process control of variables, the sample size is usually less than ten, and it becomes possible to use the alternative measure of spread of the process, the mean range of samples $\bar{R}$, to calculate the control chart limits. Use may then be made of Hartley's conversion constant (dn) for estimating the process standard deviation: $\sigma = \bar{R}/dn$.

Range charts

A process is only in control when both the accuracy (mean) and precision (spread) of the process are in control. A separate chart for control of process variability is required, and the sample standard deviation could be plotted. More conveniently the ranges of samples are plotted on a range chart which is very similar to the mean chart, the difference between the highest and lowest values in the sample being plotted and compared to predetermined limits. The development of a more serious fault than incorrect setting can lead to the situation illustrated in Figure 11.4, where the process collapses from form A to form B, e.g. due to failure of a part of the process. The ranges of the samples from B will have higher values than ranges in samples taken from A. If a range chart is plotted in conjunction with the mean chart, similar action and warning lines can be drawn to indicate trouble.

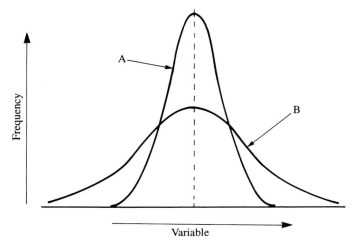

Figure 11.4   *Increase in spread of a process*

Stepwise procedure

The statistical concepts behind control charts for variables may seem a little complex, but the steps in setting up the charts for mean and range are very simple:

(a) Select 20 or so random samples of size n (n between 4 and 10)
(b) Measure the variable for each of the sample items.
(c) Calculate each sample mean and range.
(d) Calculate the grand or process mean $\overline{X}$ and the mean range $\overline{R}$.
(e) Look up the values of certain statistical constants.
(f) Calculate action and warning lines for the mean and range charts, following simple formulae.

Figure 11.5 shows mean and range control charts plotted for a process which is in-control. The detailed methods and constants for calculation of the control chart limits may be found in *Statistical Process Control* by the author.

Process 'in-control'

It was stated earlier that samples should be taken from the process when it is believed that the process is under control. Before the charts are used to control the process, the initial data is plotted on the mean and range charts to confirm that the distribution of the individual items is stable. A process is 'in-statistical-control' when all the variations have been shown

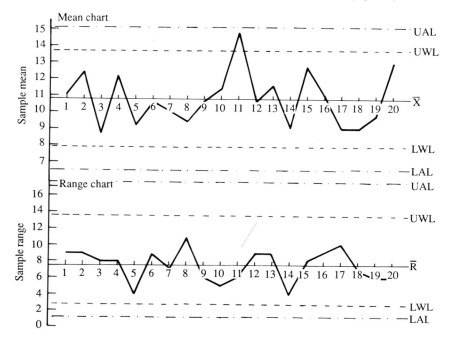

Figure 11.5   *Mean and range charts from samples of* n = 5

to arise from random or common causes and none attributable to assignable or special causes. The randomness of the variations may be shown by the plotted mean and range charts when there are:

- No mean or range values lying outside the action limits.
- No more than about 1 in 40 values lying between the warning and action limits.
- No incidences of two consecutive mean or range values lying in the same warning zone.
- No runs of more than six sample means or ranges which lie either above or below the average control chart line.
- No trends of more than six values of mean or range which are continuously either rising or falling.

The data plotted on the mean and range charts in Figure 11.5 clearly demonstrate that this process is in-control, since all the above requirements are met. If the process examined in this way is not in-statistical-control, the assignable causes must be identified and eliminated. The process may then be re-examined to test for stability.

2 Is the process capable of meeting the requirements?

Having demonstrated that only random causes of variation are present, the next task is to compare the precision of the process with the required specification tolerances. Calculation of the process capability indices Cp and Cpk allows this to be done quickly and quantitatively (see Chapter 10). If the process, as operated, is incapable of meeting the specified requirements, then the variability of the process must be reduced.

Controlling the process

When the process is shown to be in-control then the mean and range charts may be used to make decisions about the state of the process during production. For example, Figure 11.6 shows mean and range charts for 20 samples taken from a process producing steel shafts. The process is well under control, i.e. within the action lines, until sample 8, when the mean

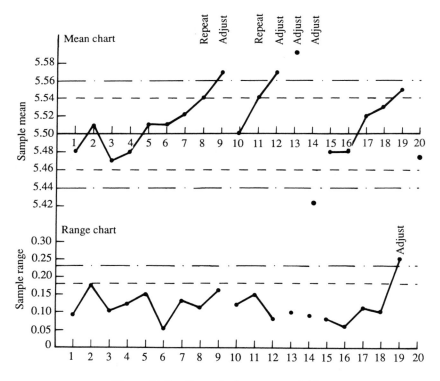

Figure 11.6   *Control of process variables*

reaches the upper warning line – a repeat sample required here. Sample 9 shows a mean plotted above the upper action line and corrective action must be taken.

Vital components of any process control system are the instructions given to the operator concerning what action should follow such a signal. Neglect of this aspect will generate at best confusion and at worst increases in process variability. The instructions, which need to be part of the documented quality system, should be clear, precise, and based on either technical knowledge of the process operation or past experience of similar occurrences.

The action taken following the results from sample 9 brings the process back into control but only until sample 11, where the sample mean is again in the warning zone; another sample should be taken immediately, rather than wait for the next sampling period. This sample (12) gives a mean above the action line; corrective action forthwith. But the action appears to be in the wrong direction, and the response results in over-correction with sample mean 14 well below the lower action line. The process continues to drift upwards out of control between samples 15 and 19, at which point the range goes out of control indicating a serious malfunctioning of the process. The process clearly requires investigation to establish the assignable causes of change in the variability. This situation would not have been identified as quickly in the absence of the process control charts and this simple example illustrates the power of the charts in both quality control and in early warning of trouble.

It will be noted that 'adjust' and 'repeat' samples have been marked on the control charts. In addition, any alterations in materials, the process, operators or any other technical changes should be recorded in code form on the charts when they take place. This practice, when linked with other process records, is extremely useful in helping to track down causes of shifts in mean or variability. It is only by tenaciously enquiring about all unexpected results that the move towards better control and never-ending improvement can be achieved.

SPC in batch and continuous processes (or for infrequent data)

SPC is based on a number of basic principles, all of which apply to both batch and continuous processes commonly found in manufacturing and service industries. One of these principles is that within all processes variations are inevitable due to either random or assignable causes of variation. There is a need to separate the two types of variation when interpreting data. If it is known that the difference between an individual result and the target value is simply a part of the inherent randomness, there is clearly no point in trying to adjust or correct for it. If the observed difference is known to be due to an assignable cause then correction or control of this cause is possible and probably desirable.

This principle and the ensuing use of mean and range control charts is often understood and accepted where data is available on a large scale, but the use of such control procedures is often thought not to apply to situations in which a new item of data is available either in isolation or infrequently. This is the case in batch processes where analysis of the final product may reveal for the first time the characteristics of what has been produced. In continuous processes, data is also often available on a one-result-per-period basis, e.g. one analysis per hour or per shift.

If it is accepted that variation is an inevitable part of all processes, it must equally be accepted that stability should be part of such processes. Apart from a very limited range of processes which are explosive in nature, only those processes which should be stable and reproducible are generally used. For batch processes this means that each time a new batch is produced, the whole recipe of materials, equipment, skills, and the methods of operation are reproduced in the expectation that the output of successive batches will be similar and lie within predetermined limits. In continuous processes, stability of the output is also sought either by holding conditions constant or by seeking to change them in a way which will hold the output constant. The output may either be the product or a parameter important to the product or process control.

The key to the separation of random and assignable causes lies in grouping results together and using this grouping to assess changes both in the average value and the scatter of results – reflections of the centring of the process (accuracy) and the spread due to random causes (precision). Many attempts have been made to avoid grouping results but there is no known way of segregating changes in centring from changes in spread without doing so. This applies to all processes including batch and continuous processes.

When only one result is available at the conclusion of a batch process, or when an isolated estimate of an important parameter is obtained on an infrequent basis, clearly the result cannot be ignored until more data is available with which to form a group. Equally it is impractical to contemplate taking, say, four samples instead of one and repeating the measurement or analysis several times in order to form a group, the costs of doing this would be prohibitive in many cases, and statistically this is different from grouping less frequent results. The answer lies in the use of 'moving mean' and 'moving range charts' in which the latest item of data is grouped with a number of the previous items of data in order to assess whether the process is still adequately centred and of acceptable spread. The setting up of such charts and their interpretation is slightly more complicated than the simple mean and range charts, but a full description will be found in the textbook on SPC by the author. It is recommended that appropriate training of all personnel likely to be involved in using any SPC techniques is carried out to ensure correct interpretation.

11.3 Process control of attributes (or counting things)

In the case of attributes, e.g. colour, general appearance, surface finish, absenteeism, when it is not possible to measure a product except in terms of 'good' or 'bad', present or absent, the control process is effectively that of determining which one, out of two possible decisions, is appropriate. When this two-way decision involves the classification of whole items or units as defective, the sampling process is governed by the laws of the 'binomial distribution'.

Number-defective (*np*) charts

If the proportion of the output which is not acceptable is p, when a large number of samples, each of size n is taken, then the average number of defectives which will be found in each sample is np. The control chart for number-defective, or np chart, operates in a similar way to those for variables, with warning and action lines. These lines are again set by reference to the average and standard deviation of the number of defectives in the samples. Figure 11.7 shows a control chart for number-defective (np) for the situation in which the sample size $n = 20$, and the proportion defective $p = 0.1$.

Proportion-defective (*p*) charts

In some situations it is not convenient to take samples of constant size and so the proportion of defectives in a sample is used as the quality indicator.

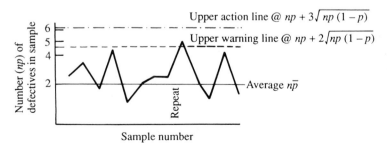

Figure 11.7   *An* np *chart for number defective*

In these proportion-defective or *p* charts, warning and action limits are calculated from the average and standard deviation of the proportion defective.

Control charts for number of errors or defects (c and u charts)

The control charts for attributes considered so far have applied to defectives. There are situations, however, where the number of errors or defects in the product or service is being counted. In these cases the binomial distribution does not apply because there are no values of n. The Poisson distribution describes the results obtained from counting defects and is used in the calculation of warning and action lines for these types of chart.

Lower action and warning lines on attribute charts

It is sometimes useful to insert lower warning and action limits on attribute charts. If points appear below the lower action limit, there is only a slight chance of this happening unless there has been a significant improvement in the process. In this case, it would be worthwhile investigating the cause of such a change, to discover how the improvement could be made permanent. The only other reason for a point plotting below the action limit would be inaccurate inspection or defectives being passed as good.

Cusum charts

The cusum (cumulative sum) chart is a graph which takes a little longer to draw than the conventional control chart, but which gives a lot more information. It is particularly useful for plotting the evolution of processes because it presents data in a way that enables the eye to separate true trends and changes from a background of random variation. Cusum charts can detect small changes in data very quickly and may be used for the control of variables and attributes. In essence, a reference or 'target value' is subtracted from each successive sample observation and the results cumulated. Values of this cumulative sum are plotted and 'trend lines' may be drawn on the resulting graphs. If this is approximately horizontal, the value of the variable is about the same as the target value. An overall slope downwards shows a value less than the target, and if the slope is upwards it is greater.

Figure 11.8 shows a comparison of an *np* chart and a cusum chart which have been plotted using the same data – errors in samples of 100 invoices. The change, which is immediately obvious on the cusum chart, is difficult to detect on the conventional control chart.

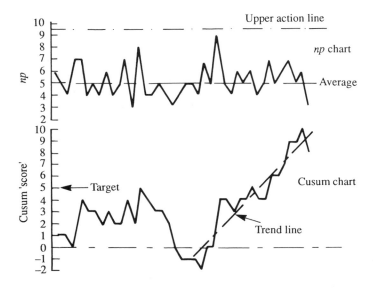

Figure 11.8 *Comparison of cusum and* np *charts for the same data*

11.4 Acceptance sampling (or sorting out things)

The techniques dealt with so far in this chapter are directed towards process control activities. Some organizations, however, carry out a further final check on each batch of finished product or documents before they are sent to the consumer. Alternatively, material or services may be purchased where it is not possible to ensure that the appropriate process control activities are taking place in the supply chain. In these situations, some form of inspection or check for acceptance or sorting out, is often used.

Such inspection schemes are concerned primarily with making sure that product which passes the inspection point meets the requirements. For this to be possible, it must be quite clear what is required. There are two aspects to a specification with regard to inspection for acceptance, and there must be specific information on both of these if sensible decisions are to be made. The specification must contain a statement of what constitutes nonconformance. This is an extremely complex issue and demands careful thought before any inspection or checking process gets underway. The various techniques of acceptance inspection will not resolve the problem of an ill-conceived definition of nonconformance, nor can they cope with the absence of one. Unfortunately the latter situation exists in far too many organizations, where high levels of expenditure on inspection or checking result in frustration and conflict.

Sometimes, in cases of subjective assessment, it is necessary to provide samples of acceptable and unacceptable material to aid the decision process.

In addition to the requirement for a definition of nonconformance, there is a need to stipulate, quite categorically the quantity or proportion which is allowed, if the batch of product is to be considered satisfactory. This clearly contradicts the tenets of TQM and zero defects and illustrates the undesirability of acceptance sampling schemes. Organizations will, however, encounter their use and it is important to know how they are usually operated, how the results should be used and interpreted, and what risks are involved.

Depending on the end use of the product or service, there is often a classification of errors or defects. For example, it may be considered that there are critical, major and minor errors or defects which demand different quantification if customer satisfaction is to be ensured. In the production of medical equipment, there are obviously different requirements from those found in the manufacture of cast-iron garden furniture. Similarly, in the assembly of a motor car, one fault, such as a deep scratch on a polished surface, may cause great distress, whereas other, slight imperfections will pass unnoticed by many purchasers; an error in a hospital might be fatal or merely create a nuisance for the staff. These factors must be considered in the design of the check or inspection system. Sometimes it is necessary to design different schemes for different error or fault classifications to operate in parallel.

100 per cent inspection is a time-consuming, costly, and unreliable method of control. There are, however, some situations in which this method is deemed to be essential. A process where life is at stake may rely very heavily on this approach. Wherever it can, the system should move away from human inspection towards automated methods and indeed towards process control. This is not always immediately possible or economical and some form of human checking activity may be required. In these cases, and where life or death consequences prevail, the only answer is to perform 100 per cent human checking or inspection several times.

Acceptance sampling procedures, if they are applied correctly, will allow the quantification and limitation of risks of making incorrect decisions. In many cases, a properly designed and effectively administered sampling scheme is the most economical and practical way of making acceptance decisions. In cases of destructive testing some form of sampling is the only acceptable alternative.

In deciding which type of scheme to use, it is first necessary to examine the nature of the quality characteristics which will be employed in the inspection process. Will the product quality be presented in the form of attribute data or variables? There are methods of acceptance sampling for both. Where only attribute data is available there is no choice, but when variables can be measured, two general approaches may be employed – acceptance sampling by variables, or convert the variable data into attribute form and use acceptance sampling by attributes. The advantages associated with using variables are similar to those found in process control – increased sensitivity and smaller sample sizes. The disadvantages concern the extra costs of obtaining the measured data and performing the necessary calculations and in some situations these may be considerable.

Acceptance sampling techniques are used to decide whether to accept or reject a batch of items based on random sample(s). If a decision is taken to accept, then the remainder of the batch is accepted without further inspection. It must be clear that such a procedure gives no guarantee of the actual quality of the whole batch, it simply provides a decision making process. If a decision to reject the batch is taken, the remainder may be sentenced in several possible ways, depending upon the use of the product and any associated technological or economic factors. A rejected batch may be destined for:

- 100 per cent screening to rectify or replace all errors or defectives;
- further inspection;
- use for lower quality requirements;
- return to supplier;
- acceptance at discounted price, etc.

Operating characteristics

A characteristic of the mechanism of all sampling plans is that they are associated with risks. There are basically two types of risk derived from the sample or samples not being representative of the lot, batch or run. There is a risk that a decision may be taken to reject a batch which should have been accepted, i.e. of acceptable quality. This is referred to by statisticians as a 'type 1 error'. Another term, which is more meaningful perhaps, is 'producer's risk'. The 'type 2 error' or 'consumer's risk' is associated with the acceptance of goods the quality of which is unacceptable.

The efficiency of any sampling plan as a detector of acceptable and unacceptable batches is shown by means of its operating characteristics (OC) curve. This curve, which should be known for every sampling plan used, is derived by plotting:

the chance (or probability) of a batch being accepted   versus   the quality offered for inspection (usually measured in percentage defective)

Further principles of acceptance sampling will not be explained here since they are well documented. The reader is referred to further reading for the details of acceptance sampling for attributes and variables.

Quality index

The quality of a product or service may be monitored by reference to a quality index. The product is 'awarded' a mark of, say, 100 and marks ('demerits') subtracted for nonconformances found; for example, 4 demerits for a major, 2 for a minor and 1 for a trivial defect or problem. Clearly, these classes must be carefully predefined. The resulting figure is then compared either with an agreed 'acceptable' figure, with a figure derived from serious competitors, or with previous figures as a monitor of the quality performance.

11.5 SPC techniques in the non-manufacturing areas

Organizations which embrace the TQM concepts should recognize the value of SPC techniques in areas such as sales, purchasing, invoicing, finance, distribution, training, etc., which are outside production or operations – the traditional area for SPC use. A Pareto analysis, a histogram, a flow chart, or a control chart is a vehicle for communication. Data is data, and whether the numbers represent defects or invoice errors, the information relates to machine settings, process variables, prices, quantities, discounts, customers, or supply points is irrelevant, the techniques can always be used.

In the author's experience, some of the most exciting applications of SPC have emerged from departments which, when first introduced to the methods, could see little relevance to their own activities. Following appropriate training, however, they have learned how to, for example:

- Pareto analyse errors on invoices to customers (Figure 11.9) and industry injury data (Figure 11.10).
- Brainstorm and cause-and-effect analyse reasons for late payment (Figure 11.11) and poor purchase invoice matching (Figure 11.12).
- Histogram defects in invoice matching (Figure 11.13) and arrival of trucks at certain times during the day (Figure 11.14).
- Control chart the weekly demand of a product (Figure 11.15).

Distribution staff have used *p* charts to monitor the proportion of deliveries which are late, and Pareto analysis to look at complaints involving the distribution system. Word processor operators have been seen using cause-and-effect analysis and histograms to represent errors in

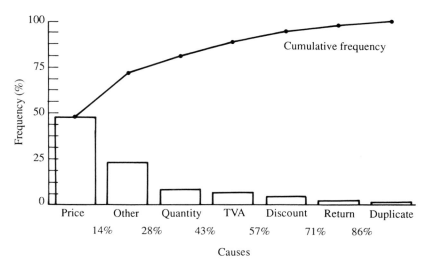

Figure 11.9   *Pareto analysis, errors in invoices to customers*

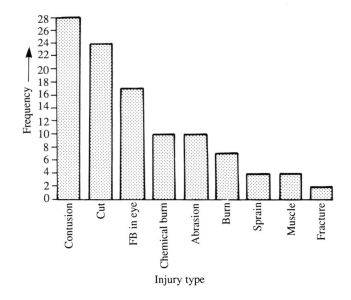

Figure 11.10   *Pareto analysis, injury data*

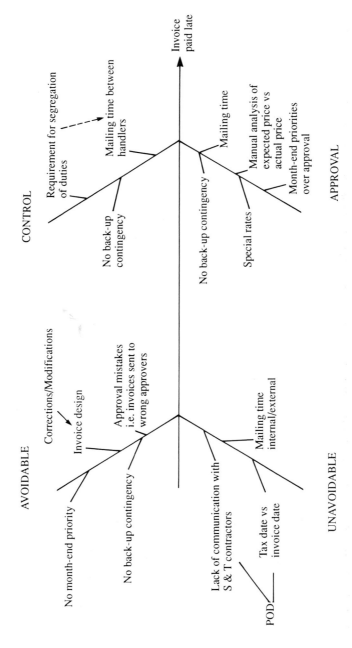

Figure 11.11   *Basic cause-and-effect analysis, reasons for late payment*

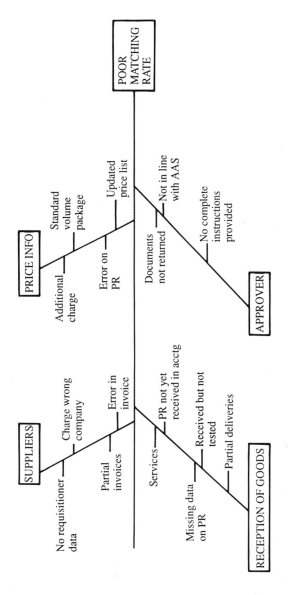

Figure 11.12 *Poor matching process, cause and effect*

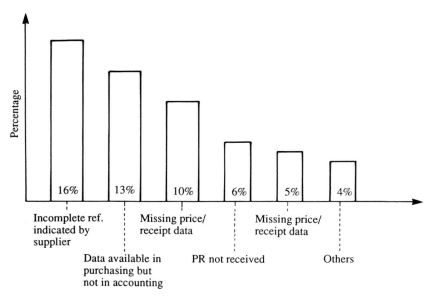

Figure 11.13   *Defects in matching process*

the output from their service. Moving average and cusum charts have immense potential for improving forecasting in the marketing area.

Those organizations which have made most progress in implementing TQM have recognized at an early stage that SPC is for the whole organization. Restricting it to traditional manufacturing or operations activities means that a window of opportunity for improvement has been closed. Applying the methods and techniques outside manufacturing will make it easier, not harder, to gain maximum benefit from an SPC programme.

Sales and marketing is one area which often resists training in SPC on the basis that it is difficult to apply. Personnel in this vital function need to be educated in SPC methods for two reasons:

1 They need to understand the way the manufacturing or service-producing processes in their organizations work. This will enable them to have more meaningful and involved dialogues with customers about the whole product service system capability and control. It will also enable them to influence customers' thinking about specifications and create a competitive advantage from improving process capabilities.
2 They will be able to improve the marketing processes and activities. A significant part of the sales and marketing effort is clearly associated with building relationships, which are best built on facts (data) and not

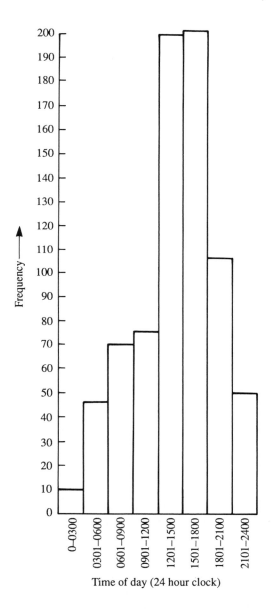

Figure 11.14 *Arrival of trucks at certain times during day*

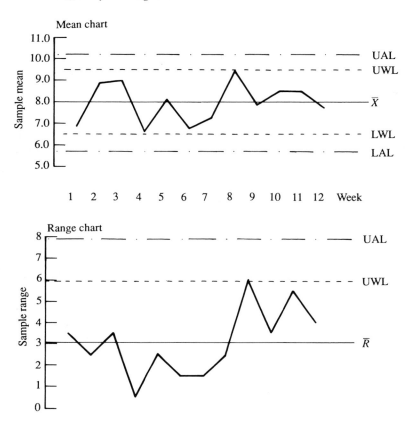

Figure 11.15   *Weekly demand of product 1102*

opinions. There are also opportunities to use SPC techniques directly in such areas as forecasting demand levels and market requirements, monitoring market penetration, marketing control, and product development, all of which must be viewed as processes.

SPC has considerable applications for non-manufacturing organizations, including universities! Data and information on patients in hospitals, students in universities, polytechnics, colleges and schools, people who pay (and do not pay) tax, draw social security benefit, shop at Sainsbury's or Macy's, is available in abundance. If it were to be used in a systematic way, and all operations treated as processes, far better decisions could be made concerning past, present, and future performances of certain non-manufacturing parts of industry.

11.6 Improvements in the process

The emphasis which must be placed on never-ending improvement has important implications for the way in which process control charts are applied. They should not be used purely for control, but as an aid in the reduction of variability by those at the point of operation capable of observing and removing assignable causes of variation. The identification and gradual elimination of random causes of variation are, moreover, the responsibility of management who may well require the involvement of the 'technical' experts – the engineers, chemists, etc.

The process of continuous improvement may be charted, and adjustments made to the control charts in use to reflect the improvements. This

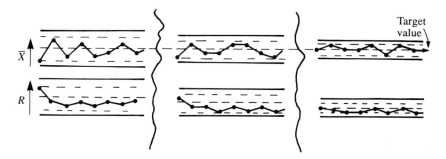

Figure 11.16   *Continuous process improvement, reductions in variability*

is shown in Figure 11.16 where progressive reductions in the variability of piston diameters has led to decreasing sample range values. If the control limits on the mean and range charts are recalculated periodically or after a step change, their positions will indicate the improvements which have been made over a period of time, and ensure that the new level of process capability is maintained. Similarly attribute or cusum charts may be used, to show a decreasing level of number of errors, or proportion of defects and to indicate improvements in capability.

Often in process control situations, action signals are given when the assignable cause results in a desirable event, such as the reduction of an impurity level, a decrease in error rate, or an increase in demand or sales. Clearly assignable or special causes which result in deterioration of the process must be investigated and eliminated, but those that result in improvements must also be sought out and managed so that they become part of the process operation. Significant variation between batches of material, operators, or differences between suppliers are frequent causes of action signals on control charts. The continuous improvement philosophy demands that these are all investigated and the results used to take another step on the long ladder to perfection. Action signals and assignable or special causes of variation should stimulate enthusiasm for solving a problem or understanding an improvement, rather than gloom and despondency.

Poka-yoke

Shigeo Shingo is the inventor of the single-minute exchange of die (SMED) system in which set-up times are reduced from hours to minutes, and the poka-yoke (mistake proofing) system. He was a key developer of the Toyota Production System and likes to be known as 'Dr Improvement'.

Shingo teaches three interrelated aspects of quality control. *Zero quality control* is the ideal production system in which no defects or errors are produced. To achieve this two things are required: *'poka-yoke'* and *source inspections*.

1 In poka-yoke, defects are examined, the production system stopped and immediate feedback given so that the root causes of the problems may be identified and prevented from occurring again.

   Poka-yoke recognizes that people are human, fallible and will, on occasions, inadvertently forget things. To counter this characteristic of the human being, Shingo suggests the incorporation of 'checklists' (i.e. a poka-yoke) into the operation, so that if a worker forgets something, the device will signal that fact, thereby preventing errors or defects from occurring. This is similar to the checklist the author uses to make sure he has all the equipment necessary when leaving for the golf-course!

   The poka-yoke concept is based on the same idea as 'foolproofing', an approach often used for preserving the safety of operations and in which assembly, manufacture, or operation can be performed in only one way – the correct way. This clearly has large implications for product and process design.

2 In source inspections, errors are looked at before they become defects and the system is either stopped for correction or the error condition automatically adjusted to prevent it from becoming a defect.

   Ordinary inspection systems stimulate feedback and action in response to defects which have been produced. Source inspections are based on discovering errors in conditions that can give rise to defects, feeding back, and taking action at the error stage to prevent the errors from turning into defects. This requires the clear distinction between errors and defects. Defects arise because errors are made and there is a cause-and-effect relationship between the two. If this is so then clearly errors will not turn into defects if feedback and action take place at the error stage.

Zero QC systems are set up by combining source inspections with 100 per cent inspections and providing immediate feedback and action. According to Shingo, a zero quality control system is based on the following basic ideas:

(a) use source inspections to prevent defects, by applying control functions at the error stage where defects originate, and eliminate them completely;
(b) use 100 per cent inspections rather than sampling inspections;
(c) minimize the time it takes to carry out corrective action when abnormalities appear;
(d) recognize that human workers are not infallible and set up poka-yoke devices accordingly.

Using poka-yoke and source inspection systems has enabled companies such as Toyota to virtually eliminate the need for acceptance sampling methods.

12 Teamwork for quality

12.1 The need for teamwork in quality management

The complexity of most of the processes which are operated in industry, commerce and the services places them beyond the control of any one individual. The only way to tackle problems concerning such processes is through the use of some form of teamwork. The use of the team approach to problem solving has many advantages over allowing individuals to work separately on problems:

- a greater variety of problems may be tackled, which are beyond the capability of any one individual, or even one department;
- the problem is exposed to a greater diversity of knowledge, skill and experience;
- the approach is more satisfying to team members and boosts morale;
- problems which cross departmental or functional boundaries can be dealt with more easily;
- the recommendations are more likely to be implemented than in- dividual suggestions.

Most of these rely on the premise that people are most willing to support any effort in which they have taken part or helped to develop.

When properly managed, teams improve the process of problem solving, producing results quickly and economically. Teamwork through- out any organization is an essential component of the implementation of TQM for it builds up trust, improves communications and develops interdependence. Much of what has been taught previously in manage- ment has led to a culture in the West of independence, with little sharing of ideas and information. Knowledge is very much like organic manure – if it is spread around it will fertilize and encourage growth, if it is kept closed in, it will eventually fester and rot. Teamwork devoted to quality improvement changes the independence to interdependence through improved communications, trust and the free exchange of ideas, know- ledge, data and information (Figure 12.1). The use of the face-to-face interaction method of communication, with a common goal, develops over time the sense of dependence on each other. This forms a key part of

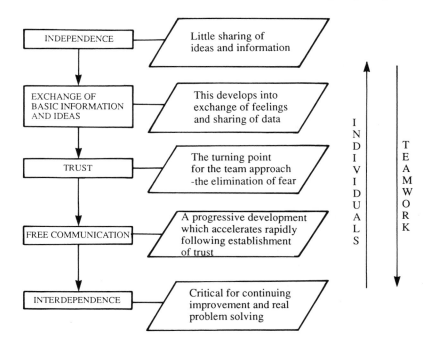

Figure 12.1   *Independence to interdependence through teamwork*

any quality improvement process, and provices a methodology for employee recognition and involvement, through active encouragement in
group activities.

A full discussion of the theory of motivation is outside the scope of this
book and there are many excellent texts on the subject. It is worth
pointing out, however, that employees will not be motivated towards
continual improvement in the absence of:

- commitment to quality from top management;
- the organizational quality 'climate';
- a team approach to quality problems.

All these are focused essentially at enabling people to feel, accept, and
discharge responsibility. More than one organization has made this part
of their quality strategy – to 'empower people to act'. If one hears from
employees comments such as 'we know this is not the best way to do this
job, but if that is the way management want us to do it, that is the way we
will do it', then it is clear that the expertise which exists at the point of
operation has not been harnessed and the people do not feel responsible

for the outcome of their actions. Responsibility and accountability foster pride, job satisfaction, and better work.

Empowerment to act is very easy to express conceptually, but it requires real effort and commitment on the part of all managers and supervisors to put into practice. Recognition that only partially successful but good ideas or attempts are to be applauded and not criticized is a good way to start. Encouragement of ideas and suggestions from the work-force, particularly through their involvement in team or group activities, requires investment but the rewards are total involvement, both inside the organization and outside through the supplier and customer chains.

There are essentially two types of teams associated with quality management:

quality improvement teams, and
quality circles.

These are quite separate entities, which can operate successfully together in one organization, or they may be used quite independently. They are described in sections 12.3 and 12.4.

12.2 Communication

People's attitudes clearly can be influenced by communication – one only has to look at the media or advertising to understand this. The essence of changing attitudes to quality is to gain acceptance for the need to change, and for this to happen it is essential to provide relevant information, convey good practices, and generate interest, ideas and awareness through a two-way communication process. This is possibly the most neglected part of many companies' operations, yet failure to communicate effectively creates unnecessary problems resulting in confusion, loss of interest and eventually in declining quality through apparent lack of guidance and stimulus.

It may be useful to contemplate why people learn. They do so for several major reasons:

- self-betterment;
- self-preservation;
- need for responsibility;
- saving time or effort;
- sense of achievement;
- pride in work;
- curiosity.

So communication and training can be a powerful stimulus to personal development at the workplace, as well as achieving improvements for the organization. This may be useful in the selection of the appropriate method(s) of communication, the principal ones are:

- Verbal communication either between individuals or groups using direct or indirect methods, such as public address and other broadcasting systems, and tape recordings.
- Written communication in the form of notices, bulletins, information sheets, reports and recommendations.
- Visual communication such as posters, films, video tapes, exhibitions, demonstrations, displays and other promotional features. Some of these also involve verbal communication.
- Example through the way people conduct themselves and adhere to established working codes and procedures; through their effectiveness as communicators and ability to 'sell' good quality practices.

The characteristics of each of these methods should be carefully examined before they are used in communicating the quality messages.

1 Direct verbal communication

The requirements of this method are for:

- careful preparation;
- good individual communication and presentation skills;
- a broad knowledge of the subject matter;
- ability to control and answer questions or seek answers;
- credibility with the audience or group;
- the encouragement of participation and involvement.

Its strengths are:

- direct impact on individuals or the group;
- permits assessment of reactions and allows discussion or presentations to be modified accordingly;
- permits use of plain words easily understood by groups or individuals;
- audience can ask questions and get answers;
- permits presenter to check assimilation through, for example, asking questions;
- allows for reiteration, recapitulation, and special emphasis as necessary;
- 'personalizes' quality and improvement;
- aids the process of participation and involvement;
- can secure commitment from groups and individuals.

But it has limitations, it:

- depends upon the individuals' ability to communicate effectively;
- uses only one of the senses through which people acquire knowledge;
- requires time to prepare carefully in proportion to the complexity of the subject;
- does not guarantee uniformity of content and understanding between groups unless based on a common agenda;
- is time-consuming and usually most effective for small groups.

The art of speaking to people effectively should be learned and practised at all levels of the communication framework.

2 Indirect verbal communication

This method is limited in its effectiveness in communicating quality. It suffers from many deficiencies, for example, many internal broadcasting systems are periodically overwhelmed by noise so there is no guarantee that the message has been even received – much less understood. It is often difficult to check that everyone has heard the message and checking understanding is often impractical. Furthermore, it is inflexible and cannot adapt easily to individual requirements.

3 Written communication

The requirements of written methods are:

- ability to express the message in words clearly and concisely;
- ability to make words interesting to read;
- ability to say exactly what is meant, unambiguously;
- sense of 'timing' – good administrative arrangements for circulation;
- awareness of limitations and deployment only in appropriate situations.

Its strengths are:

- same message goes to everyone;
- speedy;
- careful timing of 'release' can ensure that message is received by everyone at the same time;
- useful for dealing with large numbers in a short span of time;
- useful for giving 'non-critical' information;
- can be circulated by a number of routes (e.g. in pay packets, individual letters, notices, etc.) simultaneously;
- helpful, and sometimes essential, in backing up verbal communication, particularly if subject is involved;

- regularizes and records actions, procedures, systems, rules, etc.;
- usual form for submitting reports and recommendations.

The limitations are:

- not everyone chooses to – or can – read; therefore no guarantee that message has 'got through';
- written words may mean different things to different people according to vocabulary;
- words may be ambiguous and create confusion and misunderstanding;
- no opportunity for clarification, cannot easily ask questions, get replies or discuss;
- difficult to convey relative importance and emphasis and give topic 'light and shade';
- lacks animation, depersonalizes communication processes, and reduces opportunity for personal contact;
- reduces sense of involvement and precludes exchanges of information and views.

4 Visual communication

People learn through their senses but by far the highest percentage of what they take in is through sight. It is estimated that the five senses contribute to the learning process as follows:

sight (visible)	75%
hearing (audible)	13%
feeling (tactile)	6%
smell (olfactory)	3%
taste (gustatory)	3%

This clearly means that visible methods of communication can be extremely successful, especially when combined with other methods, such as verbal in the form of films, video tapes, or demonstrations. It also has implications for training sessions and group discussions in which visual aids should be used as liberally and dramatically as possible.

5 Communication by example

Showing videos, displaying posters, discussion groups, speaking, or writing are not the only ways of communicating quality. Personal example is a powerful medium for getting across the messages. This can be done by:

- people's general positive attitude and alertness to quality;
- the way people conduct themselves at the workplace;

- adherence to rules, procedures, systems, standard operations, and practices;
- standards of housekeeping and hygiene;
- the way in which people are inclined to help others appreciate and avoid potential problems;
- people learning how to relate to, communicate with, and influence others to gain their commitment to quality;
- the way in which people exude enthusiasm, pride, and confidence in themselves and the organization for which they work.

Counselling and coaching

If people do have to be corrected at work, it is important for managers and supervisors to remember that the objective is to help staff to understand and identify with their problems and prevent recurrence of mistakes. It is necessary to be objective always and supervision should try to find out *what* has gone wrong rather than *who* has gone wrong. This will lead to a reliance on facts rather than opinions and 'hunches'. Managers and supervisors should be trained to create a good atmosphere, be patient, listen, and be prepared to respond to other ideas and initiatives. When correction of operating staff is necessary, supervision should:

- choose the place and the time carefully;
- 'talk straight', but not humiliate the listener especially in front of an audience;
- never be punitive or retaliatory;
- be open and adapt to changing situations;
- recapitulate progress and gain commitment to any improvement and anticipated future steps agreed.

Communicating interest in quality – a few ideas

1 Suggestion schemes

If one already exists it may be used for periods when only quality suggestions can be accepted. Such an event, which should be used sparingly to gain maximum impact, must be given lively publicity. If special prizes can be awarded, presentations to the best suggestions should be made, with the appropriate publicity.

2 'Departmental' talk-ins

This method, often known descriptively as 'huddles' in the USA, involves the gathering together for brief, but organized, periods to discuss quality issues relevant to the department. Time is usually short (by arrangement it may be attached to a tea or meal break or shift change for administrative simplicity) so an 'agenda' should be prepared and the sessions should be 'punchy' to make significant points with impact.

3 Induction and vocational training

'Quality consciousness' begins when a new employee enters the organization. Induction training in quality alerts people to the requirements, codes of practice, conduct, procedures, and the quality culture. It should also capture interest and imagination, make people take quality seriously, and encourage them to hear more about it.

Vocational training for specific jobs should satisfy the employees' interest in quality created during the induction phase. Further training in methods and techniques for problem solving may need to be formal and off-the-job but quality training should be integrated with operational training as the opportunities occur by relating the consequences of mal-operation to quality as well as production and safety.

4 Poster campaigns

Some companies have found that posters or similar devices can form an important part of the quality communication message from the very beginning. The first poster should be simple and may carry very straightforward statements such as:

Quality starts here

The next person who checks your work
will be your customer

Get it right the first time and avoid waste

with suitable animated cartoon drawings or photographs, if appropriate. Some examples of the types of posters used by various organizations are given in Figure 12.2.

There are literally hundreds of available quality posters and many are often displayed with less effect than is possible. It is useless to simply stick them up at random. A poster campaign must be carefully planned, organized and 'managed'. The key question is 'what do you want to achieve with the campaign?' When answered, carefully select the most relevant and impact-provoking posters. Next, look at the locations. Will people stop, look and think? A well-lit and prominent location which does not interfere with traffic is required. Posters should be centred at

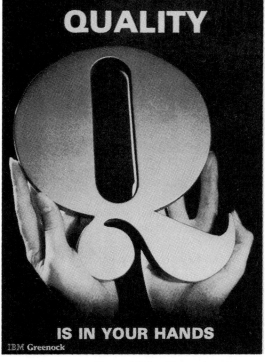

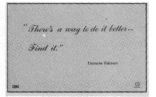

Figure 12.2   *Examples of posters for quality*

about eye-level but a few gimmicky locations sometimes arouse interest. Keep quality posters separate and away from competition or 'clutter'. Integrate posters with other interests, particularly at holiday times. Holiday posters or notices can often be made to carry quality messages with some added impact. Home-made posters can be even more effective than 'bought-in' ones and a 'quality poster' competition may stimulate even more interest.

The posters should change to match the changing awareness, as the quality poster campaign matures. They may begin to reflect the breadth of the subject by referring to computer-integrated-manufacture, just-in-time concepts, and quality in the 'non-producing' areas. The success of a quality poster campaign will be enhanced by continually freshening the communication messages with new posters, say, every three months.

5 Point-of-work reminders

The energy crisis gave birth to a good example of the point-of-work reminder with the 'save it' stickers. This idea may be developed for highlighting special problems and to encourage careful working practices, particularly where these have been neglected in the past.

6 Competitions

A competition may be at the company level with, say, a determined attempt to win a national 'quality pennant' or arranged internally on an inter-departmental basis. Quality competitions are no substitute for training, they simply raise interest and levels of awareness. If they fail to generate interest they are worthless. Mostly quality competitions are based on error or defect rates over a finite period of time. To make the competition even between departments with dissimilar risks, some 'modifier' must be brought into the calculations. To take account of uneven effects, results could be judged on, say:

(a) the percentage reduction in each department's defect rates from a previous base-period;
(b) error frequencies modified by a 'handicap' based on the relativity of the risk weightings between departments. Thus 'high risk' areas would not be disadvantaged in the competition by those with a lower risk.

Some organizations have experience of quality competitions in which each department is 'inspected' by a team on a set number of occasions within the duration of the competition at random intervals. Marks are allocated under a number of different headings relative to the customer requirements being met.

7 Prizes and formal presentations

If presentations to steering committees, quality improvement teams, or quality circles are part of the recognition process, it is a good idea to award some sort of certificate of recognition to allow people to display their success. Photographs and reports of such award 'ceremonies' provide a colourful method of publicity. Different organizations have used various reward devices from copper-etched plaques to weekends in Paris for successful individual contributions. If lunches and 'external' senior executives are used as the medium for transfer of these rewards, the commitment and support from the top are visually demonstrated. A 'chief executive's award' may be the major glittering prize for the best presentation made during the year.

8 Demonstrations and exhibitions

Static exhibitions of certain aspects of quality can be a focal point of interest and this can be a powerful way of making an impact.

9 House magazines or newsletters/papers

Local or organization-specific newspapers have a role to play if regular communication is to be achieved on a broad scale. These may feature articles on quality success stories and, in particular, should be used as a 'shop window' for quality improvement teams and/or quality circles. Publication of project findings, changes resulting from them, and measured improvements or savings, in newsletter form, is a powerful motivator which should not be underestimated. If done properly it also encourages the 'me-too' syndrome which can generate the excitement and momentum so essential for successful TQM. There are a considerable number of possibilities for getting the message across by taking space in the company publication. But it must be interesting, eye-catching and newsworthy. If it is not read or fails to make an impact it is worthless.

10 Opinion surveys

In some companies, employee opinion surveys are conducted by questionnaire, as part of TQM. If these are designed carefully, they should measure the employee perception of the programme. It is the author's experience that, in companies which have embraced TQM and carried out surveys properly, the results confirm a positive response. In one company:

- 83 per cent of the workforce were in favour of their manager's attitude to quality;

- 86 per cent believed that the quality of service provided by their department had increased;
- 73 per cent were convinced that the output of their department had improved.

The only danger with this sort of counting is the development of complacency. TQM demands that continuous improvement is an ongoing activity and each achievement should set targets for further improvement in the future.

It is not intended that this list should be exhaustive, relevant to every situation, or the most important way of communicating quality. It is given only as an indicator to the sort of possibilities there are for bringing the quality message 'alive' – even for the cynics.

Summarizing communication

If TQM is to succeed in any organization it is important for all managers, supervisors and staff to recognize the value and influence of good communication as a vital link in creating and maintaining standards for quality. Moreover, they must learn the characteristics of the various methods of communication and select the one most appropriate for the situation. This process is very much accelerated by an appreciation of how people learn to assimilate knowledge, since this will encourage people to make use of all the senses when communicating.

All communication and training exercises must be planned like a military operation, leaving nothing to chance. When dealing with people, particularly when checking or counselling, managers and supervisors must be sensitive to the effect they have. They may need to be trained to communicate with people in a way that will help everyone feel more capable, more necessary and more worthwhile.

Effective communication is a two-way exercise. We were designed with two ears and one tongue. Could it be we were meant to listen twice as much as we speak? Listening with attention, interest, and courtesy and carrying on listening does not come naturally to many people and they may need to be reminded, in their training, teamwork, or counselling activities, to listen 'openly'.

12.3 Quality improvement teams

A quality improvement team (QIT) is a group of people with the appropriate knowledge, skills, and experience who are brought together by management specifically to tackle and solve a particular problem, usually on a project basis. They are cross-functional and often multi-disciplinary.

The 'task force' has long been a part of the culture of many organizations at the 'technology' and management levels. But quality improvement teams go a step further, they expand the traditional definition of 'process' to include the entire production or operating system. This includes paperwork, communication with other units, operating procedures, and the process equipment itself. By taking this broader view new problems can be addressed.

The actual running of quality improvement teams involves several factors:

Team selection and leadership
Team objectives
Team meetings
Team assignments
Team dynamics
Team results and reviews

Team selection and leadership

The most important element of a QIT is its members. People with knowledge and experience relevant to solving the problem are clearly required, but there should be a limit of five to ten members to keep the team small enough to be manageable, but allow a good exchange of ideas. Membership should include appropriate people from groups outside the operational and technical areas directly 'responsible' for the problem, if their involvement is relevant or essential. In the selection of team members, it is often useful to start with just one or two people concerned directly with the problem. If they try to draw flow charts (see Chapter 5) of the processes involved, the requirement to include other people, in order to understand the process and complete the charts, will aid the team selection. This method will also ensure that all those who can make a significant contribution to the improvement process are represented.

The team leader has a primary responsibility for team management and maintenance and his/her selection and training are crucial to success. The leader need not be the highest-ranking person in the team, but must be concerned about accomplishing the team objectives (this is sometimes described as 'task concern') and the needs of the members (often termed 'people concern'). Weakness in either of these areas will lessen the effectiveness of the team in solving problems. Team leadership training should be directed at correcting deficiencies in these crucial aspects.

Team objectives

At the beginning of any QIT project and at the start of every meeting, the objectives should be stated as clearly as possible by the leader. This can take the simple form, 'this meeting is to continue the discussion from last Tuesday on the provision of current price data from salesmen to invoice preparation, and to generate suggestions for improvement in its quality.' Project and/or meeting objectives enable the team members to focus thoughts and efforts on the aims, which may need to be restated if the team becomes distracted by other issues.

Team meetings

An agenda should be prepared by the leader and distributed to each team member before every meeting. This should include the following information:

● meeting place, time and how long it will be;
● a list of members (and coopted members) expected to attend;
● any preparatory assignments for individual members or groups;
● any supporting material to be discussed at the meeting.

Early in a project the leader should orient the team members in terms of the approach, methods, and techniques they will use to solve the problem. This may require a review of the:

● systematic approach (Chapter 10);
● procedures and rules for using some of the basic tools, e.g. brainstorming – no judgement of initial ideas;
● role of the team in the overall continuous improvement process;
● authority of the team.

A team secretary should be appointed to take the minutes of meetings and distribute them to members as soon as possible after each meeting. The minutes should not be formal, but reflect decisions and carry a clear statement of the action plans together with assignments of tasks. They may be handwritten initially, copied, and given to team members at the end of the meeting, to be followed later by a more formal document which will be seen by any member of staff interested in knowing the outcome of the meeting. In this way the minutes form an important part of the communication system involving other teams or people involved in some way with the process.

Team assignments

It is never possible to solve problems by meetings alone. What must come out of those meetings is a series of action plans which assign specific tasks to team members. This is the responsibility of the team leader. Agreement must be reached regarding the responsibilities for individual assignments, together with the timescale, and this must be made clear in the minutes. Task assignments must be decided while the team is together and not by separate individuals in after-meeting discussions.

Team dynamics

In any team activity the interactions between the members are vital to success. If solutions to problems are to be found, the meetings and ensuing assignments should assist and harness the creative thinking process. This is easier said than done because many people have not either learned or been encouraged to be innovative. The team leader clearly has a role here to:

- create a 'climate' for creativity;
- encourage all team members to speak out and contribute their own ideas or build on others;
- allow differing points of view and ideas to emerge;
- remove barriers to idea generation, e.g. incorrect preconceptions which are usually destroyed by asking 'why?';
- support all team members in their attempts to become creative.

In addition to the team leader's responsibilities, the members have roles to:

- prepare themselves well for meetings, by collecting appropriate data or information (facts) pertaining to a particular problem;
- share ideas and opinions;
- encourage other points of view;
- listen 'openly' for alternative approaches to a problem or issue;
- help the team determine the best solutions;
- reserve judgement until all the arguments have been heard and fully understood;
- accept individual responsibility for assignments and group responsibility for the efforts of the team.

Team results and reviews

A QIT approach to problem-solving functions most effectively when the results of the projects are communicated and acted upon. Regular feedback to the teams, via their leaders, will assist them to focus on project objectives and review progress.

Reviews also help to deal with certain problems which may arise in teamwork. For example, certain members may be concerned more with their own personal objectives than those of the team. This may result in some manipulation of the problem-solving process to achieve different goals, resulting in the team splitting apart through self-interests. If recognized, the review can correct this effect and demand greater openness and honesty.

A different type of problem is the failure of certain members to contribute evenly and take their share of individual and group responsibility. Allowing other people to do their work results in an uneven distribution of effort and bitterness. The review should make sure that all members have been assigned specific tasks, and perhaps lead to the documentation of duties in the minutes. A team roster may even help.

A third area of difficulty, which may be improved by reviewing progress, is the ready, fire, aim syndrome of action before analysis. This often results from team leaders being too anxious to deal with a problem. A review should allow the problem to be redefined adequately and expose the real cause(s). This will release the trap the team may be in of doing something before they really know what should be done. The review will provide the opportunity to rehearse the steps in the systematic approach:

record data	all processes can and should be measured
	all measurements should be recorded
use data	if data is recorded and not used it will be abused
analyse data	data analysis should be carried out using the seven
systematically	basic tools (Chapter 10)
act on the results	recording and analysis of data without action leads to frustration

Organization for quality improvement teams (see also Chapter 3)

Part of the systematic approach to continuous improvement is the establishment of a team of senior managers which can provide the commitment, direction, and resources necessary to eliminate problems so that they do not recur. This team, council, or steering committee will control the QITs and have responsibility for:

- the selection of projects for the QITs;
- providing an outline and scope for each project to give to the QITs;
- the appointment of team members and leaders;
- monitoring and reviewing the progress and results from each QIT project.

As the focus of the work of this committee will be the selection of projects, some attention will need to be given to the sources of nominations. Projects may be suggested by:

1 committee members, representing their own departments, their suppliers or their customers, internal and external;
2 quality improvement teams;
3 quality circles (if in existence);
4 suppliers;
5 customers.

The committee members must be given the responsibility and authority to represent their part of the organization and every part must have a person on the committee representing it. The members must also feel that they represent the committee to the rest of the organization, and in particular their own part(s). In this way the committee will gain knowledge and respect and be seen to have the authority to act in the best interests of the organization.

12.4 Quality circles

One of the most publicized aspects of the Japanese approach to quality has been quality circles. The quality circle may be defined as a group of workers doing similar work who meet:

- voluntarily;
- regularly;
- in normal working time;
- under the leadership of their 'supervisor';
- to identify, analyse, and solve work-related problems;
- to recommend solutions to management.

Where possible quality circle members should implement the solutions themselves.

The quality circle concept first originated in Japan in the early 1960s, following a post-war reconstruction period during which the Japanese placed a great deal of emphasis on improving and perfecting their quality control techniques. As a direct result of work carried out to train foremen during that period, the first quality circles were conceived, and the first three circles registered with the Japanese Union of Scientists and Engineers (JUSE) in 1962. Since that time, the growth rate has been phenomenal. The concept has spread to Taiwan, the USA and Europe, and circles in many countries have become successful. Many others have failed.

It is very easy to regard quality circles as the magic ointment to be rubbed on the affected spot and unfortunately many managers in the West have seen them as a panacea which will cure all ills. There are no panaceas and to place this concept into perspective, Juran, who has been an important influence in Japan's improvement in quality, has stated that quality circles represent only 5–10 per cent of the canvas of the Japanese success. The rest is concerned with understanding quality, its related costs and the organization and techniques necessary for achieving customer satisfaction.

Given the right sort of commitment by top management, introduction, and environment in which to operate, quality circles can produce the shop floor motivation to achieve quality performance at that level. Circles should develop out of an understanding and knowledge of quality on the part of senior management. They must not be introduced as a desperate attempt to do something about poor quality.

The structure of a quality circle organization

The unique feature about quality circles is that people are asked to join and not told to do so. Consequently it is difficult to be specific about the structure of such a concept. It is, however, possible to identify four elements in a circle organization:

- Members
- Leaders
- Facilitator or coordinator
- Management

Members, the prime element of the programme. They will have been taught the basic problem-solving and quality control techniques and, hence, possess the ability to identify and solve work-related problems.

Leaders, usually the immediate supervisors or foremen of the members. They will have been trained to lead a circle and bear the responsibility for its success. A good leader, who develops the abilities of the circle members, will benefit directly by receiving valuable assistance in tackling nagging problems.

Facilitator, the overall manager of the quality circle programme. This person, more than anyone else, will be responsible for the success of the concept, particularly within an organization. The facilitator must coordinate the meetings, the training and energies of the leaders and members, and form the link between the circles and the rest of the organization. Ideally, the facilitator will be an innovative industrial teacher, capable of communicating at all levels and with all departments within the organization.

Management, without whose open support and commitment quality circles, like any other concept, will not succeed. Management must retain its prerogatives, particularly regarding acceptance or non-acceptance of recommendations from circles, but the quickest way to kill a programme is to ignore a proposal arising from it. One of the most difficult facts for management to accept, and yet one which forms the corner-stone of the quality circle philosophy, is that the real 'experts' on performing a task are those that do it day after day.

Training quality circles

The training of circle leaders and members is the foundation of all successful programmes. The whole basis of the training operation is that the ideas must be easy to take in and be put across in a way which facilitates understanding. Simplicity must be the key word, with emphasis being given to the basic techniques. Essentially there are eight segments of training:

1 Introduction to Quality Circles
2 Brainstorming
3 Data Gathering and Histograms
4 Cause and Effect Analysis
5 Pareto Analysis
6 Sampling
7 Control Charts
8 Presentation Techniques

Management should also be exposed to some training in the part they are required to play in the quality circle philosophy. A quality circle programme can only be effective if management believes in it and is supportive and, since changes in management style may be necessary, their training is essential.

Operation of quality circles

There are no formal rules governing the size of a quality circle. Membership usually varies from three to fifteen people with an average of seven to eight. It is worth remembering that as the circle becomes larger than this, it becomes increasingly difficult for all members of the circle to participate.

Meetings must be held away from the work area where members are free from interruptions, and are mentally and physically at ease. The room should be arranged in a manner conducive to open discussion and any situation which physically emphasizes the leader's position should be avoided.

Meeting length and frequency are variable but new circles meet for approximately one hour, once per week. Thereafter, when training is complete, many circles continue to meet weekly, others extend the interval to two or three weeks. To a large extent, the nature of the problems selected will determine the interval between meetings, but this should never extend to more than one month, otherwise members will lose interest and the circle will cease to function.

Great care is needed to ensure that every meeting is productive, no matter how long it lasts or how frequently it is held. Any of the following activities may take place during a circle meeting:

- Training – initial or refresher
- Problem identification
- Problem analysis
- Preparation and recommendation for problem solution
- Management presentations
- Quality circle administration

A quality circle usually selects a project to work on through discussion within the circle. The leader then advises management of this choice and assuming that no objections are raised, the circle proceeds with the work. Other suggestions for projects come from management, quality assurance staff, the maintenance department, various staff personnel, and other circles.

It is sometimes necessary for quality circles to contact experts in a particular field, for example, engineers, quality experts, safety officers, maintenance personnel. This communication should be strongly encouraged and the normal company channels should be used to invite specialists to attend meetings and offer advice. The experts may be considered to be 'consultants', the quality circle retaining responsibility for solving the particular problem. The overriding purpose of quality circles is to provide the powerful motivation of allowing people to take some part in deciding their own actions and futures.

12.5 Tips on communication skills for team leaders and chairmen

The starting point for any problem solving team is brainstorming, during which a team member records all the ideas on a chart, possibly as a cause-and-effect diagram (see Chapter 10). The purpose and rules of brainstorming are directed at achieving agreement on action plans. The agreement to be reached among team members with regard to action plans will force the consideration of all aspects of a problem, and will make everyone alert to possible objections to the chosen courses of action. A useful device along this path to consensus of opinion is to allow the team some 'thinking time' before, during and after brainstorming sessions.

If conflict occurs, as is inevitable in any teamwork, it must be managed so that it assists rather than hinders the team to achieve its objectives. The team leader has an important role in such situations and it will help to:

- recognize all contributors of ideas, not just those whose ideas are used;
- stress that both the organization and the individuals benefit, if improvements are made;
- clarify what is expected of each team member, in terms of the common goals and individually assigned tasks;
- mediate when dominating members cause others to feel inadequate or suppressed;
- remind members who make personal references that the group is in existence to reach agreement and find solutions;
- endorse the positive traits of members, such as cooperation, openness, listening, contribution, etc.;
- discourage criticism, defensiveness, aggressiveness, closed mindedness, interrupting, etc.

Talking to people

If anyone has to speak to a group of people, they should use the following 'checklist' as an aid to structuring and presenting the talk:

1 What is the *objective* of the talk – what has to be conveyed?
2 What *key points* must be included to achieve the objective?
3 In what *sequence* should these be arranged for maximum impact and smooth 'flow'?
4 Who will comprise the *audience*? What is their occupation, status level, experience, etc.? And how many will there be?
5 What *method* of presentation will be most effective for the particular purpose to be achieved and audience to be addressed? For example, will it be a talk or a discussion?
6 Will *visual aids* be required and if so how will they be used? The saying 'one picture is worth 1000 words' should remind people of the value of illustrating talks or discussions.
7 How much *time* is available and how will it be allocated?
8 In which *location* is the talk to be given? Is it suitable? Is it correctly appointed?
9 How will *assimilation* of the message be checked? Will tests and questions be used to check *understanding*?

10 What *follow-up* is planned to reinforce the message and ensure *implementation*?

In presenting a case or point of view in a meeting, people will need to be shown how to perform to maximum effect. The key points here are to encourage presenters to:

- try, by taking a little time and by making introductions, to take the stress out of any 'negotiating' situation and create the right 'atmosphere';
- speak slowly, simply and with variation in pitch and tone, using pauses to aid assimilation, and avoiding jargon and clichés;
- present points of view logically and with clarity and precision so that all understand the substance of the case;
- interest the audience through the content and presentation style, involving them whenever possible;
- keep an open mind and an open ear, listen carefully to what other people are saying;
- keep alert and try to read the 'language' of the situation;
- be flexible in outlook, adapt to new situations and take advantage of new avenues of approach;
- build on the best points of any particular case and diminish the weaknesses;
- make constructive proposals but prevent people from being 'cornered' inextricably;
- maintain discipline over the team or group to control discussions, cover the agenda, keep to the point, and keep cool;
- keep the objective in mind throughout;
- 'manage' the time of the meeting;
- be sure that all parties understand what has been agreed before the meeting closes;
- communicate outcomes quickly and accurately to all interested parties.

Reports and writing generally

There are some general ground rules for effective presentation of written material and reports. A good report should be readable, interesting, informative, well presented and be no longer than is necessary. Recipients are likely to be busy people and will welcome a concise report from which they can grasp the essentials. Therefore, when constructing a report the following questions should be considered:

- Why has the report been requested?
- What are the terms of reference and objectives?

- What messages need to be conveyed?
- What type of information is required? For example, is it factual information based on observation or research, conclusions drawn from facts, or recommendations as to future courses of action?
- Is it arranged in a logical sequence, such as:

  Title
  Contents
  Introduction or terms of reference
  Summary
  Data and information
  Analysis/discussion
  Conclusions and recommendations
  Action plans
  Supplementary information (e.g. appendices)?

- Will the subject and presentation capture the interest of the reader?
- Is it as short and easy to read as possible?
- Can some of the text be explained in diagrammatic form where this will aid understanding?
- Is it intelligible to the reader?
- Is it free of 'shorthand' expressions, departmental 'code words' and technical jargon?
- Does it take account of minority views or dissenting opinions?
- Have factual information and personal comments been distinguished to provide a sufficiently objective report?
- Do the conclusions and recommendations match the requirements of the terms of reference? Do they follow logically from the information and analysis contained in the main body of the report?

Good report writing requires a particular skill in expression and some experience. These notes are only a few clues to the more obvious considerations and are not exhaustive. There are many full texts on this subject.

Leading discussions

For those who have to lead discussions, including quality council chairmen, and leaders of quality improvement teams and quality circles, this plan may help:

Make an outline: Determine the objectives and what is to be covered.

Decide the 'key points' for discussion and how much time there will be available.

	Select areas of priority from 'key points' relative to the time available. Plan the session in the imagination.
Plan the approach:	Decide how the topic will be introduced. Move the discussion along from one point to the next. Determine how people will be brought into the discussion.
Plan the physical arrangements:	Make sure everyone can be made comfortable. Ensure that everyone can see and hear. Check the heating, ventilation, lighting, etc. Make sure all the necessary visual aids are available and that they are all serviceable.
Introduce the session:	Review the background to the discussion. Announce the topic briefly and concisely and emphasize the relevance to the background. Explain how the discussion should proceed and gain commitment to this approach. Lead into the discussion smoothly and logically.
Control the discussion:	Encourage participation; draw out ideas by asking questions, encouraging the exchange of views and opinions. Encourage the reluctant contributors and prevent monopolization by the more vocal members. Distribute the questions evenly and avoid bias. Keep the discussions to the point and always moving forward. Stimulate thought and discussion if necessary. Handle irrelevancies tactfully. Summarize frequently, particularly at key stages of the discussion.
Summarize the discussion and document:	Summarize the various outputs from the discussion; the ideas and experiences etc. which came to light. Restate the objective. Arrive at conclusions or solutions and restate as an achievement. Give credit for effective contributions. Issue a written statement of the main points and conclusions, with action plans, if appropriate.

Chairing meetings

Many factors make a good chairman of a meeting. The following points should help people charged with such tasks to improve their performance:

1 Initiate introductions if members of the group do not know each other.
2 Create a good 'atmosphere' in which the meeting can proceed smoothly. Remain calm and cool. Be impartial.
3 State the intentions of the meeting and 'ground rules' for its conduct. Gain tacit acceptance of this 'methodology'.
4 Maintain a good-natured discipline over the meeting; control casual conversations and damp down emotional outbursts. Involve all members present.
5 Be courteous, patient and understanding. Not all individuals are articulate; help them to overcome their problems of self-expression so that their views, ideas and experience are not disregarded.
6 Keep an eye on the clock and make sure that time is allocated usefully.
7 Be flexible. If the meeting is getting 'bogged down', allow discussions a little freedom but do not lose sight of the objectives or the time in the process. A little humour applied at the right time might help to revive a flagging meeting. Adjust the speed of debate up or down according to the situation.
8 Cover the agenda and achieve the intentions. Make interim summaries. Indicate progress; refocus off-track discussions; highlight or confirm important points; clarify and restate points which are not clear.
9 Involve the group as much as possible; generate discussion to reach solutions and decide options, according to requirements.
10 Summarize the consensus views.

12.6 Implementing teamwork for quality

The idea of introducing problem-solving groups, quality circles or quality improvement teams often makes its way into an organization through the awareness of successful results in other organizations or companies. There is no fixed methodology for starting a teamwork programme, but there are certain key points which must be considered:

1 The concept should be presented to (or come from) management and supervision and their commitment and support enlisted. It should be possible at this stage to engage the interest and support of potential team leaders.

2 Projects should be started slowly and on a small scale. Ideally a pilot scheme, involving the most enthusiastic candidates and areas, should be launched. Early teething troubles, doubts and worries may then be identified and resolved.

3 Selected or volunteer team or circle leaders must be trained in all aspects of group leadership and the appropriate techniques and they should be subsequently involved in the training of the team members in the techniques required in effective problem solving. The techniques of statistical process control (SPC) should be introduced, particularly charting and Pareto analysis. These concepts lay the groundwork for analysing problems in a systematic fashion, and show that the majority of the problems are concentrated into a few areas.

4 Based on the results of the Pareto, teams address the important problem areas. The objective of the team should be to aggressively find problem causes, determine corrective action and implement the solution as quickly as possible.

5 One of the first steps is to define the system by drawing a process flow chart, including information flow, communications channels, procedures and training. The flow chart is essential for visualizing the system under study.

6 The next step is to list all of the problems within the process. This brainstorming session helps answer the question 'what problems are people having?'.

7 The next stage is to sort and prioritize the problems. The rough magnitude of each problem can be determined through discussion. Data gathering and plotting may begin at this point to determine the frequency of a problem. A few of the most important problems are then selected for solution. Criteria for solution are also selected and data collected and used to chart progress in obtaining a solution.

8 In order to solve a problem, the root cause must first be determined. Another brainstorming session is used to list all of the possible cause-and-effect relationships involved in the process. Again, the ideas are sorted and prioritized. Experiments may be performed on the process to verify relationships. The end result is the most likely cause or causes of the problem under study.

9 Once the causes have been determined, a solution can be proposed. This solution may involve any of the components of the process: equipment, procedures, training, input requirements, or output requirements. The proposed solution should be tested by the team or circle, particularly if it involves procedures.

10 If the test of a solution proves successful, full-scale implementation can then be carried out. In the case of procedures, full documentation of the solution and management approval should be obtained. The

new procedure can then be communicated to all personnel involved. Full-scale changes in equipment and other processes should occur in the same manner. The team should monitor implementation of the solution, plotting the appropriate data until the criteria for solution are met.

With the initial problems declared solved, the circle or team may then tackle another problem, and another, or be disbanded and new teams formed. The record of successful solutions will motivate other teams within the organization and ideas should spread. As the number of teams in a company grows, new opportunities arise for stimulating interest. Some large companies organize in-house conferences of their quality improvement teams and quality circles, providing the opportunity for the publication of results and for recognition. Experience has shown that very significant improvements in areas such as energy reduction, productivity, and cost-effectiveness, in addition to quality, may be achieved using the project team approach.

One of the problems of the team approach to problem identification and solving is that sometimes the teams are organized because it is the fashionable thing to do. They either exist on paper only, or the meetings are social gatherings where nothing is learned and no projects are initiated. Another common problem is that the teams attempt to solve problems without first obtaining knowledge of the necessary techniques – enthusiasm outruns ability. Quality improvement teams and quality circles have enormous potential for helping to solve an organization's problems, but for them to be successful they must follow a disciplined approach to problem solving using proven techniques.

The team approach to problem solving works. It taps the skills and initiative of all personnel involved in a process. This may mean a change in culture which must be supported by management through the quality improvement team or quality circle activities.

13 Training for quality

13.1 It's Tuesday – it must be training

It is the author's belief that training is the single most important factor in actually improving quality, once commitment to do so is present. For training to be effective, however, it must be planned in a systematic and objective manner. Quality training must be continuous to meet not only changes in technology, but also changes involving the environment in which an organization operates, its structure, and perhaps most important of all the people who work there.

Quality training activities can be considered in the form of a cycle (Figure 13.1), the elements of which are:

Ensure training is part of the quality policy

Every organization should define its policy in relation to quality (see Chapter 2). The policy should contain principles and goals to provide a framework within which training activities will be planned and operated. This should be communicated to all levels.

Allocate responsibilities for training

Quality training must be the responsibility of line management, but there are also important roles for the quality manager and his function.

Define training objectives

The following questions are useful first steps when identifying training objectives:

- How are the customer requirements transmitted through the organization?
- Which areas demand improved performance?
- What changes are planned for the future?
- What new procedures and provisions need to be drawn up?

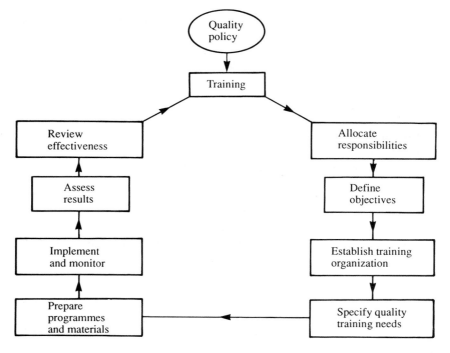

Figure 13.1 *The quality training cycle*

When attempting to set training objectives, three essential require-ments must be met:

1 senior management must ensure that objectives are clarified and priorities set:
2 defined objectives must be realistic and attainable;
3 the main problems should be identified for all functional areas in the organization; the large organization may find it necessary to promote a phased plan to identify these problems.

Establish training organization

In every organization, the overall responsibility for seeing that quality training is properly organized must be assumed by one or more desig-nated senior executives. All managers have a responsibility for ensuring that personnel reporting to them are properly trained and competent in their job. This responsibility should be written into every manager's job description. The question of whether line management require special-ized help should be answered when objectives have been identified. It is often necessary to use specialists who may be internal or external to the organization.

Specify quality training needs

The next step in the cycle is to assess and clarify specific quality training needs. The following questions need to be answered:

Who needs to be trained?
What levels of performance are required?
How long will the training take?
What are the expected benefits?
Is the training need urgent?
How many people are involved?
Who will undertake the actual training?
What resources are needed, e.g. money, people, equipment, accommodation, outside resources?

Prepare training programmes and materials

Quality management should participate in the creation of draft programmes, although line management should retain the final responsibility for what is implemented, and they will often need to create the training programmes themselves.

Quality training programmes should include:

1 the training objectives expressed in terms of the desired behaviour;
2 the actual training content;
3 the methods to be adopted;
4 who is responsible for the various sections of the programme.

Implement and monitor training

The effective implementation of quality training programmes demands considerable commitment and adjustment by the trainers and trainees alike. Training is a progressive process which must take into account the learning problems of the trainees.

Assess the results

In order to determine whether further training is required, line management should themselves review performance when training is completed. However good the quality training may be, if it is not valued and built upon by managers and supervisors its effect can be severely reduced.

Review the overall effectiveness

Senior management require a system whereby decisions are taken at regular fixed intervals on:

- the quality policy;
- the quality training objectives;
- the training organization.

Even if the quality policy remains constant, there is a continuing need to ensure that new quality training objectives are set either to promote work changes or to raise the standards already achieved.

The purpose of system audits and reviews is to assess the effectiveness of an organization's quality effort. Clearly, adequate and refresher training in these methods is essential if such checks are to be realistic and effective. Audits and reviews can provide useful information for the identification of changing quality training needs.

The training organization should similarly be reviewed in the light of the new objectives, and here again it is essential to aim at continuous improvement. Training must never be allowed to become static. Similarly, the effectiveness of the organization's quality training programmes and methods must be assessed systematically.

13.2 A systematic approach to quality training

Training for quality in any organization should have, as its first objective, an appreciation of the personal responsibility for meeting the 'customer' requirements, by everyone from the most senior executive to the newest and most junior employee. Responsibility for the training of employees in quality rests with management at all levels and, in particular, the person nominated for the coordination of the organization's quality effort. Quality training will not be fully effective, however, unless responsibility for the quality policy rests clearly with the chief executive. One objective of this policy should be to develop within the organization a climate in which everyone is quality conscious and acts with the needs of the immediate customer in mind. Quality objectives should be stated in relation to the overall activities and the place of training in their achievement.

The main elements of effective and systematic quality training may be considered under four broad headings:

Error/defect/problem prevention
Error/defect/problem reporting and analysis

Error/defect/problem investigation
Review

The emphasis should obviously be on error/defect/problem prevention and, hopefully, what is said under the other headings maintains this objective.

Error/defect/problem prevention

The following contribute to effective and systematic training for prevention of problems in the organization:

- an issued quality policy;
- a written quality system;
- job specifications which include quality requirements;
- an effective quality council or committee, which includes representation of both senior management and employees;
- efficient housekeeping standards;
- preparation and display of flow diagrams and charts for all processes.

Error/defect/problem reporting and analysis

It will be necessary for management to arrange the necessary reporting procedures and ensure that those concerned are adequately trained in these procedures. All errors, rejects, defects, defectives, problems, waste, etc., should be recorded and analysed in a way that is meaningful for each organization, bearing in mind the corrective action programmes that should be arising at appropriate times.

Error/defect/problem investigation

The investigation of errors, defects, and problems, can provide valuable information which can be used in their prevention. Participating in investigations offers an opportunity for training. The following information is useful for the investigation:

- nature of problem;
- date, time, and place;
- people involved;
- product/service involved;
- description of problem;
- causes and reasons behind causes;
- action advised;
- action taken to prevent recurrence.

Effective problem investigation requires appropriate follow-up and monitoring of recommendations.

Review of quality training

Review of the effectiveness of quality training programmes should be a continuous process. However, the measurement of their effectiveness is a complex problem. One way of reviewing the content and assimilation of a training course or programme is to monitor behaviour during quality audits. This review can be taken a stage further by comparing employees' behaviour with the objectives of the quality training programme.

Training records

All organizations should establish and maintain procedures for the identification of training needs and the provision of the actual training itself. These procedures should be designed (and documented) to include all personnel. In many situations it is necessary to employ professionally qualified people to carry out specific tasks, e.g. accountants, lawyers, engineers, chemists, etc. But it must be recognized that all other employees, including managers, must have or receive from the company the appropriate education, training and/or experience to perform their jobs. This leads to the establishment of training records.

Once an organization has identified the special skills required for each task, and developed suitable training programmes to provide competence for the tasks to be undertaken, it should prescribe how the competence is to be demonstrated. This can be by some form of examination, test, or certification, which may be carried out in-house or by a recognized external organization (such as the Institute of Quality Assurance, the British Institute of Management, or the Royal Society of Chemistry in the UK). In every case, records of personnel qualifications, training, and experience, should be developed and maintained.

At the simplest level this may be a record of tasks and a date placed against each employee's name as he/she acquires the appropriate skill through training. Details of attendance on external short courses, in-house induction or training schemes complete such records. What must be clear and easily retrievable is the status of training and development of any single individual, related to the tasks that they are likely to encounter. For example, in a factory producing contact lenses which has developed a series of well-defined tasks for each stage of the manufacturing process, it should be possible, by turning up the appropriate records, to decide whether a certain operator is competent to carry out a lathe-turning process. Clearly, as the complexity of jobs increases and managerial activity replaces direct manual skill, it becomes more difficult to make decisions on the basis of such records alone. Nevertheless they should document the basic requirements and assist the selection procedure.

13.3 Starting where and for whom?

Training needs occur at four levels of an organization:

Very senior management	strategic decision makers
Middle management	tactical decision makers or implementers of policy
First level supervision and quality team leaders	on-the-spot decision makers
All other employees	the doers

It is important that training is provided for all levels and neglect in any of these areas will, at best, delay the implementation of TQM. The provision of training for each group will be considered in turn, but it is important to realize that an integrated training programme is required, which includes follow-up activities and encourages exchange of ideas and experience, to allow each transformation process to achieve quality at the supplier/customer interface.

Very senior management

The chief executive and his team of strategic policy makers are of primary importance and the role of training here is to provide awareness and gain commitment to quality. The importance of developing real commitment must be established and often this can only be done by a free and frank exchange of views between trainers and trainees. This has implications for the choice of the trainers themselves and the fresh-faced graduate, sent by the 'package consultancy' operator into the lion's den of a board room, will not make much impression with the theoretical approach that he or she is obliged to bring to bear. The author recalls thumping many a U-shaped arrangement of tables and using all his experience, and whatever presentation skills he could muster, to convince senior managers that without the TQM approach they would fail. It is a sobering fact that the pressure from competition and customers has a much greater record of success than enlightenment, although dragging a team of senior managers down to the shop floor to show them the results of poor management was successful on one occasion.

Executives responsible for marketing, sales, finance, design, operations, purchasing, personnel, distribution, etc., must all be helped to understand quality. They must be shown how to define the quality policy and objectives, establish the appropriate organization for quality, clarify authority, and generally create the atmosphere in which total quality will thrive. This is the only group of people in the organization which can ensure that adequate resources are provided and they must be directed at:

- meeting customer requirements – internally and externally;
- setting standards to be achieved – zero failure;
- monitoring of overall quality performance – quality costs;
- introducing a good quality management system – prevention;
- implementing process control methods – SPC;
- involving the whole workforce – TQM.

Middle management

The basic objectives of management quality training should be to make managers conscious and anxious to secure the benefits of the total quality effort. One particular 'staff' manager will require special training, the quality manager, who will carry the responsibility for management of the quality system, including its design, operation, and review.

Training for quality managers

The selection of a person of the right calibre to be able to advise management on quality is a key part of any TQM programme. Their training must be related to the kind of job they are expected to do, the number of people employed, and the nature of the processes and materials handled. In smaller companies, a senior manager may perform the function of 'quality manager' as part of his/her normal duties.

The quality manager and subordinates will require training in how to assist colleagues in the design and operation of management systems within their own functions, which allow them to discharge their duties adequately and to liaise effectively with other parts of the organization. For example, the purchasing manager may require assistance with setting up a system of receiving certificates of conformity from suppliers. The quality manager should be shown how to provide this help without assuming responsibility for the system itself. Similarly the quality manager should be shown how to encourage the 'ownership' of an SPC system within production. Usually the most effective way to train a quality manager in these tasks is to enlist the services of a good specialist quality management consultant to carry out a quality system advisory project and provide almost 'on-the-spot' training through the implementation phase of the consultancy.

Other middle management

The building-in of quality requires the commitment of the direct operating managers. This can only be engaged if the most senior management communicate effectively their own feelings and devotion to total quality. Only then will it be possible to bring to life the quality policy through an effective management system.

The middle managers should be provided with the technical skills required to design, implement, review, and change the part of the quality system which will be under their direct operational control. It will be useful, through the training programmes, to ensure the responsibilities for the various activities in each of the functional areas are clarified. The presence of a highly qualified and experienced quality manager must not allow abdication of these responsibilities, for the internal 'consultant' can easily create the not-invented-here feelings by writing out procedures without adequate consultation of those charged with implementation.

The middle management must receive comprehensive training on the philosophy, concepts, techniques, and applications of statistical process control (SPC). Without this 'tool kit', the quality system will lie dormant and lifeless. It will be relegated to a paper generating system fulfilling the needs of only those who thrive on the keeping of meticulous bureaucracy.

First level supervision

There is a layer of personnel in many an organization which plays a vital role in its inadequate performance – the foreman, supervisor – the forgotten men and women of industry and commerce. Frequently promoted from the 'shop floor' (or recruited as graduates in a flush of conscience and wealth!) these people carry one of the most crucial managerial roles, often with no idea of what they are supposed to be doing, without an identity, and without training. If this behaviour pattern is familiar and is continued, then TQM ends here.

The first level of supervision is where the implementation of total quality is actually 'managed'. Their training should include an explanation of the principles of TQM, a convincing exposition on the commitment to quality of the senior management, and an explanation of what the quality policy means for them. The remainder of their training should then be devoted to explaining their role in the operation of the quality system, SPC etc., and to gaining their commitment to the concepts and techniques of total quality.

It is often desirable to involve the middle managers in the training of first-line supervision to:

- ensure that the message they wish to convey through their tactical manoeuvres is not distorted;
- indicate to the foreman level that the organization's whole management structure is serious about quality, and intends that everyone is suitably trained and involved. One display of arrogance towards the training of supervisors and the workforce can destroy such careful planning, and will certainly undermine the educational effort.

All other employees

Awareness and commitment at the point of production or operation is just as vital as at the very senior level. If it is absent from the latter, the TQM programme will not begin; if it is absent from the shop-floor, total quality will not be implemented. The training here must include the basics of quality and particular care should be given to using easy reference points for the explanation of the terms and concepts. Most people can relate to quality and how it should be managed, if they can think about the applications in their own lives and their home lives. Quality is really so much common sense that, with sensitivity and regard to various levels of intellect and experience, little resistance should be experienced.

All employees should receive detailed training in the quality procedures relevant to their own work. Obviously they must have appropriate technical or 'job' training, but they must also understand the requirements of their customers. This is frequently a difficult concept to introduce, particularly in the non-manufacturing areas, and time and follow-up assistance must be given if TQM is to take hold. It is always bad management to ask people to follow instructions without understanding why and where they fit into their own scheme of things.

13.4 Training programmes and their design

The series of integrated training programmes described in this section are centred around the basic principles of defining quality and taking it into account throughout all the activities of the organization. Training in TQM does not lend itself to conference-style, mass-education methods and the number of people attending each of the seminars or workshops should be limited to about twenty. Six is rather a small number and thirty is far too many. Somewhere in between allows a U-shape arrangement of seating so that the tutor can get 'close' to the participants, and the group can begin to knit together through face-to-face discussions as the training progresses.

Senior management (8–20 hours seminar(s))

The following recommendations represent the minimum requirement for an introduction of TQM to the most senior executives of an organization:

1 The foundations necessary for an effective quality management and control system should be examined by means of a free-ranging discussion. This may take the form of a case study which illustrates the relationships between organization, quality and cost.
2 A presentation should be made of the case for a company-wide approach to the control of quality, showing how the functions of marketing, finance, research and development, production and distribution must interface well for good management. There should be some discussion on the effects of quality on market share.
3 An understanding of quality and its costs is essential for good marketing–operations relations. A consideration of the economics of quality together with the indirect and direct costs of controlling quality should provide the basis for further discussions. Some discussion should also take place at this stage on quality management systems, using an international standard as the foundation.
4 A brief introduction to the systematic techniques associated with good quality management should be given. These techniques are the essential tool kit for senior managers interested in the introduction of TQM.
5 Understanding of the meaning of a 'process' and knowledge of process capabilities is an essential requirement for senior management, if the needs of the customers are to be met. A brief introduction to the control of variables and attributes using various types of control charts should be given, including the basic techniques such as mean and range charts, attribute and cumulative sum (cusum) charts, and an explanation of process capability indices.

The tutors should have considerable experience with similar organizations in the design and implementation of total quality management programmes so that in a brief final session, the recommended training programmes and action plans can be discussed to ensure that the senior management of the organization benefit to the full from the brief exposure to the latest thinking in quality management.

Middle management (20–30 hours seminar(s))

This 'workshop' should introduce, through a series of practical case studies and exercises, the concepts of quality management. It should illustrate the importance and application of quality systems, teamwork and statistical methods of process control (SPC) using simple concepts and elementary statistics. The seminars should include a wide range of applications of TQM concepts and techniques, and give guidance on how they might be introduced, most effectively and with least resistance. The emphasis should be on practical problem solving rather than acquiring theoretical perfection, and the course should be very participative.

The course programme should include the following:

1 An introduction to quality and total quality management – understanding, commitment, policy, costs, supplier–customer interface, etc.
2 Quality systems – content, design, implementation, operation, etc.
3 Systematic quality control – basic tools and techniques such as Pareto and cause–effect analysis, flow charting, and their introduction.
4 Process capability and market requirements – a 'process', measurement of capability, concept of in-control, capability indices, etc.
5 Process control charts for variables and attributes – grouping of data, mean and range, np, p, c, u, charts, etc.
6 Metrology and variability – precision of measurement and relationship to total process variation.
7 Cumulative sum (cusum) techniques – detection of slight changes.
8 Special control chart methods – individual results, infrequent data, moving average and moving range, etc.
9 Product control – use of sampling schemes, risks, assessment of performance, etc.
10 Control of organization's own processes – application of the technqiues to local data.
11 Quality improvement teams – their role, use, establishment, training requirements, etc.
12 Implementation of TQM – recommended programmes, follow-up workshops, projects, action plans, reading, etc.

Throughout the programme, exercises, video tapes, etc., should be used to illustrate the application of the principles, concepts and techniques introduced in the workshop sessions. Suitable periods of time should also be devoted to applying the methods and techniques to the participants' own processes and data. To derive maximum benefit from the programme, the delegates should bring with them to the sessions flow charts of operations which highlight data collection points, typical data, and descriptions of current sampling, testing, and inspection procedures.

First-level supervision and quality team leaders (30–40 hours seminar(s) with follow-up workshops)

Supervisors should be trained in the correct, efficient, and safe operation and maintenance of plant and processes, the management of people and the establishment of the correct work procedures. They must know and accept their role in ensuring that these are understood and adhered to by their managers, colleagues and subordinates. This, of course, requires that people should be allocated to jobs for which they are mentally and physically suitable.

Quality training for first-level supervisors should include knowledge and appreciation of the quality policy, error and waste prevention and investigation, methods of communicating with and motivating the workforce, and the quality system and procedures. The 'foreman' is the key link in the training that is given to all the other employees. They must be given intensive training, perhaps over forty hours, that is designed not only to teach them about the control of quality, but also to equip them to communicate their knowledge to the 'shop-floor'.

The seminars should illustrate the importance and application of TQM methods in the supervisors' own environment. Using simple concepts and examples it should indicate, through the practical nature of the seminars, the wide range of applications of TQM techniques and give guidance on how they might be introduced. The purpose of the course should be to provide practical training and to place the emphasis on process control.

A quality team leader or facilitator training programme should be developed which must avoid the twin dangers of becoming too simplistic or over-specialized. Once again the emphasis should be on practice. In addition to problem-solving methods, group dynamics, meetings management, and team leadership will need to be addressed specifically. A course programme should include the following modules:

1 Quality philosophy, in which is covered all the relevant theories, concepts, and definitions pertinent to a competent working knowledge in the field of quality. It may be necessary to explain why change is needed and to explain the organization's quality policy. The basic ideas of customer focus, design, detection versus prevention, consistency, continuous improvement, and quality system protocol will require detailed attention.

2 Quality tools, in which will be explained the array of tools available for quality management and improvement. The topics must include the seven basic tools (Chapter 10), control charts, process capability studies and indices, and any special topics required such as FMECA, statistical inference, regression, analysis of variance, and Taguchi methods.

3 Team leadership, to provide knowledge of elements of 'group processes', and corresponding skills to ensure a quick start-up of the team work. Specific topics include:

(a) Leadership skills and style
  - skills needed for team leaders and members
  - assessment of team leader's style
  - assessment of team members' styles
  - fitting the styles and skills together

(b) Forming new teams
  - defining projects
  - selecting appropriate teams
  - team organization and role of members
  - starting up tasks or assignments
  - stages of team development

(c) Running effective meetings
  - clarifying terms of reference and objectives
  - gaining commitment to the involvement in projects
  - sharing leadership
  - managing the agenda and other documentation
  - assuring follow-up

(d) Managing group dynamics
  - predicting behaviour (natural and expected)
  - characteristics of effective teams
  - managing the group 'process' and problem-solving skills
  - action planning

(c) Leading teams through difficult situations
  - handling conflict
  - difficult behaviour
  - team leader traps and their release
  - problems originating outside the team

Other course possibilities include 'whole team' training which provides the opportunity for the leader to practise training skills and strengthen his/her capability to manage. Good team leadership skills training is essential if an organization is to integrate TQM throughout.

All other employees

It is difficult to set down here specific training programmes for this group, since it is vital that their quality education process is closely related to their jobs. The people in the typing pool will require a different approach and content for their introduction to TQM from, say, the chemical process operators. Clearly, there is a need to train every employee in the general principles of company-wide quality achievement, and much of the first part of the training given to first-level supervision is appropriate for this purpose. It is recommended, however, that the training of the workforce is spread over a period of time, perhaps a half day per week for six weeks, and that the formal sessions are interspersed with small projects or assignments which involve the participants in activities such as:

1 listing their immediate 'customers' and the corresponding requirements;
2 listing their immediate 'suppliers' and their own requirements;
3 identifying the various processes with which they are involved and listing the inputs and outputs for each;
4 flow charting the processes;
5 designing checksheets for gathering data;
6 collecting data from processes and about inputs and outputs;
7 analysing data using simple methods, such as histograms, Pareto and cause/effect analysis, and recommending action for improvement;
8 using simple charts and process capability analysis techniques for control and improvement.

These projects almost create their own training programme, which must be very relevant to the individuals involved. This aspect cannot be overemphasized. The improvement projects outlined above help employees to acquire the necessary technical expertise, and sow the seeds of quality improvement teams, which are such an essential component of the successful TQM effort.

Analysis of jobs and tasks will identify the specific quality training needs. Where such analysis has not been completed, and there is an appreciable risk of errors or defects being produced, an analysis should be prepared as a priority. The quality aspects of the analysis should be kept under continuous review, and retraining undertaken when the nature of a job changes.

Operating instructions should cover the use of materials, plant and equipment (including maintenance). Operators should receive instruction about the potential risks for errors and waste which have been realized from either past operation of the process or customer feedback.

One aspect of quality training which is all too often missing from TQM, quality system, and SPC implementation programmes is corrective action. Written procedures are introduced, control charts are explained, and posters appear but when things do not go according to plan, nobody is sure what to do. The involvement of the workforce at this stage is absolutely vital for it is here that their training and expertise have to be used to the full to design corrective action procedures and controls which will rapidly analyse and remove the causes of failure. These principles apply equally to people employed in offices, laboratories, warehouses, computer rooms, etc.

New entrants

The acceptance and understanding of the total quality philosophy and practices by new entrants to the organization is of paramount importance. Quality should be included in all training and induction programmes for new employees.

Shift workers

Where it is difficult to obtain the release of a sufficient number of people to form a group of a reasonable size for training, it may be possible to release people singly for programmed learning sessions. Various institutions and organizations specialize in these methods and advice and information may be obtained directly from them.

13.5 Follow-up and quality counselling

Follow-up

For the successful implementation of TQM, the training must be followed up during the early stages of the programme. Follow-up can take many forms, but the managers must provide the lead through the design of implementation programmes.

In introducing statistical methods of process control, the most satisfactory strategy is to start small and build up a bank of knowledge and experience. For example, sometimes it is necessary to introduce SPC techniques alongside existing methods of control (if they exist), thus allowing comparisons to be made between the new and old methods. When confidence has been established from these comparisons, the SPC methods will almost take over the control of the processes themselves. Improvements in one or two areas of the organization's operations, using this approach, will quickly establish the techniques as reliable methods of controlling quality.

The author and his colleagues have found that a successful formula is the in-company training course plus follow-up workshops. Typically a 20-hour seminar on TQM is followed within a few weeks by an 8–10-hour workshop. At this, participants on the initial training course present the results of their efforts to introduce TQM and use the methods. The various presentations and specific implementation problems may be discussed. A series of such workshops will add continually to the follow-up and can be used to initiate quality improvement teams. Wider company presence and activities should be encouraged by the follow-up activities.

As quality improvement teams become established, there will be a number of quality problems all requiring attention. Pareto analysis should be used to decide the order in which to tackle the problems. It is then important for each team to choose *one* problem and work on it until satisfactory progress has been achieved, before passing on to a second problem. The coordination of the activities of the QITs is clearly an important task.

Counselling

It will usually be found that external help is required to introduce and establish the necessary components of TQM. The author has lost count of the number of occasions on which, following a presentation in a board room of a company, he has been challenged by the quality manager, who claims that he has been repeating for years all the points and suggestions that he has just heard the 'outsider' pronounce with such authority. The difference, of course, is that the company is now going to do something about it. It is not clear why this happens, perhaps it is about presentation skills, perhaps the prophet is never accepted in his own land, but the fact remains that external advice is often heeded and, therefore, needed.

If external consultants and trainers are used, and both large and small companies buy in skills in this field, it is essential to carefully select and control the counselling. The dangers of not doing so are:

- the creation of a paperwork system which is not operational;
- the 'not-invented-here' effect of buying in someone else's methods;
- a mismatch of the consultant's approach and the unique requirements of the company, its style, operations and the business environment in which it lives.

Any of these will render the system unworkable.

The fact that a consultant is 'known to operate' in an industry is not quite the same as the consultant knowing what the quality requirements of the industry or company are and how they differ from those of other industries. There are many consultancy organizations which have failed to provide good advice because they did not possess the depth of knowledge of both quality management issues and their application in special processes. For example, the application of statistical process control (SPC) methods in continuous polymer production is not simply a question of changing widgets for polyolefins, it requires a fundamentally different approach, which derives from the direct experience of the consultant and his/her understanding of the nature of the process or industry involved.

The two requirements, for knowledge of the industry and for knowledge of quality management, should give rise to a crude initial filter which perhaps could operate on the basis of qualifications and membership of professional bodies. For example, a consultant with a technical or professional qualification and membership of a learned society devoted to quality should pass the first hurdle for inclusion on the shortlist.

The 'consultants' should have worked with many different companies in the industry, helping them to implement total quality management. This does not prevent the introduction of new consultants into the field, provided their training is adequate and supervised by experienced professionals. The acquisition of outside help can become a minefield for the unsuspecting organization, but the establishment of professional bodies, such as the Association of Quality Management Consultants (AQMC) in the UK, which carefully vets and qualifies its members with designatory letters, should enable clients to acquire the correct expertise and skills – whether in seminar presentation or direct consultancy.

14 Implementation of TQM

14.1 A guide to the American gurus

A small group of American quality experts or gurus has been advising industry throughout the world on how it should manage quality, and it may be useful to consider their approaches, their similarities and differences. The most notable quality gurus from the USA are Philip B. Crosby, W. Edwards Deming, and Joseph M. Juran. A fourth, William E. Conway, is perhaps less widely known, but has acted as teacher to some very large organizations. They have all formed consultancy-type operations which use their philosophies and methods.

One thing that they all have in common is they recognize that there are no short-cuts to quality, no quick fixes, and that improvement requires full commitment and support from the top, extensive training and participation of all employees. Their ideas and approaches are discussed below:

Phil Crosby

Phil Crosby is best known for the concept of 'zero defects' which he developed in the early 1960s whilst in charge of quality for various missile projects, and later as Quality Director of ITT. In 1979 he formed Crosby Associates, a large consultancy operation. He has written several books, perhaps the most famous of which is *Quality is Free*, which has sold over a million copies.

Crosby's definition of quality is 'conformance to requirements' which he says can only be measured by the cost of nonconformance. He prefers people to talk of conformance and nonconformance rather than low quality and high quality. This leads to the existence of only one standard of performance – zero defects. Crosby sums up quality management in one word, *prevention*, which should replace the conventional view that quality is achieved through inspection, testing, and checking. Prevention is the only system that can be utilized according to Crosby, and by this he means 'perfection'. There is no place in his philosophy for statistically acceptable levels of quality, for this leads to the belief that errors are inevitable and are planned for.

Crosby has coined the term 'quality vaccine' which companies may use to prevent nonconformance, and which comprises three ingredients:

- determination;
- education;
- implementation.

He points out that quality improvement is a process not a programme, since nothing permanent will arise from a programme.

Like all gurus, Crosby is strong on the responsibility of management for quality and encourages them to be as concerned about quality as they are about profit. He observes that committed management can obtain a 40 per cent reduction in error rates very quickly from a committed workforce. Eliminating the remaining error may take a little more work. Crosby feels that many companies compound quality problems by 'hassling' their employees, and demotivating them by using 'thoughtless, irritating, unconcerned' ways of dealing with people.

There is perhaps a misconception about Crosby – that he is primarily advocating pushing employees into performing better. But he explains, 'unfortunately, zero defects was picked up by industry as a "motivation" program', when it should be used, as the Japanese have used it, as a management performance standard.

Crosby's view of purchased materials is that at least half the quality problems associated with them are caused by not clearly stating what the requirements are. Again the Japanese model is used to stress that the supplier should be treated as an extension of the business. Most of the faults concerning purchased material in the West, according to Crosby, are the fault of the purchaser. For this reason he recommends rating buyers as well as vendors to remove the 'built-in defect rate'. Visiting a potential supplier to conduct a quality audit is next to useless, unless it is a 'complete and obvious disaster area'; it is impossible to know whether their quality system will provide the proper control or not.

So, Crosby has four absolutes of quality:

- Definition – conformance to requirements
- System – prevention
- Performance standard – zero defects
- Measurement – price of nonconformance

and offers management 14 steps to improvement.

Crosby's 14 steps to quality improvement

1 Make it clear that management is committed to quality.
2 Form quality improvement teams with representatives from each department.

3 Determine where current and potential quality problems lie.
4 Evaluate the cost of quality and explain its use as a management tool.
5 Raise the quality awareness and personal concern of all employees
6 Take actions to correct problems identified through previous steps.
7 Establish a committee for the zero defects programme.
8 Train supervisors to actively carry out their part of the quality improvement programme.
9 Hold a 'zero defects day' to let all employees realize that there has been a change.
10 Encourage individuals to establish improvement goals for themselves and their groups.
11 Encourage employees to communicate to management the obstacles they face in attaining their improvement goals.
12 Recognize and appreciate those who participate.
13 Establish quality councils to communicate on a regular basis.
14 Do it all over again to emphasize that the quality improvement programme never ends.

The Crosby consultancy organization offers company-wide training based on these principles.

Bill Conway

Bill Conway is the least-known of the American gurus and is a relative newcomer. He spent some years in the US Naval Academy before starting an industrial career that led him to become President and Chairman of Nashua Corp. In 1979 he invited Deming to Nashua to help him improve quality. After the visit, which lasted three years, he founded his own consultancy. Conway is often described as a 'Deming disciple' because of this association, but he has developed his own plan for quality improvement.

Conway does not have a specific definition of quality, but incorporates it into his broad description of quality management, 'development, manufacture, administration, and distribution of consistent low-cost products and services that customers want and/or need'. He believes also that it means constant improvement in all areas of operations, including suppliers and distributors to eliminate waste of material, capital, and time. He claims that the wasting of time is by far the biggest waste that occurs in most organizations. Another important category of waste is excess inventory which, says Conway, occupies space, 60 per cent of which is not really required but must be paid for and maintained.

Conway tends to talk less of quality than of the 'right' or 'new way to manage'. He shares the views of other gurus that top management is often lacking in conviction that quality increases productivity and lowers costs. This leads to the conclusion that, 'the bottleneck is located at the top of the bottle'. Conway talks of a 'new system of management', the primary task of which is continuous improvement in all areas. He believes that this is the most important change required for it means changing all the unwritten company rules and giving people positive reinforcement.

Conway advocates strongly the use of statistical methods to achieve waste reduction, on the grounds that attempts to improve quality and productivity with generalities always fail. 'The use of statistics is a commonsense way of getting into specifics', but he adds that statistics alone do not solve problems, they simply identify where the problems are and point managers and employees towards solutions. He distinguishes between simple and sophisticated statistical techniques which he calls 'tools'. The simple tools are: flow charts, fishbone charts, histograms, Pareto charts, run charts, correlation charts, surveys of customers, which according to Conway can be used to solve 85 per cent of a company's problems. The more sophisticated SPC methods are needed only for the remaining 15 per cent.

Conway actually defines six 'tools' for quality improvement:

Conway's six tools for quality improvement

1 Human relations skills – the responsibility of management to create at every level, among all employees, the motivation and training to make the necessary improvements in the organization.
2 Statistical suveys – the gathering of data about customers (internal as well as external) employees, technology, and equipment, to be used as a measure for future progress and to identify what needs to be done.
3 Simple statistical techniques – clear charts and diagrams that help identify problems, track work flow, gauge progress, and indicate solutions.
4 Statistical process control – the statistical charting of a process, whether manufacturing or non-manufacturing, to help identify and reduce variation.
5 Imagineering – a key concept in problem solving, involves the visualization of a process, procedure, or operaton with all waste eliminated.
6 Industrial engineering – common techniques of pacing, work simplification, methods analysis, plant layout, and material handling to achieve improvements.

It is perhaps useful to explain briefly Conway's concept of 'imagineering', which is based on images of the desired future being used to shape thoughts and guide actions. The power of the method lies in its ability to generate creativity and energy and extend the problem-solving framework. Imagineering works well in problem identification when used to create a flow chart of what the ideal process should look like and in generating improvement projects. The technique can lead to a brief 'vision statement' which provides the group with a goal. The images then become measures to be used as the basis of brainstorming to generate ideas which are prioritized and translated into actions, projects, and programmes.

Conway believes that once a process is in-control, the people responsible for it become more creative in eliminating variations because they know that they are personally capable of improving the system. In fact, people at the bottom make the most improvement because they learn 'how to be logical all the time'. He claims that, using these concepts, it is possible to continually improve the productivity and quality performance of everyone in an organization on a monthly basis. In his talks, Conway does not dwell on functional areas because he believes the principles apply to all areas, and that focusing efforts on one area is not sufficient to change the management 'system' of a company. He does accept, however, that the creation and implementation of the 'new system' should be customized for each department.

Like the other gurus, Conway's call for constant improvement in all areas of operations is intended to include the suppliers, and here too he advocates the use of statistics. 'It is just as vital to achieve statistical control of quality from your vendors as it is to have it internally.' He is also critical of overspecification – another form of waste. Here he blames engineers, purchasing, and anyone concerned with the design of a product, and warns that specifications, like work standards, sometimes 'cap' improvements.

Dr Deming

Dr Deming is a statistician who gained fame by helping Japanese companies to improve quality after the second world war. In the 1950s he lectured on statistical quality control to business leaders in Japan. The results of his efforts have been recognized in that country by the award of the Deming Prize which is given on the basis of the degree of dissemination, state of application, and future promise in statistical methods of quality control. He is author of several books on quality and productivity improvement.

Deming has defined quality as, 'a predictable degree of uniformity and dependability, at low cost and suited to the market'. He recognizes that the quality of any service or product has many scales – a product may achieve a low mark on one scale, but a high mark on another. This clearly fits in with the view that quality is whatever the customer needs or requires. Since customer tastes and requirements are always changing, a major part of the quality effort must be devoted to market research.

Deming's basic philosophy is that quality and productivity increase as variability decreases and, because all things vary, that is why statistical methods of quality control must be used. He explains, 'statistical control does not imply absence of defective items. It is a state of random variation in which the limits of variation are predictable.' He then goes on to explain the difference between chance and assignable causes of variation (see Chapter 10) but Deming claims that the difference between these is one of the most difficult concepts to understand. According to Deming, many companies waste time and money looking for causes of chance or random variation in attempting to solve quality problems without using statistical methods. He advocates the use of statistics to measure performance in all areas, not just conformance to product or service specifications. Moreover, he points out that it is not enough to meet specifications, continued efforts must be made to reduce the process variation still further.

Deming is an advocate of employee participation in decision making. He claims that management is responsible for 94 per cent of quality problems and that their first step should be to dismantle the barriers that prevent employees doing a good job, by encouraging them to work smarter, not harder. He is also somewhat critical of motivational programmes, including zero defects. He has pointed out that everyone simply doing their best is not the answer because it is also necessary for people to know what to do. He uses the illustration of a man trying to do a job 'right first time' when the material he is using is outside the requirements of the process, or the machinery has not been maintained properly.

Inspection, whether of incoming or outgoing goods is, according to Deming, too late, ineffective, and costly. It neither guarantees nor improves quality, since it is usually designed to allow a certain number of defects to enter the system through acceptable quality levels (AQLs). He says that to judge quality 'statistical evidence' is required and that companies which deal with suppliers under statistical control can eliminate inspection. This evidence is obtained from the control charts delivered with the product, which give information about parameter distributions and what they will be tomorrow. This leads to predictability, measures of improvement, and a dialogue in 'statistical language' between customer and supplier. The simple checking of material against specifications is not enough – the supplier must know what the material is to be used for. Deming is critical of most vendor rating systems.

Deming has laid down 14 points for management to abide by which can be used internally, or for qualifying suppliers.

Deming's 14 points for management

1 Create constancy of purpose towards improvement of product and service.
2 Adopt the new philosophy. We can no longer live with commonly accepted levels of delays, mistakes, defective workmanship.
3 Cease dependence on mass inspection. Require, instead, statistical evidence that quality is built in.
4 End the practice of awarding business on the basis of price tag.
5 Find problems. It is management's job to work continually on the system.
6 Institute modern methods of training on the job.
7 Institute modern methods of supervision of production workers. The responsibility of foremen must be changed from numbers to quality.
8 Drive out fear, so that everyone may work effectively for the company.
9 Break down barriers between departments.
10 Eliminate numerical goals, posters, and slogans for the workforce asking for new levels of productivity without providing methods.
11 Eliminate work standards that prescribe numerical quotas.
12 Remove barriers that stand between the hourly worker and his right to pride of workmanship.
13 Institute a vigorous programme of education and retraining.
14 Create a structure in top management that will push every day on the above 13 points.

In addition to following these 'rules' suppliers should, according to Deming, use statistical process control (SPC) and be willing to cooperate on measurements, tests, and use of measuring equipment and gauges. The best recognition that can be given to a supplier is to give it more business. The requirement to use SPC in the selection of vendors would reduce the number of suppliers most organizations deal with and, since Deming is an advocate of single sourcing, this gives advantages of improved commitment, elimination of variation in products caused by different suppliers of material, and simplifying paperwork and accounting. If challenged on the effects of this on price, he points out, 'the policy of forever trying to drive down the price of everything purchased, with no regard to quality and service, can drive good vendors and good service out of business.'

Joe Juran

Joe Juran's background is in inspection with the Western Electric Company, and Professor at New York University. Juran, along with Deming, is credited with part of the success of Japanese companies. He also lectured in Japan in the 1950s and is author of many books on quality control and management and editor of the *Quality Control Handbook*. He has founded the Juran Institute which conducts quality training seminars and produces training materials.

Juran first coined the term 'fitness for use or purpose' and distinguished it from the definition of quality often used, 'conformance to specifications'. He points out that a dangerous product could meet all the specifications, and not be fit for use. Juran was the first to deal with the broader management issues of quality and this distinguishes him from those who espouse specific techniques. In the 1940s he claimed that the 'technical aspects of quality control' had been well covered, but that companies did not know how to manage to achieve quality. He identified problems such as:

- organization;
- communication; and
- coordination of functions;

in other words the human element. He put it, 'an understanding of the human situations associated with the job will go far to solve the technical problems; in fact such understanding may be a prerequisite of a solution.' He gives an example of an inspector misinterpreting specifications, or knowingly protecting favoured operators or suppliers.

Juran has three basic steps to progress:

- structured annual improvements (combined with devotion and a sense of urgency);
- massive training programmes;
- upper management leadership.

In his view, less than 20 per cent of quality problems are due to workers, with the remainder caused by management (compare Deming's 94 per cent). Just as all managers need some training in finance, all should be trained in quality to enable them to manage and participate in quality improvement projects. Juran is adamant that top management need to be involved because, 'all major quality problems are interdepartmental', and he believes that pursuing departmental goals can undermine the overall company quality mission.

Juran, like Deming, believes that companies should avoid campaigns to motivate the workforce to solve quality problems by 'doing perfect work', because the exhortation-only approach fails to set specific goals, establish specific plans to meet these goals, or provide the needed resources. He also points out that top management often go for such programmes because they do not detract from their time. Juran favours the concept of quality circles because they improve communications between management and employees. He also recommends using SPC, but warns that it can lead to a 'tool-oriented' approach.

Juran has 10 steps to quality improvement.

Juran's 10 steps to quality improvement

1 Build awareness of the need and opportunity for improvement.
2 Set goals for improvement.
3 Organize to reach the goals (establish a quality council, identify problems, select projects, appoint teams, designate facilitators).
4 Provide training.
5 Carry out projects to solve problems.
6 Report progress.
7 Give recognition.
8 Communicate results.
9 Keep score.
10 Maintain momentum by making annual improvement part of the regular systems and processes of the company.

He does not believe that 'quality is free' because of the law of diminishing returns which generates an optimum point of quality, beyond which conformance is more costly than the value of the quality obtained. This is in some conflict with Deming's and Conway's continuous improvement approaches.

Like all the gurus, Juran recognizes the important role of purchasing in quality improvement, and that the tasks can be more complex than often assumed. This is illustrated by the problems of assessing the quality of contractors competing for large one-off projects. Juran is not in favour of single sourcing for critical purchases, for which he recommends multiple sources of supply, 'a single source can more easily neglect to sharpen its competitive edge in quality, cost and service.'

Juran also believes that training for purchasing managers should include techniques for rating vendors, but he adds that this is only half the process because an investment of time, effort and special skills is required to help the supplier improve. Juran thinks that purchasing should carry out formal surveys to ensure consistent achievement of specifications, Juran does not seem to be a big believer in systems-organization, written procedures, manuals, audits, etc., and prefers the Japanese approach of process capabilities, process controls, teamwork relationships, quality control training, and 'quality of prior deliveries'. The team approach should be extended to suppliers.

The Juran Institute teaches a project-by-project team problem-solving method of quality improvement, in which top management **must** be involved. He claims that 'the project approach is important. When it comes to quality there is no such thing as improvement in general. Any improvement in quality is going to come about project by project and no other way.'

A comparison

The only way to compare directly the various approaches of the four gurus is in tabular form. Table 14.1 shows the differences and similarities, classified under 12 different factors.

14.2 Planning the implementation of TQM

The task of implementing TQM can be daunting and the chief executive faced with this may draw little comfort from the quality gurus. The first decision is where to begin and this can be so difficult that many organizations never get started. This has been called TQP – total quality paralysis!

The chapters of this book have been arranged in an order which should help senior management bring total quality into existence. The preliminary stages of understanding and commitment are vital first steps which also form the foundation of the whole TQM structure (Figure 14.1). Too many organizations skip these phases, believing that they have the right

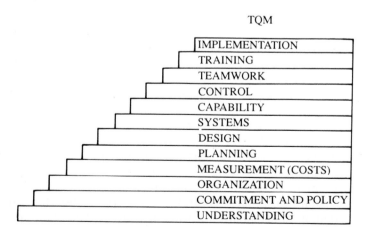

TQM

| IMPLEMENTATION |
| TRAINING |
| TEAMWORK |
| CONTROL |
| CAPABILITY |
| SYSTEMS |
| DESIGN |
| PLANNING |
| MEASUREMENT (COSTS) |
| ORGANIZATION |
| COMMITMENT AND POLICY |
| UNDERSTANDING |

Figure 14.1   *The steps to TQM*

attitude and awareness, when in fact there are some fundamental gaps in their 'quality credibility'. These will soon lead to insurmountable difficulties and collapse of the edifice.

While an intellectual understanding of quality provides a basis for TQM, it is clearly only the planting of the seed. The understanding must be translated into commitment, policies, plans and actions for TQM to germinate. Making this happen requires not only commitment, but a competence in the mechanics of quality management, and in making changes. Without a strategy to implement TQM through systems, capability, and control, the expended effort will lead to frustration. Poor quality management can become like poor gardening – a few weed leaves are pulled off only for others to appear in their place days later, plus additional weeds elsewhere. Problem solving is very much like weeding, tackling the root causes, often by digging deep, is essential for better control.

Individuals working on their own, even with a plan, will never generate optimum results. The individual effort is required in improvement but it must be coordinated and become involved with the efforts of others to be truly effective. The implementation begins with the drawing up of a quality policy statement, and the establishment of the appropriate organizational structure, both for managing and encouraging involvement in quality through teamwork. Collecting information on how the organization operates, including the costs of quality, helps to identify the prime areas in which improvements will have the largest impact on performance. Planning improvement involves all managers but a crucial early stage involves putting quality management systems in place to drive the improvement process and make sure that problems remain solved forever, using structured corrective action procedures.

Once the plans and systems have been put into place, the need for continued education, training, and communication becomes paramount. Organizations which try to change the quality culture, operate systems, procedures, or control methods without effective, honest, two-way communication, will experience the frustration of being a 'cloned' type of organization which can function but inspires no confidence in being able to survive the changing environment in which it lives.

An organization may, of course, have already taken several steps on the road to TQM. If good understanding of quality and how it should be managed already exists, there is top management commitment, a written quality policy, and a satisfactory organizational structure, then the planning stage may begin straight away. When implementation is contemplated, priorities amongst the various projects must be identified. For example, a quality system which conforms to the requirements of ISO 9000 may already exist and the systems step will not be a major task, but

Table 14.1   The quality gurus compared

	Crosby	Conway	Deming	Juran
Definition of quality	Conformance to requirements	No definition, incorporated in definition of quality management	A predictable degree of uniformity and dependability at low cost and suited to the market	Fitness for use
Degree of senior management responsibility	Responsible for quality	Bottleneck is located at the top of the bottle	Responsible for 94% of quality problems	Less than 20% of quality problems are due to workers
Performance standard/ motivation	Zero defects	Remove waste, measure on monthly basis	Quality has many 'scales'; use statistics to measure performance in all areas; critical of zero defects	Avoid campaigns to 'do perfect work'
General approach	Prevention, not inspection	'Right' or 'new way' to manage, Deming 'disciple' 'imagineering'	Reduce variability by continuous improvement; cease mass inspection	General management approach to quality, especially 'human' elements
Structure	14 steps to quality improvement	6 tools for quality improvement	14 points for management	10 steps to quality improvement
Statistical process control (SPC)	Rejects statistically acceptable levels of quality	Advocates use of simple statistical methods to identify problems and point to solutions	Statistical methods of quality control must be used	Recommends SPC but warns that it can lead to 'tool-driven' approach

Improvement basis	A 'process', not a programme; improvement goals	Constant in all areas; statistical and industrial engineering basis	Continuous to reduce variation; eliminate goals without methods	Project-by-project team approach; set goals
Teamwork	Quality improvement teams; quality councils	Human relations skills	Employee participation in decision making; break down barriers between departments	Team and quality circle approach
Costs of quality	Cost of nonconformance; quality is free.	Measure waste in all areas, including inventory	No optimum, continuous improvement	Quality is not free, there is an optimum
Purchasing and goods received	State requirements; supplier is extension of business; most faults due to purchasers themselves	Call for improvement includes suppliers; use statistics	Inspection too late; allows defects to enter system through AQLs; statistical evidence and control charts required	Problems are complex; carry out formal surveys
Vendor rating	Yes and buyers; quality audits useless	Statistical surveys	No, critical of most systems	Yes, but help supplier improve
Single sourcing of supply			Yes	No, can neglect to sharpen competitive edge

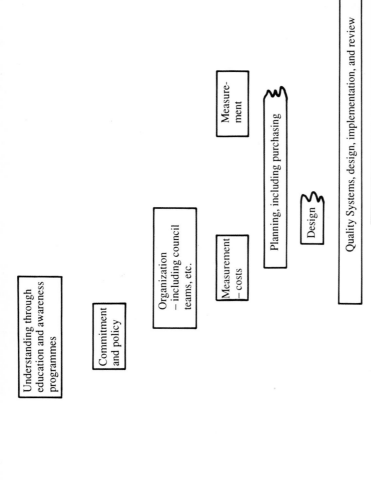

Figure 14.2   *Planning TQM implementation*

introducing a quality-related costing system may well be. It is important to remember, however, that a review of the current performance in all the areas, even when well established, should be part of normal operations to ensure continuous improvement.

These major steps may be used as an overall planning aid for the introduction of TQM, and they should appear on a planning or Gantt chart (Figure 14.2). Major projects should be time-phased to suit in-dividual organizations' requirements, but this may be influenced by outside factors, such as pressure from a customer to introduce statistical process control (SPC) or to operate a quality system which meets the requirements of a standard. The main projects may need to be split into smaller sub-projects, and this is certainly true of quality system work, the introduction of SPC, and quality improvement teams.

The education and training part will be continuous and draw together

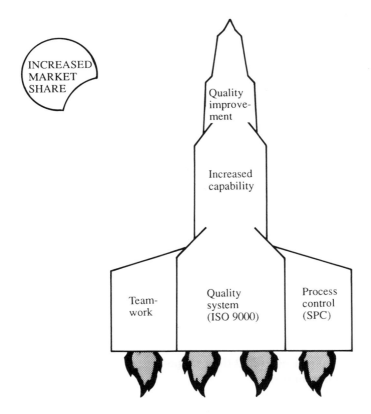

Figure 14.3 *Launching quality improvement*

the requirements of all the steps into a cohesive programme of introduction. The timing of the training inputs, follow-up sessions, and advisory work should be coordinated and reviewed, in terms of their effectiveness, on a regular basis. It may be useful at various stages of the implementation to develop checks to establish the true progress. For example, before moving from understanding to trying to obtain top management commitment, objective evidence should be obtained to show that the next stage is justified.

Following commitment being demonstrated by the publication of a signed quality policy, there should be the formation of the Quality Council, and/or Steering Committee(s). Delay here will prevent real progress being made towards TQM through teamwork activities.

The launch of quality improvement requires a balanced approach and the three major components must be 'fired' in the right order to lift the campaign off the ground (Figure 14.3). If teams are started before the establishment of a good system of management, there will be nothing to which they can adhere. Equally, if SPC is introduced without a good system of data recording and standard operating procedures, the techniques will simply measure how bad things are. A quality system on its own will give only a weak thrust which must have the boost of improvement teams and SPC to make it come 'alive'.

An effective coordination of these three components will result in quality improvement through increased capability. This should in turn lead to consistently satisfied customers and, where appropriate, increase or preservation of market share.

14.3 Continuous improvement and the TQM model

Never-ending or continuous improvement is probably the most powerful concept to guide management. It is a term not well understood in many organizations, although that must begin to change if those organizations are to survive. To maintain a wave of interest in quality, it is necessary to develop generations of managers who not only understand but are dedicated to the pursuit of never-ending improvement in meeting external and internal customer needs.

The concept requires a systematic approach to quality management which has the following components:

- *planning* the processes and their inputs;
- *providing* the inputs;
- *operating* the processes;
- *evaluating* the outputs;
- *examining* the performance of the processes;

- *modifying* the processes and their inputs.

This system must be firmly tied to a continuous assessment of customer needs, and depends on a flow of ideas on how to make improvements, reduce variation, and generate greater customer satisfaction. It also requires a high level of commitment, involvement, and a sense of personal responsibility accepted by those operating the processes.

The never-ending improvement cycle ensures that the organization learns from results, standardizes what it does well in a documented quality management system, and improves operations and outputs from what it learns. But the emphasis must be that this is done in a planned, systematic, and conscientious way to create a climate, a way of life, that permeates the whole organization.

There are three basic principles of never-ending improvement:

1 Focus on the customer
2 Understand the process
3 Involve the people

1 Customer focus

An organization must recognize, throughout its ranks, that the purpose of all work and all efforts to make improvements is to serve better the customers. This means that it must always know how well its outputs are performing, in the eyes of the customer, through measurement and feedback. The most important customers are the external ones that purchase products or services, but the quality chain can break down at any unit in the flow of work. Internal customers, therefore, must also be well served if the external ones are to be satisfied.

2 Process understanding

In the successful operation of any process, it is essential to understand what determines its performance and outputs. This means intense focus on the design and control of the inputs, working closely with suppliers, and understanding process flows to eliminate bottlenecks and reduce waste. If there is one difference between management and supervision in the Far East and the West, it is that the former are closer to and more involved themselves in the processes. It is not possible to stand aside and manage in never-ending improvement. TQM in an organization means that everyone has the determination to make improvements using their detailed knowledge of the processes, together with information derived from them, and the appropriate statistical methods to analyse and create action plans.

3 People involvement

Everyone in the organization, from top to bottom, from offices to technical service, from headquarters to local sites, must be involved. People are the source of ideas and innovation and their expertise, experience, knowledge, and cooperation have to be harnessed to get those ideas implemented.

When people are treated like machines, work becomes uninteresting and unsatisfying. Under such conditions, it is not possible to expect quality services and reliable products. The rates of absenteeism and of staff turnover are measures that can be used in determining the strengths and weaknesses of management style and worker morale in any company.

The first step is to convince everyone of their own role in total quality. Employers and managers must, of course, take the lead and one senior executive should have a personal responsibility for quality. The degree of management's enthusiasm and drive will determine the ease with which the whole workforce is motivated.

Most of the work in any organization is done away from the immediate view of mangement and supervision, and often with individual discretion. If the cooperation of some or all of the people is absent, there is no way that managers will be able to cope with the chaos that will result. This principle is extremely important at the points where the processes 'touch' the outside customer. Every phase of these operations must be subject to continuous improvement, and for that total involvement is required.

Never-ending improvement is the process by which is achieved greater customer satisfaction. Its adoption recognizes that quality is a moving target, but its operation actually results in quality.

A model for total quality management

The concept of total quality management is basically very simple. Each part of an organization has customers, whether within or without, and the need to identify what the customer requirements are, and then set about meeting them, forms the core of a total quality approach. This requires several things including a good quality management system, statistical process control (SPC), and teamwork. These are complementary in many ways and they share the same requirement for an uncompromising commitment to quality. This must start with the most senior management and flow down through the organization. Having said that, either SPC or the quality system or both may be used as a spearhead to drive TQM through an organization. The attention to many aspects of a company's

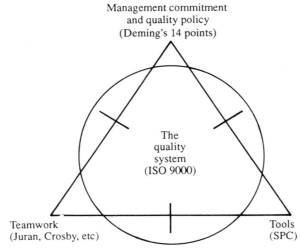

Figure 14.4 *The TQM model*

operations – from purchasing through to distribution, from data recording to control chart plotting – which are required for the successful introduction of a good quality system, or the implementation of SPC, will have a 'Hawthorne effect'[1] concentrating everyone's attention on the customer/supplier interface, both inside and outside the organization.

A good quality management system involves consideration of all the major areas: marketing, design, materials, plant, process, skills, distribution, etc. Clearly, these each require considerable expansion and thought but if attention is given to all areas using the concepts of TQM then very little will be left to chance. A well-operated, documented quality management system provides the necessary foundation for the successful application of SPC and teamwork. It is not possible simply to 'graft' these onto a poor quality system.

Much of industry and commerce would benefit from the improvements in quality brought about by the approach represented in Figure 14.4. This will ensure the implementation of the management commitment represented in the quality policy, and provide the environment and information base on which teamwork, perhaps through Juran and/or Crosby methods, thrives.

[1] The term 'Hawthorne effect' was coined following work by Mayo on the shop floors of Western Electric's Hawthorne plant. In attempts to demonstrate that improved conditions of work would have a direct and positive effect on productivity, he installed increased lighting and productivity went up as predicted. However, as he routinely returned the lights to their original intensity, it was observed that the productivity went up again. Clearly the attention paid to the employees, not the conditions *per se*, had a beneficial effect.

A systematic, structured approach to the launch of quality improvement through a balanced introduction of a quality system, SPC, and teamwork will provide a powerful spearhead with which to improve capability, and thereby market share. The importance of the use of SPC and improvements in quality management systems cannot be over-emphasized. With increases in automation and the use of flexible manufacturing systems (FMS), optimized production technology (OPT) and the adoption of operations management methods such as just-in-time (JIT) inventory systems, the requirement for a total approach to quality is paramount. To compete locally, nationally or internationally, all organizations and their parts must adopt a professional approach to the collection, analysis and use of quality data throughout.

14.4 How long can TQM survive?

During the introduction of TQM, or several years into its implementation, problems may arise. Companies have experienced different types of difficulty but the major ones are:

- management is not fully committed and reverts to meeting short-term gains;
- scepticism due to lack of organizational focus on quality;
- loss of credibility for TQM which becomes last month's or last year's flavour;
- teams become bogged down in trivia instead of tackling the important problems.

After several years of TQM, organizations may find it useful to carry out surveys to ensure that real commitment at the top is still present. Departmental managers may find the check list in Table 14.2 useful in reviews. Moreover, the quality council should be interrogated regarding its:

commitment;
strategies;
teamwork;
problems and results;
development.

Commitment

The survey should examine the success of the initial drive towards management commitment and its current level. Senior management may be, or perceive themselves to be, fully committed, at least to the TQM ideology, but middle management need to have the right attitude, and be sure of the practical implications. This approach should draw attention to a number of problems, including staff struggling due to lack of direction.

The workforce may be committed to the concept to a far greater degree than management believe, but they may doubt the sincerity of management's application. Work in companies using the survey approach has shown that:

- communication is the key to the programme;
- commitment from the workforce is tied to the amount of training they receive;
- involvement is linked directly to the training emphasis.

Strategies

The strategy for TQM implementation is often underdeveloped. This can lead to intermittent tactics and 'add-on' fads which contribute greatly to a 'flavour of the month' reputation for TQM. The lack of long-term strategies, objectives, and targets will cause the scheme to lose credibility with the workforce. If, for example, teams are formed, meet and make presentations to management without really knowing the ultimate purpose or aims of their operation, or the goal-posts are moved during a project, frustration and even anger will destroy the TQM drive very quickly.

It helps if part of the strategy is to develop proper measurement indices for all departments, including administration. Another valuable aid is to obtain an outside independent view to help with and develop the strategy. This will usually be seen, by top management and the workforce, as a positive step to keep up the momentum.

Teamwork

Some basic misconceptions may develop during the first few years of operating TQM. The perception of the status of the various teams, QITs and quality circles, may become distorted. In one organization, for example, it was found that the workforce felt that QITs were for professional staff and quality circles for the rest of the workforce. There was also a belief that teams worked best in a production environment because the progress of results could be measured against definite parameters. This led to teams not being formed in the administration departments as quickly as hoped. Communications were also poor in those areas, since half the staff did not know about the scheme, or had not been asked to join a team. When people did find out about the teams, they asked for training and wanted to become involved.

Table 14.2   A TQM check list for departmental managers

		Comments *Proposed action*
Commitment		
Do you accept that meeting customer requirements and error/ waste prevention is an essential part of your managerial responsibilities?	YES/NO	
Do you make this clear to your supervisors?	YES/NO	
Do your supervisors accept that meeting the requirements and error/waste prevention is an essential part of their function?	YES/NO	
Do they make this clear to their operators?	YES/NO	
Communications		
How often do you discuss customer requirements and error/waste prevention with supervisors?	DAILY WEEKLY MONTHLY QUARTERLY	
Do your supervisors discuss error and waste prevention and the customer/supplier relationship with operators?	YES/NO	
How effective are communications on customer requirements and error/waste prevention in your department?	POOR FAIR GOOD	
What percentage of your department is involved in quality-related teams?	. . . . . %	
Do you have good methods of recognizing contributions to improvement?	YES/NO	
Quality training		
Is quality training an integral part of all job instruction?	YES/NO	
Is quality training carried out by: quality management? supervisors? other operators? outsiders?	YES/NO YES/NO YES/NO YES/NO	

Table 14.2   A TQM check list for departmental managers – contd

		Comments Proposed action
Is there any follow-up?	YES/NO	
What percentage of your operators have attended special quality courses?	. . . . . %	
Have all operators received training in the use of problem-solving techniques?	YES/NO	
If no, what percentage have been trained?	. . . . . %	
When did this take place? This year? Last year? Year before last?	YES/NO YES/NO YES/NO	
Is refresher and updating training required?	YES/NO	

Problems and results

Everyone in an organization which is, say, five years into TQM will realize that it is not without its problems. The application of measurement to administrative practices, for example, will cause a number of headaches. Other problems that have been seen blocking the road to TQM include:

- no formal strategy;
- failure to provide incentives by recognition;
- lack of effective communication;
- narrowly based training.

These can be major causes of lack of penetration within the workforce. One approach which should definitely not be used to try to correct these difficulties is a financial incentive; it does not form part of the TQM culture, and would defeat many of the objectives. Recognition and involvement are the only effective incentives.

The successes of TQM will be measured by a number of features:

- the involvement and recognition by external customers;
- reductions in complaints;
- improved attitudes at and to work;

- reductions in errors, scrap, rework, etc.;
- increased productivity;
- improved conditions.

Development

Following a review of progress using surveys or other means, thought must be given to how TQM is to develop in the organization. Suggestions for consideration may include:

- Development of the long-term TQM strategies.
- Re-emphasis of the TQM culture.
- Reorganization of the TQM structure.
- Increase in QITs and quality circles membership.
- Additional training and resources.
- Improvements in measurements – especially for administration areas.
- Improvements in communication of progress, results, and successes.
- Improvements in the recognition process.

The most important thing is that management and the workforce must want TQM to continue because they recognize the benefits. The organization may realize through progress reviews that, although it is getting a number of things right, it has a long way to go before the quality management can be considered to be total. The emphasis may, for example, move from achieving assessment of the quality system by an independent body to new initiatives aimed at getting the involvement of all the people.

The basic lessons that those companies with most success in TQM have learned can be summarized:

- TQM is hard work.
- To establish TQM takes longer than first thought.
- TQM needs to be driven through the whole business.
- Top and middle management commitment is vital.
- TQM champions must balance their enthusiasm with practicability.
- Sceptics are not always a hindrance – they can be beneficial.

14.5 Caution – this concept can damage your wealth

The author has forgotten who first said that there is nothing as inevitable as an idea whose time has come. TQM is in this fortunate situation. But, there is also nothing as inevitable as the rejection of ideas that do not fulfil their promise. In the 1990s this is the greatest danger facing TQM.

TQM, or any other good idea, will not succeed by itself, it must be carefully managed. To avoid TQD – total quality disillusionment – several things must be done by all concerned:

- Avoid overstating the benefits of TQM (disillusionment is often caused by unrealistic expectations – anyone who has played golf will certainly know this!).
- Avoid understating the commitment required when trying to gain acceptance for the quality strategy.
- Emphasize the long, slow journey to TQM to avoid it being consigned to the scrap heap of discarded magic management ointments or fads.
- Avoid creating the impression that quality is a finite task, that once installed will last forever, with only minimum maintenance.
- Prevent TQM being used as an instant solution to a particular problem.
- Emphasize that quality improvement requires an ongoing, never-ending commitment to reap the lasting benefits.

Above all, ensure it is understood that TQM is a new operational philosophy which is vital to pursue the continuation of most organizations in the world.

Appendix TQM bibliography

Crosby Philip B. (1979). *Quality is Free*. New York: McGraw-Hill Book Company.

Crosby Philip B. (1984). *Quality Without Tears*. New York: McGraw-Hill Book Company.

Crosby Philip B. (1986). *Running Things*. New York: McGraw-Hill Book Company.

Cullen Joe, Hollingham (1987). *Implementing Total Quality*. London: IFS (Publications) Ltd.

Deming Walter E. (1982). *Quality, Productivity, and Competitive Position*. MIT Center for Advanced Engineering Study, Cambridge, Mass.

Deming Walter E. (1986). *Out of the Crisis*. MIT Center for Advanced Engineering Study, Cambridge, Mass.

Feigenbaum A. V. (1983). *Total Quality Control* 3rd edn. New York: McGraw-Hill Book Company.

Gitlow Howard S., Gitlow Shelly J. (1987). *The Deming Guide to Quality and Competitive Position*. Englewood Cliffs, NJ: Prentice-Hall Inc.

Ishikawa Kaoru (1976). *Guide to Quality Control*. Asian Productivity Organisation, Tokyo.

Ishikawa Kaoru (translated by David J. Lu) (1985). *What is Total Quality Control? – the Japanese Way*. Englewood Cliffs, NJ: Prentice-Hall.

Juran Joseph M. (1979). *Quality Control Handbook* 3rd edn. New York: McGraw-Hill Book Company.

Juran Joseph M., Gryna F. M. (1980). *Quality Planning and Analysis* 2nd edn. New York: McGraw-Hill Book Company.

Mann N. R. (1985). *The Keys to Excellence: The Story of the Deming Philosophy*. Los Angeles, California: Prestwick Books.

Murphy John A. (1986). *Quality in Practice*. Dublin: Gill and MacMillan.

Oakland John S. (1986). *Statistical Process Control*. London: Heinemann.

Peters Thomas J., Waterman Robert H. Jr (1982). *In Search of Excellence*. New York: Harper and Row Publishers.

Price Frank (1985). *Right First Time*. London: Gower.

Scherkenbach W. W. (1986). *The Deming Route to Quality and Productivity: Road Maps and Road Blocks*. Rockville, Md: Mercury Press/Fairchild Publications.

Shaw John C. (1978). *The Quality-Productivity Connection in Service Sector Management*. New York: Van Nostrand Reinhold Company.

Shingo Shigeo (1986). *Zero Quality Control: Source Inspection and the Poka-yoke System*. Stamford, Conn.: Productivity Press.

Taguchi G. (1979). *Introduction to Off-line Quality Control*. Central Japan Quality Control Assoc., Magaya, Japan.

Taguchi G. (1981). *On-line Quality Control during Production*. Japanese Standards Association, Tokyo.

Townsend Patrick L., Gebhart Joan E. (1986). *Commit to Quality*. New York: John Wiley and Sons Inc.

Index